THE INNOVATOR'S SOLUTION

THE
INNOVATOR'S
SOLUTION

CREATING AND SUSTAINING
SUCCESSFUL GROWTH

CLAYTON M. CHRISTENSEN
MICHAEL E. RAYNOR

HARVARD BUSINESS SCHOOL PRESS
BOSTON, MASSACHUSETTS

Library of Congress Cataloging-in-Publication Data
Christensen, Clayton M.
    The innovators solution : creating and sustaining successful growth / Clayton M.
Christensen, Michael E. Raynor.
        p. cm.
Includes bibliographical references and index.
    ISBN 1-57851-852-0 (alk. paper)
    1. Creative ability in business. 2. Industrial management. 3. Customer service.
4. Succcess in business. I. Raynor, Michael E. II. Title.
    HD53.C495 2003
    658.4'063—dc21

                                                                2003014328

CONTENTS

IN GRATITUDE

I have spent much of the past decade puzzling over two questions. The first: It is easy to explain why poorly run companies fail; but many of history's most successful and best-run firms have lost their positions of leadership, too. Why is it so hard to sustain success? *The Innovator's Dilemma* summarized what I learned about this puzzle. It's not just management mistakes that cause failure. Certain practices that are essential to a company's success—like catering to the needs of your best customers and focusing investments where profitability is most attractive—can cause failure too.

The second centered on the opportunity in the dilemma: If I wanted to start a company that could become significant and successful and ultimately topple the firms that now lead an industry, how could I do it? If indeed there are predictable reasons why businesses stumble, we might then help managers avoid those causes of failure and help them make decisions that predictably lead to successful growth. This is *The Innovator's Solution.*

The challenge of this research quickly outstripped my abilities; and I have relied upon some extraordinary people to help me complete it. Michael Raynor, who has tutored me from the day he arrived as a doctoral student at Harvard, has been an exceptional colleague. To describe Michael's integrated grasp of arts, letters, philosophical discourse, and history as "incisive" would understate his intellect.

Confident that I could expose and rectify the gaps in my evidence and logic by examining my rough ideas through the lenses of the varied academic disciplines that Michael's mind has mastered, I asked him to join me as coauthor. Michael has balanced this work with his duties as a husband, father, and director of research at Deloitte Consulting, all the while shuttling between Toronto and Boston. I deeply appreciate his selfless, humble, and persistent hammering to get these ideas shaped right. He has become a great friend.

Scott Anthony, Mark Johnson, and Matt Eyring each have forsaken or postponed far more lucrative careers to join me in this effort. As my primary research associate, Scott has managed our staff of researchers, written crucial case studies, helped me teach and explain complicated concepts, and reviewed and refined every draft of this book. Mark and Matt, through our firm *Innosight,* have translated these concepts into practical tools and processes to help managers build businesses that will be significant and successful—and in so doing have taught me how our findings can interface with managerial reality. My office manager, Christine Gaze, and research partners Sally Aaron, Mick Bass, Will Clark, Jeremy Dann, Tara Donovan, Taddy Hall, John Kenagy, Michael and Amy Overdorf, Nate Redmond, Erik Roth, and David Sundahl each have helped me stay atop the huge volume of interesting ideas, opportunities for inquiry and authorship, and requests for assistance that flow into and out of my office. They have painstakingly helped us get the data, logic, and language right for every purpose.

I have a profound debt to Harvard Business School and my colleagues here. The insightful research of Professors Clark Gilbert and Steve Spear has been exceptionally valuable. Other faculty, including Kent Bowen, Joseph Bower, Hank Chesbrough, Kim Clark, Tom Eisenmann, Lee Fleming, Frances Frei, Alan MacCormack, Gary Pisano, Richard Rosenbloom, Bill Sahlman, Don Sull, Richard Tedlow, Stefan Thomke, Michael Tushman, and Steve Wheelwright have also shaped what we have come to understand—as have Professors Rebecca Henderson, Paul Carlile, James Utterback, and Eric von Hippel of MIT, Robert Burgelman of Stanford, and Stuart Hart of UNC. The extraordinary benefit of Harvard's case method of teaching is that the teachers can carry issues they don't understand into the classroom, ask questions of the students in the context of a case, and then listen to and learn from some of the brightest people in the world. I express my love and my gratitude to my students for preparing so hard every day to teach each other and their teacher in so many ways. It is a learning system without parallel.

I also have sought the advice of some the most capable business thinkers and executives in the world. Matt Verlinden and Steve King of Integral, Geoffrey Moore of the Chasm Group, Tony Ulwick of Strategyn, Crawford del Prete of IDC, Andy Grove of Intel, Ken Dobler of Johnson & Johnson, Dan Carp and Willy Shih of Kodak, Dennis Hunter of Applied Materials, Michael Putz of Cisco, Chris Rowen of Tensilica, Bill George of Medtronic, Meir Weinstein of EMC, Michael Packer and Kelly Martin of Merrill Lynch, Mark Ross of Cypress Semiconductor, and Ron Dollens, Ginger Graham, and Rod Nash of Guidant have all tutored me.

I owe the deepest debt to my family. My children, Matthew, Ann, Michael, Spencer, and Katie, each have discussed, used, and bettered my understanding through their own work and schooling. My wife, Christine, is the smartest person I have known. Her standards for clarity and completeness are uncompromising, and her language and intellect are imprinted on *every* concept in this book—which is remarkable, given that much of her advice came at the end of long days that were filled with the pressures of motherhood and her selfless service to others. She brings love and light to me and everyone she meets, every day.

Academia for some can be an enterprise of solitary pursuits. I am blessed in contrast to work within a community of selfless, humble, smart, and intellectually courageous men and women who as a group have made the substantial progress that is summarized in this book. I am grateful to have been able to play my role in this effort.

Clayton M. Christensen
Boston, Massachusetts

Like Clayton, I offer my thanks to the many people who have shared their experiences and talents with us. Without their willingness to be part of our learning processes, neither this book nor our respective careers would be possible.

The latitude I have enjoyed within Deloitte Research is, as far as I know, unparalleled in the consulting industry. The firm has gone beyond simply tolerating my idiosyncratic undertakings—of which this book is certainly one—to actively encouraging them, making possible the exploration of a different way to create and share knowledge. I am especially grateful to Ann Baxter, the head of Deloitte Research, and Larry Scott, global leader of Deloitte Consulting's Strategy and Operations practice, for making it possible for the ball to start rolling, and to innumerable others in Deloitte Consulting and Deloitte & Touche for their enthusiasm and support that has maintained and accelerated that momentum.

These few sentences are one of the few opportunities I shall have to acknowledge for posterity my intellectual debt to Clayton. My first contact with Clayton's work was as a doctoral student at Harvard Business School. In his writings I found a rare combination of theoretical elegance, intellectual rigor, creative data analysis, and managerial relevance. When I read *The Innovator's Dilemma,* I, like so many others, felt that a mote had been removed from my eye, and that what I had previously seen only dimly, if at all, was suddenly brought into the light. Clayton's work has become for me a standard to which I continue to aspire, and so it is truly a privilege to have had the opportunity to contribute to and be part of the continued development and elaboration of those ideas. During the course of my doctoral studies, I was lucky enough to have Clayton as a teacher. In the course of our work together on this book, he has become a mentor, colleague, and friend.

I save for last the one to whom I owe the most: my wife, Annabel. Her love and support have been unconditional through the years of doctoral studies, through the inevitable absences attendant to a career in consulting, through my preoccupation with this and other projects (but mostly this one!), and through the various other challenges resulting from the somewhat oddball path I have chosen. Without her, I could not pursue my dreams. Without her, and without our daughter, Charlotte, I wouldn't have any worth pursuing.

Michael E. Raynor
Mississauga, Ontario

THE INNOVATOR'S SOLUTION

CHAPTER ONE

THE GROWTH IMPERATIVE

Financial markets relentlessly pressure executives to grow and keep growing faster and faster. Is it possible to succeed with this mandate? Don't the innovations that can satisfy investors' demands for growth require taking risks that are unacceptable to those same investors? Is there a way out of this dilemma?

This is a book about how to create new growth in business. Growth is important because companies create shareholder value through profitable growth. Yet there is powerful evidence that once a company's core business has matured, the pursuit of new platforms for growth entails daunting risk. Roughly one company in ten is able to sustain the kind of growth that translates into an above-average increase in shareholder returns over more than a few years.[1] Too often the very attempt to grow causes the entire corporation to crash. Consequently, most executives are in a no-win situation: equity markets demand that they grow, but it's hard to know *how* to grow. Pursuing growth the wrong way can be worse than no growth at all.

Consider AT&T. In the wake of the government-mandated divestiture of its local telephony services in 1984, AT&T became primarily a long distance telecommunications services provider. The break-up agreement freed the company to invest in new businesses, so management almost immediately began seeking avenues for growth and the shareholder value that growth creates.

The first such attempt arose from a widely shared view that computer systems and telephone networks were going to converge. AT&T first tried to build its own computer division in order to position itself at that intersection, but was able to do no better than annual losses of $200 million. Rather than retreat from a business that had proved to be unassailable from the outside, the company decided in 1991 to bet bigger still, acquiring NCR, at the time the world's fifth-largest computer maker, for $7.4 billion. That proved only to be a down payment: AT&T lost another $2 billion trying to make the acquisition work. AT&T finally abandoned this growth vision in 1996, selling NCR for $3.4 billion, about a third of what it had invested in the opportunity.

But the company *had* to grow. So even as the NCR acquisition was failing, AT&T was seeking growth opportunities in technologies closer to its core. In light of the success of the wireless services that several of its spun-off local telephone companies had achieved, in 1994 the company bought McCaw Cellular, at the time the largest national wireless carrier in the United States, for $11.6 billion, eventually spending $15 billion in total on its own wireless business. When Wall Street analysts subsequently complained that they were unable to properly value the combined higher-growth wireless business within the lower-growth wireline company, AT&T decided to create a separately traded stock for the wireless business in 2000. This valued the business at $10.6 billion, about two-thirds of the investment AT&T had made in the venture.

But that move left the AT&T wireline stock right where it had started, and the company *had* to grow. So in 1998 it embarked upon a strategy to enter and reinvent the local telephony business with broadband technology. Acquiring TCI and MediaOne for a combined price of $112 billion made AT&T Broadband the largest cable operator in the United States. Then, more quickly than anyone could have foreseen, the difficulties in implementation and integration proved insurmountable. In 2000, AT&T agreed to sell its cable assets to Comcast for $72 billion.[2]

In the space of a little over ten years, AT&T had wasted about $50 billion and destroyed even more in shareholder value—all in the hope of *creating* shareholder value through growth.

The bad news is that AT&T is not a special case. Consider Cabot Corporation, the world's major producer of carbon black, a compound that imparts to products such as tires many of their most important properties. This business has long been very strong, but the core markets haven't grown rapidly. To create the growth that builds shareholder value, Cabot's executives in the early 1980s launched several aggressive growth initiatives in advanced materials, acquiring a set of promising specialty metals and high-tech ceramics businesses. These constituted operating platforms into which the company would infuse new process and materials technology that was emerging from its own research laboratories and work it had sponsored at MIT.

Wall Street greeted these investments to accelerate Cabot's growth trajectory with enthusiasm and drove the company's share price to triple the level at which it had languished prior to these initiatives. But as the losses created by Cabot's investments in these businesses began to drag the entire corporation's earnings down, Wall Street hammered the stock. While the overall market appreciated at a robust rate between 1988 and 1991, Cabot's shares dropped by more than half. In the early 1990s, feeling pressure to boost earnings, Cabot's board brought in new management whose mandate was to shut down the new businesses and refocus on the core. As Cabot's profitability rebounded, Wall Street enthusiastically doubled the company's share price. The problem, of course, was that this turnaround left the new management team no better off than their predecessors: desperately seeking growth opportunities for mature businesses with limited prospects.[3]

We could cite many cases of companies' similar attempts to create new-growth platforms after the core business had matured. They follow an all-too-similar pattern. When the core business approaches maturity and investors demand new growth, executives develop seemingly sensible strategies to generate it. Although they invest aggressively, their plans fail to create the needed growth fast enough; investors hammer the stock; management is sacked; and Wall Street rewards the new executive team for simply restoring the *status quo ante*: a profitable but low-growth core business.[4]

Even expanding firms face a variant of the growth imperative. No matter how fast the growth treadmill is going, it is not fast enough. The reason: Investors have a pesky tendency to discount into the *present* value of a company's stock price whatever rate of growth they *foresee* the company achieving. Thus, even if a company's core business is growing vigorously, the only way its managers can deliver a rate of return to shareholders in the future that exceeds the risk-adjusted market average is to grow *faster* than shareholders expect. Changes in stock prices are driven not by simply the *direction* of growth, but largely by *unexpected* changes in the *rate of change* in a company's earnings and cash flows. Hence, one company that is projected to grow at 5 percent and in fact keeps growing at 5 percent and another company that is projected to grow at 25 percent and delivers 25 percent growth will both produce for future investors a market-average risk-adjusted rate of return in the future.[5] A company must deliver the rate of growth that the market is projecting just to keep its stock price from falling. It must *exceed* the consensus forecast rate of growth in order to boost its share price. This is a heavy, omnipresent burden on every executive who is sensitive to enhancing shareholder value.[6]

It's actually even harder than this. That canny horde of investors not only discounts the expected rate of growth of a company's *existing* businesses into the present value of its stock price, but also discounts the growth from new, yet-to-be-established lines of business that they expect the management team to be able to create in the future. The magnitude of the market's bet on growth from unknown sources is, in general, based on the company's track record. If the market has been impressed with a company's historical ability to leverage its strengths to generate new lines of business, then the component of its stock price based on growth from unknown sources will be large. If a company's past efforts to create new-growth businesses have not borne fruit, then its market valuation will be dominated by the projected cash flow from known, established businesses.

Table 1-1 presents one consulting firm's analysis of the share prices of a select number of *Fortune* 500 companies, showing the proportion of each firm's share price on August 21, 2002, that was attributable to cash generated by existing assets, versus cash that investors expected to be generated by new investments.[7] Of this sample, the company that was on the hook at that time to generate the largest percentage of its total growth from future investments was Dell Computer. Only 22 percent of its share price of $28.05 was justified by cash thrown off by the company's present assets, whereas 78 percent of Dell's valuation reflected investors' confidence that the company would be able to invest in new assets that would generate whopping amounts of cash. Sixty-six percent of Johnson & Johnson's market valuation and 37 percent of Home Depot's valuation were grounded in expectations of growth from yet-to-be-made investments. These companies were on the hook for *big* numbers. On the other hand, only 5 percent of General Motors's stock price on that date was predicated on future investments. Although that's a chilling reflection of the track record of GM's former management in creating new-growth businesses, it means that if the present management team does a better job, the company's share price could respond handsomely.

Probably the most daunting challenge in delivering growth is that if you fail once to deliver it, the odds that you ever will be able to deliver in the future are very low. This is the conclusion of a remarkable study, *Stall Points,* that the Corporate Strategy Board published in 1998.[8] It examined the 172 companies that had spent time on *Fortune*'s list of the 50 largest companies between 1955 and 1995. Only 5 percent of these companies were able to sustain a real, inflation-adjusted growth rate of more than 6 percent across their entire tenure in this group. The other 95 percent reached a point at which their growth simply stalled, to rates at or below the rate of growth of the gross national product (GNP). Stalling is understandable, given our expectations that all growth markets become saturated and mature. What is scary is that of all these companies whose growth had stalled, only 4 percent were able to successfully reignite their growth even to a rate of 1 percent above GNP growth. Once growth had stalled, in other words, it proved nearly impossible to restart it.

The equity markets brutally punished those companies that allowed their growth to stall. Twenty-eight percent of them lost more than 75 percent of their market capitalization. Forty-one percent of the companies saw their market value drop by between 50 and 75 percent when they stalled, and 26 percent of the firms lost between 25

TABLE 1-1

Portion of Selected Firms' Market Value That Was Based on Expected Returns from New Investments on August 21, 2002

Fortune 500 rank	Company Name	Share Price	Percent of Valuation That Was Based on: New Investments	Existing Assets
53	Dell Computer	$28.05	78%	22%
47	Johnson & Johnson	$56.20	66%	34%
35	Procter & Gamble	$90.76	62%	38%
6	General Electric	$32.80	60%	40%
77	Lockheed Martin	$62.16	59%	41%
1	Wal-Mart Stores	$53.88	50%	50%
65	Intel	$19.15	49%	51%
49	Pfizer	$34.92	48%	52%
9	IBM	$81.93	46%	54%
24	Merck	$53.80	44%	56%
92	Cisco Systems	$15.00	42%	58%
18	Home Depot	$33.86	37%	63%
16	Boeing	$28.36	30%	70%
11	Verizon	$31.80	21%	79%
22	Kroger	$22.20	13%	87%
32	Sears Roebuck	$36.94	8%	92%
37	AOL Time Warner	$35.00	8%	92%
3	General Motors	$49.40	5%	95%
81	Phillips Petroleum	$35.00	3%	97%

Source: CSFB/HOLT; Deloitte Consuting analysis.

and 50 percent of their value. The remaining 5 percent lost less than 25 percent of their market capitalization. This, of course, increased pressure on management to regenerate growth, and to do so quickly—which made it all the more difficult to succeed. Managers cannot escape the mandate to grow.[9] Yet the odds of success, if history is any guide, are frighteningly low.

Is Innovation a Black Box?

Why is achieving and sustaining growth so hard? One popular answer is to blame managers for failing to generate new growth—implying that more capable and prescient people could have succeeded. The solve-the-problem-by-finding-a-better-manager approach might have credence if failures to restart growth were isolated events. Study after study, however, concludes that about 90 percent of all publicly traded companies have proved themselves unable to sustain for more than a few years a growth trajectory that creates above-average shareholder returns.[10] Unless we believe that the pool of management talent in established firms is like some perverse Lake Wobegon, where 90 percent of managers are below average, there has to be a more fundamental explanation for why the vast majority of good managers has not been able to crack the problem of sustaining growth.

A second common explanation for once-thriving companies' inability to sustain growth is that their managers become risk averse. But the facts refute this explanation, too. Corporate executives often bet the future of billion-dollar enterprises on an innovation. IBM bet its farm on the System 360 mainframe computer, and won. DuPont spent $400 million on a plant to make Kevlar tire cord, and lost. Corning put billions on the line to build its optical fiber business, and won big. More recently it sold off many of its other businesses in order to invest more in optical telecommunications, and has been bludgeoned. *Many* of the executives who have been unable to create sustained corporate growth have evidenced a strong stomach for risk.

There is a third, widely accepted explanation for why growth seems so hard to achieve repeatedly and well, which we also believe does not hold water: Creating new-growth businesses is simply unpredictable.

Many believe that the odds of success are just that—odds—and that they are low. Many of the most insightful management thinkers have accepted the assumption that creating growth is risky and unpredictable, and have therefore used their talents to help executives manage this unpredictability. Recommendations about letting a thousand flowers bloom, bringing Silicon Valley inside, failing fast, and accelerating selection pressures are all ways to deal with the allegedly irreducible unpredictability of successful innovation.[11] The structure of the venture capital industry is in fact a testament to the pervasive belief that we cannot predict which new-growth businesses will succeed. The industry maxim says that for every ten investments—all made in the belief they would succeed—two will fail outright, six will survive as the walking wounded, and two will hit the home runs on which the success of the entire portfolio turns. Because of this belief that the process of business creation is unfathomable, few have sought to pry open the black box to study the *process* by which new-growth businesses are created.

We do not accept that most companies' growth stalls because the odds of success for the next growth business they launch are impossibly low. The historical results may indeed seem random, but we believe it is because the process for creating new-growth businesses has not yet been well understood. In this book we intend to pry open the black box and study the processes that lead to success or failure in new-growth businesses.

To illustrate why it is important to understand the processes that create those results, consider these strings of numbers:

1, 2, 3, 4, 5, 6
75, 28, 41, 26, 38, 64

Which of these would you say is random, and which is predictable? The first string looks predictable: The next two numbers should be 7 and 8. But what if we told you that it was actually the winning numbers for a lottery, drawn from a drum of tumbling balls, whereas the second is the sequence of state and county roads one would follow on a scenic tour of the northern rim of Michigan's Upper Peninsula on the way from Sault Ste. Marie, Ontario to Saxon, Wisconsin?

Given the route implied by the first six roads, you can reliably predict the next two numbers—2 and 122—from a map. The lesson: You cannot say, just by looking at the result of the process, whether the process that created those results is capable of generating predictable output. You must understand the process itself.

The Forces That Shape Innovation

What can make the process of innovation more predictable? It does *not* entail learning to predict what *individuals* might do. Rather, it comes from understanding the *forces* that act upon the individuals involved in building businesses—forces that powerfully influence what managers choose and cannot choose to do.

Rarely does an idea for a new-growth business emerge fully formed from an innovative employee's head. No matter how well articulated a concept or insight might be, it must be shaped and modified, often significantly, as it gets fleshed out into a business plan that can win funding from the corporation. Along the way, it encounters a number of highly predictable forces. Managers as individuals might indeed be idiosyncratic and unpredictable, but they all face forces that are similar in their mechanism of action, their timing, and their impact on the character of the product and business plan that the company ultimately attempts to implement.[12] Understanding and managing these forces can make innovation more predictable.

The action and impact of these forces in shaping ideas into business plans is illustrated in a case study of the Big Idea Group (BIG), a company that identifies, develops, and markets ideas for new toys.[13] After quoting a senior executive of a multibillion-dollar toy company who complained that there have been no exciting new toy ideas for years, the case then chronicles how BIG attacks this problem—or rather, this opportunity.

BIG invites mothers, children, tinkerers, and retirees who have ideas for new toys to attend "Big Idea Hunts," which it convenes in locations across the country. These guests present their ideas to a panel of experts whose intuition BIG executives have come to trust. When the panel sees a good idea, BIG licenses it from the inventor and over the next several months shapes the idea into a business plan with a working prototype that they believe will sell. BIG then licenses the product to a toy company, which produces and markets it through its own channels. The company has been extraordinarily successful at finding, developing, and deploying into the market a sequence of truly exciting growth products.

How can there be such a flowering of high-potential new product opportunities in BIG's system, and such a dearth of opportunities in the large toy company? In discussing the case, students often suggest that the product developers in the toy company just aren't as creative, or that the executives of the major company are just too risk averse. If these diagnoses were true, the company would simply need to find more creative managers who could think outside the box. But a parade of people has cycled through the toy company, and none has been able to crack the apparent lack of exciting toy ideas. Why?

The answer lies in the process by which the ideas get shaped. Midlevel managers play a crucial role in *every* company's innovation process, as they shepherd partially formed ideas into fully fledged business plans in an effort to win funding from senior management. It is the middle managers who must decide which of the ideas that come bubbling in or up to them they will support and carry to upper management for approval, and which ideas they will simply allow to languish. This is a key reason why companies employ middle managers in the first place. Their job is to sift the good ideas from the bad and to make good ideas so much better that they readily secure funding from senior management.

How do they sift and shape? Middle managers typically hesitate to throw their weight behind new product concepts whose market is not assured. If a market fails to materialize, the company will have wasted millions of dollars. The system therefore mandates that midlevel managers support their proposals with credible data on the size and growth potential of the markets that each idea targets. Opinions and feedback from significant customers add immeasurably to the credibility of claims that an idea has potential. Where does this evidence come from, given that the product hasn't yet been fully developed? It typically comes from existing customers and markets for similar products that have been successful in the past.

Personal factors are at work in this shaping process, too. Managers who back ideas that flop often find their prospects for promotion effectively truncated. In fact, ambitious managers hesitate even to propose ideas that senior managers are not likely to approve. If they favor an idea that their superiors subsequently judge to be weak, their reputation for good judgment can be tarnished among the very executives they hope to impress. Furthermore, companies' management development programs rarely leave their most talented middle managers in a position for longer than a few years—they move them to new assignments to broaden their skills and experience. What this means, however, is that middle managers who want a reputation for delivering results will be inclined to promote only those new-growth ideas that will pay off within the time that they reside in that particular job.

The process of sorting through and packaging ideas into plans that can win funding, in other words, shapes those ideas to resemble the ideas that were approved and became successful in the past. The processes have in fact evolved to weed out business proposals that target markets where demand might be small. The problem for growth-seeking managers, of course, is that the exciting growth markets of tomorrow are small today.

This is why the senior managers at the major toy company and at BIG can live in the same world and yet see such different things. In every sizable company, not just in the toy business, the set of ideas that has been processed and packaged for top management approval is *very* different from the population of ideas that is bubbling at the bottom.

A dearth of good ideas is rarely the core problem in a company that struggles to launch exciting new-growth businesses. The problem is in the shaping process. Potentially innovative new ideas seem inexorably to be recast into attempts to make existing customers still happier. We believe that many of the ideas that emerge from this packaging and shaping process as me-too innovations could just as readily be shaped into business plans that create truly disruptive growth. Managers who understand these forces and learn to harness them in making key decisions will develop successful new-growth businesses much more consistently than historically has seemed possible.[14]

Where Predictability Comes From: Good Theory

The quest for predictability in an endeavor as complex as innovation is not quixotic. What brings predictability to any field is a body of well-researched *theory*—contingent statements of what causes what and why. Executives often discount the value of management theory because it is associated with the word *theoretical,* which connotes *impractical.* But theory is consummately practical. The law of gravity, for example, actually is a theory—and it is useful. It allows us to predict that if we step off a cliff, we will fall.[15]

Even though most managers don't think of themselves as being theory driven, they are in reality voracious consumers of theory. Every time managers make plans or take action, it is based on a mental model in the back of their heads that leads them to believe that the action being taken will lead to the desired result.[16] The problem is that managers are rarely aware of the theories they are using—and they often use the wrong theories for the situation they are in. It is the absence of conscious, trustworthy theories of cause and effect that makes success in building new businesses seem random.

To help executives to know whether and when they can trust the recommendations from management books or articles (including this one!) that they read for guidance as they build their businesses, we describe in the following sections a model of how good theories are built and used. We will repeatedly return to this model to illustrate how bad theory has caused growth builders to stumble in the past, and how the use of sound theory can remove many of the causes of failure.[17]

How Theories Are Built

The process of building solid theory has been researched in several disciplines, and scholars seem to agree that it proceeds in three stages. It begins by describing the phenomenon that we wish to understand. In physics, the phenomenon might be the behavior of high-energy particles. In the building of new businesses, the phenomena of interest are the things that innovators do in their efforts to succeed, and what the results of those actions are. Bad management theory results when researchers impatiently observe one or two success stories and then assume that they have seen enough.

After the phenomenon has been thoroughly characterized, researchers can then begin the second stage, which is to classify the phenomenon into categories. Juvenile-onset versus adult-onset diabetes is an example from medicine. Vertical and horizontal integration are categories of corporate diversification. Researchers need to categorize in order to highlight the most meaningful differences in the complex array of phenomena.

In the third stage, researchers articulate a theory that asserts what causes the phenomenon to occur, and why. The theory must also show whether and why the same causal mechanism might result in different outcomes, depending on the category or situation. The process of theory building is iterative, as researchers and managers keep cycling through these three steps, refining their ability to predict what actions will cause what results, under what circumstances.[18]

Getting the Categories Right

The middle stage in this cycle—getting the categories right—is the key to developing useful theory. To see why, imagine going to your medical doctor seeking treatment for a particular set of symptoms, and before you have a chance to describe what ails you, the physician hands you a prescription and tells you to "take two of these and call me in the morning."

"But how do you know this will help me?" you ask. "I haven't told you what's wrong."

"Why wouldn't it work?" comes the reply. "It cured my previous two patients just fine."

No sane patient would accept medicine like this. But academics, consultants, and managers *routinely* dispense and accept remedies to management problems in this manner. When something has worked for a few "excellent" companies, they readily advise all other companies that taking the same medicine will be good for them as well. One reason why the outcomes of innovation appear to be random is that many who write about strategy and management ignore categorization. They observe a few successful companies and then write a book recommending that other managers do the same things to be successful too—without regard for the possibility that there might be some circumstances in which their favorite solution is a bad idea.[19]

For example, thirty years ago many writers asserted that vertical integration was the key to IBM's extraordinary success. But in the late 1990s we read that *non*-integration explained the triumph of outsourcing titans such as Cisco and Dell. The authors of "best practices" gospels such as these are no better than the doctor we introduced previously. The critical question that these researchers need to resolve is, "What are the *circumstances* in which being integrated is competitively critical, and when is a strategy of partnering and outsourcing more likely to lead to success?"

Because theory-building scholars struggle to define the right and relevant categorization of circumstances, they rarely can define the circumstances immediately. Early studies almost always sort researchers' observations into categories defined by the *attributes* of the phenomena themselves. Their assertions about the actions or events that lead to the results at this point can only be statements about *correlation* between attributes and results, not about causality. This is the best they can do in early theory-building cycles.

Consider, for illustration, the history of man's attempts to fly. Early researchers observed strong correlations between being able to fly and having feathers and wings. Possessing these attributes had a high *correlation* with the ability to fly, but when humans attempted to follow the "best practices" of the most successful flyers by strapping feathered wings onto their arms, jumping off cliffs, and flapping hard, they were not successful—because as strong as the correlations were, the would-be aviators had not understood the fundamental causal mechanism that enabled certain animals to fly. It was not until Bernoulli's study of fluid mechanics helped him articulate the mechanism through which airfoils create lift that human flight began to be *possible*. But understanding the mechanism itself still wasn't enough to make the ability to fly perfectly *predictable*. Further research, entailing careful experimentation and measurement under various conditions, was needed to identify the *circumstances* in which that mechanism did and did not yield the desired result.

When the mechanism did not result in successful flight, researchers had to carefully decipher *why*—what it was about the circumstances in which the unexpected result occurred that led to failure. Once categories could be stated in terms of the different types of circumstances in which aviators might find themselves, then aviators could predict the conditions in which flight was and was not possible. They could develop technologies and techniques for successfully flying in those circumstances where flight was viable. And they could teach aviators how to recognize when the circumstances were changing, so that they could change their methods appropriately. Understanding the mechanism (what causes what, and why) made flight possible; understanding the categories of circumstances made flight predictable.[20]

How did aviation researchers know what the salient boundaries were between these categories of circumstance? As long as a change in conditions did not require change in the way the pilot flew the plane, the boundary between those conditions didn't matter. The circumstance boundaries that mattered were those that mandated a fundamental change in piloting techniques in order to keep the plane flying successfully.

Similar breakthroughs in management research increase the predictability of creating new-growth businesses. Getting beyond correlative assertions such as "Big companies are slow to innovate," or "In our sample of successful companies, each was run by a CEO who had been promoted from within," the breakthrough researcher first discovers the fundamental *causal* mechanism behind the phenomena of success. This allows those who are looking for "an answer" to get beyond the wings-and-feathers mind-set of copying the attributes of successful companies. The foundation for predictability only begins to be built when the researcher sees the same causal mechanism create a *different* outcome from what he or she expected—an anomaly. This prompts the researcher to define what it was about the circumstance or circumstances in which the anomaly occurred that caused the identical mechanism to result in a different outcome.

How can we tell what the right categorization is? As in aviation, a boundary between circumstances is salient only when executives need to use fundamentally different management techniques to succeed in the different circumstances defined by that boundary. If the same statement of cause and effect leads to the same outcome in two circumstances, then the distinction between those circumstances is not meaningful for the purposes of predictability.

To know for certain what circumstances they are in, managers also must know what circumstances they are *not* in. When collectively exhaustive and mutually exclusive *categories of circumstances* are defined, things get predictable: We can state what will cause what and why, and can predict how that statement of causality might vary by circumstance. Theories built on categories of circumstances become easy for companies to employ, because managers live and work in circumstances, not in attributes.[21]

When managers ask questions such as "Does this apply to my industry?" or "Does it apply to service businesses as well as product businesses?" they really are probing to understand the circumstances. In our studies, we have observed that industry-based or product/service-based categorization schemes almost never constitute a useful foundation for reliable theory. *The Innovator's Dilemma,* for example, described how the same mechanism that enabled entrant companies to up-end the leading established firms in disk drives and computers also toppled the leading companies in mechanical excavators, steel, retailing, motorcycles, accounting software, and motor controls.[22] The circumstances that mattered were not what industry you were in. Rather, there was a mechanism—the resource allocation process—that caused the established leaders to win the competitive fights when an innovation was financially attractive to their business model. The same mechanism disabled the established leaders when they were attacked by disruptive innovators—whose products, profit models, and customers were not attractive.

We can trust a theory only when its statement of what actions will lead to success describe how this will vary as a company's circumstances change.[23] This is a major reason why the outcomes of innovation efforts have seemed quite random: Shoddy categorization has led to one-size-fits-all recommendations that in turn have led to the wrong results in many circumstances.[24] It is the ability to begin thinking and acting in a circumstance-contingent way that brings predictability to our lives.

We often admire the intuition that successful entrepreneurs seem to have for building growth businesses. When they exercise their intuition about what actions will lead to the desired results, they really are employing theories that give them a sense of the right thing to do in various circumstances. These theories were not there at birth: They were learned through a set of experiences and mentors earlier in life.

If some people have learned the theories that we call intuition, then it is our hope that these theories also can be taught to others. This is our aspiration for this book. We hope to help managers who are trying to create new-growth businesses use the best research we have been able to assemble to learn how to match their actions to the circumstances in order to get the results they need. As our readers use these ways of thinking over and over, we hope that the thought processes inherent in these theories can become part of their intuition as well.

We have written this book from the perspective of senior managers in established companies who have been charged to maintain the health and vitality of their firms. We believe, however, that our ideas will be just as valuable to independent entrepreneurs, start-up companies, and venture capital investors. Simply for purposes of brevity, we will use the term *product* in this book when we describe what a company makes or provides. We mean, however, for this to encompass product *and* service businesses, because the concepts in the book apply just as readily to both.

The Outline of This Book

The Innovator's Dilemma summarized a theory that explains how, under certain circumstances, the mechanism of profit-maximizing resource allocation causes well-run companies to get killed. *The Innovator's Solution,* in contrast, summarizes a set of theories that can guide managers who need to grow new businesses with predictable success—to become the disruptors rather than the disruptees—and ultimately kill the well-run, established competitors. To succeed predictably, disruptors must be good theorists. As they shape their growth business to be disruptive, they must align every critical process and decision to fit the disruptive circumstance.

Because building successful growth businesses is such a vast topic, this book focuses on nine of the most important decisions that all managers must make in creating growth—decisions that represent key actions that drive success inside the black box of innovation. Each chapter offers a specific theory that managers can use to make one of these decisions in a way that greatly improves their probability of success. Some of this theory has emerged from our own studies, but we are indebted to many other scholars for much of what follows. Those whose work we draw upon have contributed to improving the predictability of business building because their assertions of causality have been built upon circumstance-based categories. It is because of their careful work that we believe that managers can begin using these theories explicitly as they make these decisions, trusting that their predictions will be applicable and reliable, given the circumstances that they are in.

The following list summarizes the questions we address.

- *Chapter 2:* How can we beat our most powerful competitors? What strategies will result in the competitors killing us, and what courses of action could actually give us the upper hand?
- *Chapter 3:* What products should we develop? Which improvements over previous products will customers enthusiastically reward with premium prices, and which will they greet with indifference?
- *Chapter 4:* Which initial customers will constitute the most viable foundation upon which to build a successful business?
- *Chapter 5:* Which activities required to design, produce, sell, and distribute our product should our company do internally, and which should we rely upon our partners and suppliers to provide?
- *Chapter 6:* How can we be sure that we maintain strong competitive advantages that yield attractive profits? How can we tell when commoditization is going to occur, and what can we do to keep earning attractive returns?

- *Chapter 7:* What is the best organizational structure for this venture? What organizational unit(s) and which managers should contribute to and be responsible for its success?
- *Chapter 8:* How do we get the details of a winning strategy right? When is flexibility important, and when will flexibility cause us to fail?
- *Chapter 9:* Whose investment capital will help us succeed, and whose capital might be the kiss of death? What sources of money will help us most at different stages of our development?
- *Chapter 10:* What role should the CEO play in sustaining the growth of the business? When should CEOs keep their hands off the new business, and when should they become involved?

The issues that we tackle in these chapters are critical, but they cannot constitute an exhaustive list of the questions that should be relevant to launching a new-growth business. We can simply hope that we have addressed the most important ones, so that although we cannot make the creation of new-growth businesses perfectly risk free, we *can* help managers take major steps in that direction.

Notes

1. Although we have not performed a true meta-analysis, there are four recently published studies that seem to converge on this estimate that roughly one company in ten succeeds at sustaining growth. Chris Zook and James Allen found in their 2001 study *Profit from the Core* (Boston: Harvard Business School Press) that only 13 percent of their sample of 1,854 companies were able to grow consistently over a ten-year period. Richard Foster and Sarah Kaplan published a study that same year, *Creative Destruction* (New York: Currency/Doubleday), in which they followed 1,008 companies from 1962 to 1998. They learned that only 160, or about 16 percent of these firms, were able merely to survive this time frame, and concluded that the perennially outperforming company is a chimera, something that has never existed at all. Jim Collins also published his *Good to Great* (New York: HarperBusiness) in 2001, in which he examined a universe of 1,435 companies over thirty years (1965–1995). Collins found only 126, or about 9 percent, that had managed to outperform equity market averages for a decade or more. The Corporate Strategy Board's findings in *Stall Points*

(Washington, DC: Corporate Strategy Board, 1988), which are summarized in detail in the text, show that 5 percent of companies in the *Fortune* 50 successfully maintained their growth, and another 4 percent were able to reignite some degree of growth after they had stalled. The studies all support our assertion that a 10 percent probability of succeeding in a quest for sustained growth is, if anything, a generous estimate.

2. Because all of these transactions included stock, "true" measures of the value of the different deals are ambiguous. Although when a deal actually closes, a definitive value can be fixed, the implied value of the transaction at the time a deal is announced can be useful: It signals what the relevant parties were willing to pay and accept at a point in time. Stock price changes subsequent to the deal's announcement are often a function of other, exogenous events having little to do with the deal itself. Where possible, we have used the value of the deals at announcement, rather than upon closing. Sources of data on these various transactions include the following:

NCR

"Fatal Attraction (AT&T's Failed Merger with NCR)," *The Economist*, 23 March 1996.

"NCR Spinoff Completes AT&T Restructure Plan," *Bloomberg Business News*, 1 January 1997.

McCaw and AT&T Wireless Sale

The Wall Street Journal, 21 September 1994.

"AT&T Splits Off AT&T Wireless," AT&T news release, 9 July 2001.

AT&T, TCI, and MediaOne

"AT&T Plans Mailing to Sell TCI Customers Phone, Web Services," The *Wall Street Journal*, 10 March 1999.

"The AT&T-Mediaone Deal: What the FCC Missed," *Business Week*, 19 June 2000.

"AT&T Broadband to Merge with Comcast Corporation in $72 Billion Transaction," AT&T news release, 19 December 2001.

"Consumer Groups Still Questioning Comcast-AT&T Cable Merger," Associated Press Newswires, 21 October 2002.

3. Cabot's stock price outperformed the market between 1991 and 1995 as it refocused on its core business, for two reasons. On one side of the equation, demand for carbon black increased in Asia and North America as car sales surged, thereby increasing the demand for tires. On the supply side, two other American-based producers of carbon black exited the industry because

they were unwilling to make the requisite investment in environmental controls, thereby increasing Cabot's pricing power. Increased demand and reduced supply translated into a tremendous increase in the profitability of Cabot's traditional carbon black operations, which was reflected in the company's stock price. Between 1996 and 2000, however, its stock price deteriorated again, reflecting the dearth of growth prospects.

4. An important study of companies' tendency to make investments that fail to create growth was done by Professor Michael C. Jensen: "The Modern Industrial Revolution, Exit, and the Failure of Internal Control Systems," *Journal of Finance* (July 1993): 831–880. Professor Jensen also delivered this paper as his presidential address to the American Finance Association. Interestingly, many of the firms that Jensen cites as having productively reaped growth from their investments were disruptive innovators—a key concept in this book.

   Our unit of analysis in this book, as in Jensen's work, is the individual firm, not the larger system of growth creation made manifest in a free market, capitalist economy. Works such as Joseph Schumpeter's *Theory of Economic Development* (Cambridge, MA: Harvard University Press, 1934) and *Capitalism, Socialism, and Democracy* (New York: London, Harper & Brothers, 1942) are seminal, landmark works that address the environment in which firms function. Our assertion here is that whatever the track record of free market economies in generating growth at the macro level, the track record of individual firms is quite poor. It is the performance of firms within a competitive market to which we hope to contribute.

5. This simple story is complicated somewhat by the market's apparent incorporation of an expected "fade" in any company's growth rate. Empirical analysis suggests that the market does not expect any company to grow, or even survive, forever. It therefore seems to incorporate into current prices a foreseen decline in growth rates from current levels and the eventual dissolution of the firm. This is the reason for the importance of terminal values in most valuation models. This fade period is estimated using regression analysis, and estimates vary widely. So, strictly speaking, if a company is expected to grow at 5 percent with a fade period of forty years, and five years into that forty-year period it is still growing at 5 percent, the stock price would rise at rates that generated economic returns for shareholders, because the forty-year fade period would start over. However, because this qualification applies to companies growing at 5 percent as well as those growing at 25 percent, it does not change the point we wish to make; that is, that the market is a harsh taskmaster, and merely meeting expectations does not generate meaningful reward.

6. On average over their long histories, of course, faster-growing firms yield higher returns. However, the faster-growing firm will have produced higher

returns than the slower-growing firm only for investors in the past. If markets discount efficiently, then the investors who reap above-average returns are those who were fortunate enough to have bought shares in the past when the future growth rate had not been fully discounted into the price of the stock. Those who bought when the future growth potential already had been discounted into the share price would not receive an above-market return. An excellent reference for this argument can be found in Alfred Rappaport and Michael J. Mauboussin, *Expectations Investing: Reading Stock Prices for Better Returns* (Boston: Harvard Business School Press, 2001). Rappaport and Mauboussin guide investors in methods to detect when a market's expectations for a company's growth might be incorrect.

7. These were the closing market prices for these companies' common shares on August 21, 2002. There is no significance to that particular date: It is simply the time when the analysis was done. HOLT Associates, a unit of Credit Suisse First Boston (CSFB), performed these calculations using proprietary methodology applied to publicly available financial data. The percent future is a measure of how much a company's current stock price can be attributed to current cash flows and how much is due to investors' expectations of future growth and performance. As CSFB/HOLT defines it,

> *The percent future is the percentage of the total market value that the market assigns to the company's expected future investment. Percent future begins with the total market value (debt plus equity) less that portion attributed to the present value of existing assets and investments and divides this by the total market value of debt and equity.*

CSFB/Holt calculates the present value of existing assets as the present value of the cash flows associated with the assets' wind down and the release of the associated nondepreciating working capital. The HOLT CFROI valuation methodology includes a forty-year fade of returns equal to the total market's average returns.

Percent Future = [Total Debt and Equity (market) − Present Value Existing Assets]/[Total Debt and Equity (market)]

The companies listed in table 1-1 are not a sequential ranking of *Fortune* 500 companies, because some of the data required to perform these calculations were not available for some companies. The companies listed in this table were chosen only for illustrative purposes, and were not chosen in any way to suggest that any company's share price is likely to increase or decline. For more information on the methodology that HOLT used, see <http://www. holtvalue.com>.

8. See *Stall Points* (Washington, DC: Corporate Strategy Board, 1998).

9. In the text we have focused only on the pressure that equity markets impose on companies to grow, but there are many other sources of intense pressure. We'll mention just a couple here. First, when a company is growing, there are increased opportunities for employees to be promoted into new management positions that are opening up above them. Hence, the potential for growth in managerial responsibility and capability is much greater in a growing firm than in a stagnant one. When growth slows, managers sense that their possibilities for advancement will be constrained not by their personal talent and performance, but rather by how many years must pass before the more senior managers above them will retire. When this happens, many of the most capable employees tend to leave the company, affecting the company's abilities to regenerate growth.

Investment in new technologies also becomes difficult. When a growing firm runs out of capacity and must build a new plant or store, it is easy to employ the latest technology. When a company has stopped growing and has excess manufacturing capacity, proposals to invest in new technology typically do not fare well, since the full capital cost and the average manufacturing cost of producing with the new technology are compared against the marginal cost of producing in a fully depreciated plant. As a result, growing firms typically have a technology edge over slow-growth competitors. But that advantage is not rooted so much in the visionary wisdom of the managers as it is in the difference in the circumstances of growth versus no growth.

10. Detailed support for this estimate is provided in note 1.

11. For example, see James Brian Quinn, *Strategies for Change: Logical Incrementalism* (Homewood, IL: R.D. Irwin, 1980). Quinn suggests that the first step that corporate executives need to take in building new businesses is to "let a thousand flowers bloom," then tend the most promising and let the rest wither. In this view, the key to successful innovation lies in choosing the right flowers to tend—and that decision must rely on complex intuitive feelings, calibrated by experience.

More recent work by Tom Peters (*Thriving on Chaos: Handbook for a Management Revolution* [New York: Knopf/Random House, 1987]) urges innovating managers to "fail fast"—to pursue new business ideas on a small scale and in a way that generates quick feedback about whether an idea is viable. Advocates of this approach urge corporate executives not to punish failures because it is only through repeated attempts that successful new businesses will emerge.

Others draw on analogies with biological evolution, where mutations arise in what appear to be random ways. Evolutionary theory posits that whether a mutant organism thrives or dies depends on its fit with the "selection environment"—the conditions within which it must compete against other organisms for the resources required to thrive. Hence, believing that good and bad innovations pop up randomly, these researchers advise corporate executives to focus on creating a "selection environment" in which viable new business ideas are culled from the bad as quickly as possible. Gary Hamel, for example, advocates creating "Silicon Valley inside"—an environment in which existing structures are constantly dismantled, recombined in novel ways, and tested, in order to stumble over something that actually works. (See Gary Hamel, *Leading the Revolution* [Boston: Harvard Business School Press, 2001].)

We are not critical of these books. They can be very helpful, given the present state of understanding, because if the processes that create innovations were indeed random, then a context within which managers could accelerate the creation and testing of ideas would indeed help. But if the process is *not* intrinsically random, as we assert, then addressing only the context is treating the symptom, not the source of the problem.

To see why, consider the studies of 3M's celebrated ability to create a stream of growth-generating innovations. A persistent highlight of these studies is 3M's "15 percent rule": At 3M, many employees are given 15 percent of their time to devote to developing their own ideas for new-growth businesses. This "slack" in how people spend their time is supported by a broadly dispersed capital budget that employees can tap in order to fund their would-be growth engines on a trial basis.

But what guidance does this policy give to a bench engineer at 3M? She is given 15 percent "slack" time to dedicate to creating new-growth businesses. She is also told that whatever she comes up with will be subject first to internal market selection pressures, then external market selection pressures. All this is helpful information. But none of it helps that engineer create a new idea, or decide which of the several ideas she might create are worth pursuing further. This plight generalizes to managers and executives at all levels in an organization. From bench engineer to middle manager to business unit head to CEO, it is not enough to occupy oneself only with creating a context for innovation that sorts the fruits of that context. Ultimately, every manager must create something of substance, and the success of that creation lies in the decisions managers must make.

All of these approaches create an "infinite regress." By bringing the market "inside," we have simply backed up the problem: How can managers decide which ideas will be developed to the point at which they can be subjected to the selection pressures of their internal market? Bringing the market still deeper inside simply creates the same conundrum. Ultimately, innovators must judge what they will work on and how they will do it —and what they should consider when making those decisions is what is in the black box. The acceptance of randomness in innovation, then, is not a stepping-stone on the way to greater understanding; it is a barrier.

Dr. Gary Hamel was one of the first scholars of this problem to raise with Professor Christensen the possibility that the management of innovation actually has the potential to yield predictable results. We express our thanks to him for his helpful thoughts.

12. The scholars who introduced us to these forces are Professor Joseph Bower of the Harvard Business School and Professor Robert Burgelman of the Stanford Business School. We owe a deep intellectual debt to them. See Joseph L. Bower, *Managing the Resource Allocation Process* (Homewood, IL: Richard D. Irwin, 1970); Robert Burgelman and Leonard Sayles, *Inside Corporate Innovation* (New York: Free Press, 1986); and Robert Burgelman, *Strategy Is Destiny* (New York: Free Press, 2002).

13. Clayton M. Christensen and Scott D. Anthony, "What's the BIG Idea?" Case 9-602-105 (Boston: Harvard Business School, 2001).

14. We have consciously chosen phrases such as "increase the probability of success" because business building is unlikely ever to become perfectly predictable, for at least three reasons. The first lies in the nature of competitive marketplaces. Companies whose actions were perfectly predictable would be relatively easy to defeat. Every company therefore has an interest in behaving in deeply unpredictable ways. A second reason is the computational challenge associated with any system with a large number of possible outcomes. Chess, for example, is a fully determined game: After White's first move, Black should always simply resign. But the number of possible games is so great, and the computational challenge so overwhelming, that the outcomes of games even between supercomputers remain unpredictable. A third reason is suggested by complexity theory, which holds that even fully determined systems that do not outstrip our computational abilities can still generate deeply random outcomes. Assessing the extent to which the outcomes of innovation can be predicted, and the significance of any residual uncertainty or unpredictability, remains a profound theoretical challenge with important practical implications.

15. The challenge of improving predictability has been addressed somewhat successfully in certain of the natural sciences. Many fields of science appear today to be cut and dried—predictable, governed by clear laws of cause and effect, for example. But it was not always so: Many happenings in the natural world seemed very random and unfathomably complex to the ancients and to early scientists. Research that adhered carefully to the scientific

method brought the predictability upon which so much progress has been built. Even when our most advanced theories have convinced scientists that the world is not deterministic, at least the phenomena are predictably random.

Infectious diseases, for example, at one point just seemed to strike at random. People didn't understand what caused them. Who survived and who did not seemed unpredictable. Although the outcome seemed random, however, the process that led to the results was not random—it just was not sufficiently understood. With many cancers today, as in the venture capitalists' world, patients' probabilities for survival can only be articulated in percentages. This is not because the outcomes are unpredictable, however. We just do not yet understand the process.

16. Peter Senge calls theories *mental models* (see Peter Senge, *The Fifth Discipline* [New York: Bantam Doubleday Dell, 1990]). We considered using the term *model* in this book, but opted instead to use the term *theory*. We have done this to be provocative, to inspire practitioners to value something that is indeed of value.

17. A full description of the process of theory building and of the ways in which business writers and academics ignore and violate the fundamental principles of this process is available in a paper that is presently under review, "The Process of Theory Building," by Clayton Christensen, Paul Carlile, and David Sundahl. Paper or electronic copies are available from Professor Christensen's office, cchristensen@hbs.edu. The scholars we have relied upon in synthesizing the model of theory building presented in this paper (and only very briefly summarized in this book) are, in alphabetical order, E. H. Carr, *What Is History?* (New York: Vintage Books, 1961); K. M. Eisenhardt, "Building Theories from Case Study Research," *Academy of Management Review* 14, no. 4 (1989): 532–550; B. Glaser and A. Straus, *The Discovery of Grounded Theory: Strategies of Qualitative Research* (London: Wiedenfeld and Nicholson, 1967); A. Kaplan, *The Conduct of Inquiry: Methodology for Behavioral Research* (Scranton, PA: Chandler, 1964); R. Kaplan, "The Role for Empirical Research in Management Accounting," *Accounting, Organizations and Society* 4, no. 5 (1986): 429–452; T. Kuhn, *The Structure of Scientific Revolutions* (Chicago: University of Chicago Press, 1962); M. Poole and A. Van de Ven, "Using Paradox to Build Management and Organization Theories," *Academy of Management Review* 14, no. 4 (1989): 562–578; K. Popper, *The Logic of Scientific Discovery* (New York: Basic Books, 1959); F. Roethlisberger, *The Elusive Phenomena* (Boston: Harvard Business School Division of Research, 1977); Arthur Stinchcombe, "The Logic of Scientific Inference," chapter 2 in *Constructing Social Theories* (New York: Harcourt,

Brace & World, 1968); Andrew Van de Ven, "Professional Science for a Pro-
fessional School," in *Breaking the Code of Change,* eds. Michael Beer and
Nitin Nohria (Boston: Harvard Business School Press, 2000); Karl E. Weick,
"Theory Construction as Disciplined Imagination," *Academy of Manage-
ment Review* 14, no. 4, (1989): 516–531; and R. Yin, *Case Study Research*
(Beverly Hills, CA: Sage Publications, 1984).

18. What we are saying is that the success of a theory should be measured by the
accuracy with which it can predict outcomes across the entire range of situations in which managers find themselves. Consequently, we are not seeking
"truth" in any absolute, Platonic sense; our standard is practicality and usefulness. If we enable managers to achieve the results they seek, then we will
have been successful. Measuring the success of theories based on their usefulness is a respected tradition in the philosophy of science, articulated most
fully in the school of logical positivism. For example, see R. Carnap, *Empiricism, Semantics and Ontology* (Chicago: University of Chicago Press,
1956); W. V. O. Quine, *Two Dogmas of Empiricism* (Cambridge, MA: Harvard University Press, 1961); and W. V. O. Quine, *Epistemology Natural-
ized.* (New York: Columbia University Press, 1969).

19. This is a serious deficiency of much management research. Econometricians
call this practice "sampling on the dependent variable." Many writers, and
many who think of themselves as serious academics, are so eager to prove
the worth of their theories that they studiously avoid the discovery of anomalies. In case study research, this is done by carefully selecting examples that
support the theory. In more formal academic research, it is done by calling
points of data that don't fit the model "outliers" and finding a justification
for excluding them from the statistical analysis. Both practices seriously
limit the usefulness of what is written. It actually is the discovery of phenomena that the existing theory cannot explain that enables researchers to
build better theory that is built upon a better classification scheme. We need
to do *anomaly-seeking* research, not anomaly-avoiding research.

We have urged doctoral students who are seeking potentially productive
research questions for their thesis research to simply ask when a "fad" theory won't work—for example, "When is process reengineering a bad idea?"
Or, "Might you ever want to outsource something that *is* your core competence, and do internally something that is *not* your core competence?" Asking questions like this almost always improves the validity of the original
theory. This opportunity to improve our understanding often exists even for
very well done, highly regarded pieces of research. For example, an important conclusion in Jim Collins's extraordinary book *From Good to Great*
(New York: HarperBusiness, 2001) is that the executives of these successful

companies weren't charismatic, flashy men and women. They were humble people who respected the opinions of others. A good opportunity to extend the validity of Collins's research is to ask a question such as, "Are there circumstances in which you actually *don't* want a humble, noncharismatic CEO?" We suspect that there are—and defining the different circumstances in which charisma and humility are virtues and vices could do a great service to boards of directors.

20. We thank Matthew Christensen of the Boston Consulting Group for suggesting this illustration from the world of aviation as a way of explaining how getting the categories right is the foundation for bringing predictability to an endeavor. Note how important it was for researchers to discover the circumstances in which the mechanisms of lift and stabilization did *not* result in successful flight. It was the very search for failures that made success consistently possible. Unfortunately, many of those engaged in management research seem anxious *not* to spotlight instances their theory did not accurately predict. They engage in anomaly-avoiding, rather than anomaly-seeking, research and as a result contribute to the perpetuation of unpredictability. Hence, we lay much responsibility for the perceived unpredictability of business building at the feet of the very people whose business it is to study and write about these problems. We may, on occasion, succumb to the same problem. We can state that in developing and refining the theories summarized in this book, we have truly sought to discover exceptions or anomalies that the theory would not have predicted; in so doing, we have improved the theories considerably. But anomalies remain. Where we are aware of these, we have tried to note them in the text or notes of this book. If any of our readers are familiar with anomalies that these theories cannot yet explain, we invite them to teach us about them, so that together we can work to improve the predictability of business building further.

21. In studies of how companies deal with technological change, for example, early researchers suggested attribute-based categories such as incremental versus radical change and product versus process change. Each categorization supported a theory, based on correlation, about how entrant and established companies were likely to be affected by the change, and each represented an improvement in predictive power over earlier categorization schemes. At this stage of the process there rarely is a best-by-consensus theory, because there are so many attributes of the phenomena. Scholars of this process have broadly observed that this confusion is an important but unavoidable stage in building theory. See Thomas Kuhn, *The Structure of Scientific Revolutions* (Chicago: University of Chicago Press, 1962). Kuhn chronicles at length the energies expended by advocates of various competing theories at this stage, prior to the advent of a paradigm.

In addition, one of the most influential handbooks for management and social science research was written by Barney G. Glaser and Anselm L. Strauss (*The Discovery of Grounded Theory: Strategies of Qualitative Research* [London: Wiedenfeld and Nicholson, 1967]). Although they name their key concept "grounded theory," the book really is about categorization, because that process is so central to the building of valid theory. Their term "substantive theory" is similar to our term "attribute-based categories." They describe how a knowledge-building community of researchers ultimately succeeds in transforming their understanding into "formal theory," which we term "circumstance-based categories."

22. Clayton M. Christensen, *The Innovator's Dilemma: When New Technologies Cause Great Firms to Fail* (Boston: Harvard Business School Press, 1997).

23. Managers need to know if a theory applies in their situation, if they are to trust it. A very useful book on this topic is Robert K. Yin's *Case Study Research: Design and Methods* (Beverly Hills, CA: Sage Publications, 1984). Building on Yin's concept, we would say that the breadth of applicability of a theory, which Yin calls its *external validity,* is established by the soundness of its categorization scheme. There is no other way to gauge where theory applies and where it does not. To see why, consider the disruptive innovation model that emerged from the study of the disk drive industry in the early chapters of *The Innovator's Dilemma*. The concern that readers of the disk drive study raised, of course, was whether the theory applied to other industries as well. *The Innovator's Dilemma* tried to address these concerns by showing how the same theory that explained who succeeded and failed in disk drives also explained what happened in mechanical excavators, steel, retailing, motorcycles, accounting software, motor controls, diabetes care, and computers. The variety was chosen to establish the breadth of the theory's applicability. But this didn't put concerns to rest. Readers continued to ask whether the theory applied to chemicals, to database software, and so on.

Applying any theory to industry after industry cannot prove its applicability because it will always leave managers wondering if there is something different about their current circumstances that renders the theory untrustworthy. A theory can confidently be employed in prediction only when the categories that define its contingencies are clear. Some academic researchers, in a well-intentioned effort not to overstep the validity of what they can defensibly claim and not claim, go to great pains to articulate the "boundary conditions" within which their findings can be trusted. This is all well and good. But unless they concern themselves with defining what the other circumstances are that lie beyond the "boundary conditions" of their own study, they circumscribe what they can contribute to a body of useful theory.

24. An illustration of how important it is to get the categories right can be seen in the fascinating juxtaposition of two recent, solidly researched books by very smart students of management and competition that make compelling cases for diametrically opposite solutions to a problem. Each team of researchers addresses the same underlying problem—the challenge of delivering persistent, profitable growth. In *Creative Destruction* (New York: Currency/Doubleday, 2001), Richard Foster and Sarah Kaplan argue that if firms hope to create wealth sustainably and at a rate comparable to the broader market, they must be willing to explore radically new business models and visit upon themselves the tumult that characterizes the capital markets. At the same time, another well-executed study, *Profit from the Core* (Boston: Harvard Business School Press, 2001), by Bain consultants Chris Zook and James Allen, drew upon the same phenomenological evidence—that only a tiny minority of companies are able to sustain above-market returns for a significant time. But *their* book encourages companies to focus on and improve their established businesses rather than attempt to anticipate or even respond to the vagaries of equity investors by seeking to create new growth in less-related markets. Whereas Foster and Kaplan motivate their findings in terms of the historical suitability of incrementalism in a context of competitive continuity and argue for more radical change in light of today's exigencies, Zook and Allen hold that focus is timeless and remains the key to success. Their prescriptions are mutually exclusive. Whose advice should we follow? At present, managers grappling with their own growth problems have no choice but to pick a camp based on the reputations of the authors and the endorsements on the dust jacket. The answer is that there is a great opportunity for circumstance-focused researchers to build on the valuable groundwork that both sets of authors have established. The question that now needs answering is: What are the circumstances in which focusing on or near the core will yield sustained profit and growth, and what are the circumstances in which broader, Fosteresque creative destruction is the approach that will succeed?

CHAPTER TWO

HOW CAN WE BEAT OUR MOST POWERFUL COMPETITORS?

How can we know in advance of the battle whether we're going to be able to beat the competition? Why has disruption proven to be such a consistently effective strategy for causing strong incumbent competitors to flee from their entrant attackers, rather than fight them? How can we shape our business idea into one of these disruptive strategies? Can we really predict the winners in a race for innovative growth? What if we could choose our competitive battles knowing we could win nearly every time? What if we knew in advance which growth strategies would succeed, and which would fail?

Managers have long sought ways to predict the outcome of competitive fights. Some have looked at the attributes of the companies involved, predicting that larger companies with more resources to throw at a problem will beat the smaller competitors. It's interesting how often the CEOs of large, resource-rich companies base their strategies upon this theory, despite repeated evidence that the level of resources committed often bears little relationship to the outcome.

Others have considered the attributes of the change: When innovations are incremental, the established, leading firms in an industry are likely to reinforce their dominance; however, compared with entrants, they will be conservative and ineffective in exploiting breakthrough innovation.[1] We noted in the introduction that predictions based on attribute-based categories, as these are, prove frustratingly undependable.

Our ongoing study of innovation suggests another way to understand when incumbents will win, and when the entrants are likely to beat them. *The Innovator's Dilemma* identified two distinct categories—sustaining and disruptive—based on the *circumstances* of innovation. In *sustaining circumstances*—when the race entails making better products that can be sold for more money to attractive customers—we found that incumbents almost always prevail. In *disruptive circumstances*—when the challenge is to commercialize a simpler, more convenient product that sells for less money and appeals to a new or unattractive customer set—the entrants are likely to beat the incumbents. This is the phenomenon that so frequently defeats successful companies. It implies, of course, that the best way for upstarts to attack established competitors is to disrupt them.

Few technologies or business ideas are intrinsically sustaining or disruptive in character. Rather, their disruptive impact must be molded into strategy as managers shape the idea into a plan and then implement it. Successful new-growth builders know—either intuitively or explicitly—that disruptive strategies greatly increase the odds of competitive success.

This chapter's purpose is to review the disruptive innovation model from the perspective of both the disruptee *and* the disruptor in order to help growth builders shape their strategies so that they pick disruptive fights they can win. Because disruption happens whether we want it or not, this chapter will also help managers of established companies capture disruptive growth, instead of seeing their companies get killed by it.

The Disruptive Innovation Model

The Innovator's Dilemma identified three critical elements of disruption, as depicted in figure 2-1. First, in every market there is a rate of improvement that customers can utilize or absorb, represented by the dotted line sloping gently upward across the chart. For example, the automobile companies keep giving us new and improved engines, but we can't utilize all the performance that they make available under

FIGURE 2-1

The Disruptive Innovation Model

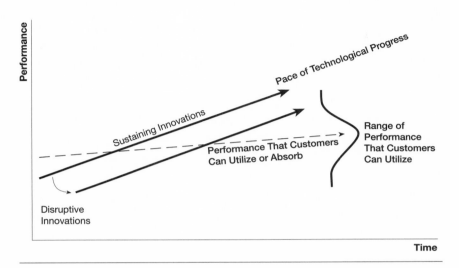

the hood. Factors such as traffic jams, speed limits, and safety concerns constrain how much performance we can use.

To simplify the chart, we depict customers' ability to utilize improvement as a single line. In reality, there is a distribution of customers around this median: There are many such lines, or tiers, in a market—a range indicated by the distribution curve at the right. Customers in the highest or most demanding tiers may never be satisfied with the best that is available, and those in the lowest or least demanding tiers can be oversatisfied with very little.[2] This dotted line represents technology that is "good enough" to serve customers' needs.

Second, in every market there is a distinctly different trajectory of improvement that innovating companies provide as they introduce new and improved products. This pace of technological progress almost always outstrips the ability of customers in any given tier of the market to use it, as the more steeply sloping solid lines in figure 2-1 suggest. Thus, a company whose products are squarely positioned on mainstream customers' current needs today will probably overshoot what those same customers are able to utilize in the future. This happens because companies keep striving to make better products that they can sell for higher profit margins to not-yet-satisfied customers in more demanding tiers of the market.

To visualize this, think back to 1983 when people first started using personal computers for word processing. Typists often had to stop their fingers to let the Intel 286 chip inside catch up. As depicted at the left side of figure 2-1, the technology was not good enough. But today's processors offer much more speed than mainstream customers can use—although there are still a few unsatisfied customers in the most demanding tiers of the market who need even faster chips.

The third critical element of the model is the distinction between sustaining and disruptive innovation. A *sustaining innovation* targets demanding, high-end customers with better performance than what was previously available. Some sustaining innovations are the incremental year-by-year improvements that all good companies grind out. Other sustaining innovations are breakthrough, leapfrog-beyond-the-competition products. It doesn't matter how technologically difficult the innovation is, however: The established competitors almost always win the battles of sustaining technology. Because this strategy entails making a better product that they can sell for higher profit margins to their best customers, the established competitors have powerful motivations to fight sustaining battles. And they have the resources to win.

Disruptive innovations, in contrast, don't attempt to bring better products to established customers in existing markets. Rather, they disrupt and redefine that trajectory by introducing products and services that are not as good as currently available products. But disruptive technologies offer other benefits—typically, they are simpler, more convenient, and less expensive products that appeal to new or less-demanding customers.[3]

Once the disruptive product gains a foothold in new or low-end markets, the improvement cycle begins. And because the pace of technological progress outstrips customers' abilities to use it, the previously not-good-enough technology eventually improves enough to intersect with the needs of more demanding customers. When that happens, the disruptors are on a path that will ultimately crush the incumbents. This distinction is important for innovators seeking to create new-growth businesses. Whereas the current leaders of the industry almost always triumph in battles of sustaining innovation, successful disruptions have been launched most often by entrant companies.[4]

Disruption has a paralyzing effect on industry leaders. With resource allocation processes designed and perfected to support sustaining innovations, they are constitutionally unable to respond. They are always motivated to go up-market, and almost never motivated to defend the new or low-end markets that the disruptors find attractive. We call this phenomenon *asymmetric motivation*. It is the core of the innovator's dilemma, and the beginning of the innovator's solution.

Disruption at Work: How Minimills Upended Integrated Steel Companies

The disruption of integrated steel mills by minimills, whose history was partially reviewed in *The Innovator's Dilemma*, offers a classic example of why established leaders are so much easier to beat if the idea for a new product or business is shaped into a disruption.

Historically, most of the world's steel has come from massive integrated mills that do everything from reacting iron ore, coke, and limestone in blast furnaces to rolling finished products at the other end. It costs about $8 billion to build a huge new integrated mill today. Minimills, in contrast, melt scrap steel in electric arc furnaces—cylinders that are approximately twenty meters in diameter and ten meters tall. Because they can produce molten steel cost-effectively in such a small chamber, minimills don't need the massive-scale rolling and finishing operations that are required to handle the output of efficient blast furnaces—which is why they are called *minimills*. Most important, though, minimills' straightforward technology can make steel of any given quality for 20 percent lower cost than an integrated mill.

Steel is a commodity. You would think that every integrated steel company in the world would have aggressively adopted the straightforward, lower-cost minimill technology. Yet as of 2000 not a single integrated steel company had successfully invested in a minimill, even as the minimills had grown to account for nearly half of North America's steel production and a significant share of other markets as well.[5]

We can explain why something that makes so much sense has been so difficult for the integrated mills. Minimills first became technologically viable in the mid-1960s. Because they melt scrap of uncertain and varying chemistry in their electric arc furnaces, the quality of the steel that minimills initially could produce was poor. In fact, the only market that would accept the output of minimills was the concrete reinforcing bar (rebar) market. The specifications for rebar are loose, so this was an ideal market for products of low and variable quality.

As the minimills attacked the rebar market, the integrated mills were happy to be rid of that dog-eat-dog commodity business. Because of the differences in their cost structures and the opportunities for investment that they each faced, the rebar market looked very different to the disruptee and the disruptor. For integrated producers, gross profit margins on rebar often hovered near 7 percent, and the entire product category accounted for only 4 percent of the industry's tonnage. It was the least attractive of any tier of the market in which they might invest to grow. So as the minimills established a foothold in the rebar market, the integrated mills reconfigured their rebar lines to make more profitable products.

In contrast, with a 20 percent cost advantage, the minimills enjoyed attractive profits in competition against the integrated mills for rebar—until 1979, when the minimills finally succeeded in driving the last integrated mill out of the rebar market. Historical pricing statistics show that the price of rebar then collapsed by 20 percent. As long as the minimills could compete against higher-cost integrated mills, the game was profitable for them. But as soon as low-cost minimill was pitted against low-cost minimill in a commodity market, the reward for victory was that none of them could earn attractive profits in rebar.[6] Worse, as they all sought profitability by becoming more efficient producers, they discovered that cost reductions meant survival, but not profitability, in a commodity such as rebar.[7]

Soon, however, the minimills looked up-market, and what they saw there spelled relief. If they could just figure out how to make bigger and better steel—shapes like angle iron and thicker bars and rods—they could roll *tons* of money, because in that tier of the market, as suggested in figure 2-2, the integrated mills were earning gross margins of about 12 percent—nearly double the margins that they had been able to earn in rebar. That market was also twice as big as the rebar segment, accounting for about 8 percent of industry tonnage. As the minimills figured out how to make bigger and better steel and attacked that tier of the market, the integrated mills were almost relieved to be rid of the bar and rod business as well. It was a dog-eat-dog commodity compared with their higher-margin products, whereas for the minimills, it was an attractive opportunity compared with their lower-margin rebar. So as the minimills expanded their capacity to make angle iron and thicker bars and rods, the integrated mills shut their lines down or reconfigured them to make more profitable products. With a 20 percent cost advantage, the minimills enjoyed significant profits in competition against the integrated mills until 1984, when they finally succeeded in driving the last integrated mill out of the bar and rod market. Once again, the minimills reaped their reward: With low-cost minimill pitted against low-cost minimill, the price of bar and rod collapsed by 20 percent, and they could no longer earn attractive profits. What could they do?

FIGURE 2-2

The Up-Market Migration of Steel Minimills

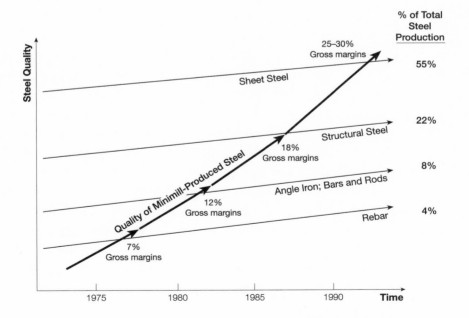

Source: American Iron and Steel Institute; interviews with company executives. Note that the tonnage percentages do not sum to 100 percent because there are other specialty categories of steel.

Continued up-market movement into structural beams appeared to be the next obvious answer. Gross margins in that sector were a whopping 18 percent, and the market was three times as large as the bar and rod business. Most industry technologists thought minimills would be unable to roll structural beams. Many of the properties required to meet the specifications for steel used in building and bridge construction were imparted to the steel in the rolling processes of big integrated mills, and you just couldn't get those properties in minimills' abbreviated facilities. What the technical experts didn't count on, however, was how desperately motivated the minimills would be to solve that problem, because it was the only way they could make attractive money. Minimills achieved extraordinarily clever innovations as they stretched from angle iron to I-beams—things such as Chaparral Steel's dog-bone mold in its continuous caster, which no one had imagined could be done. Although you could never have predicted what the technical solution would be, you *could* predict with perfect certainty that the minimills were powerfully motivated to figure it out. Necessity remains the mother of invention.

At the beginning of their invasion into structural beams, the biggest that the minimills could roll were little six-inch beams of the sort that undergird mobile homes. They attacked the low end of the structural beam market, and again the integrated mills were almost relieved to be rid of it. It was a dog-eat-dog commodity compared with their other higher-margin products where focused investment might bring more attractive volume. To the minimills, in contrast, it was an attractive product compared with the margins they were earning on rebar and angle iron. So as the minimills expanded their capacity to roll structural beams, the integrated mills shut their structural beam mills down in order to focus on more profitable sheet steel products. With a 20 percent cost advantage, the minimills enjoyed significant profits as long as they could compete against the integrated mills. Then in the mid-1990s, when they finally succeeded in driving the last integrated mill out of the structural beam market, pricing again collapsed. Once again, the reward for victory was the end of profit.

The sequence repeated itself when the leading minimill, Nucor, attacked the sheet steel business. Its market capitalization now dwarfs that of the largest integrated steel company, US Steel. Bethlehem Steel is bankrupt at the time of this writing.

This is not a history of bungled steel company management. It is a story of rational managers facing the innovator's dilemma: Should we invest to protect the least profitable end of our business, so that we can retain our least loyal, most price-sensitive customers? Or should we invest to strengthen our position in the most profitable tiers of our business, with customers who reward us with premium prices for better products?

The executives who confront this dilemma come in all varieties: timid, feisty, analytical, and action-driven. In an unstructured world their actions might be unpredictable. But as large industry incumbents, they encounter powerful and predictable forces that motivate them to flee rather than fight when attacked from below. That is why shaping a business idea into a disruption is an effective strategy for beating an established competitor. Disruption works because it is *much* easier to beat competitors when they are motivated to flee rather than fight.

The forces that propel well-managed companies up-market are *always* at work, in every company in every industry. Whether or not entrant firms have disrupted the established leaders yet, the forces are at work, leading predictably in one direction. It is not just a phenomenon of "technology companies" such as those involved in microelectronics, software, photonics, or biochemistry. Indeed, when we use the term *technology* in this book, it means the process that any company uses to convert inputs of labor, materials, capital, energy, and information into outputs of greater value. For the purpose of predictably creating growth, treating "high tech" as different from "low tech" is not the right way to categorize the world. Every company has technology, and each is subject to these fundamental forces.

The Role of Sustaining Innovation in Generating Growth

We must emphasize that we do *not* argue against the aggressive pursuit of sustaining innovation. Several other insightful books offer management techniques to help companies excel in sustaining innovations—and their contribution is important.[8] Almost always a host of similar companies enters an industry in its early years, and getting ahead of that crowd—moving up the sustaining-innovation trajectory more decisively than the others—is critical to the successful *exploitation* of the disruptive opportunity. But this is the source of the dilemma: Sustaining innovations are so important and attractive, relative to disruptive ones, that the very best sustaining companies systematically ignore disruptive threats and opportunities until the game is over.

Sustaining innovation essentially entails making a better mouse-trap. Starting a new company with a sustaining innovation isn't necessarily a bad idea: Focused companies sometimes can develop new products more rapidly than larger firms because of the conflicts and distractions that broad scope often creates. The theory of disruption suggests, however, that once they have developed and established the viability of their superior product, entrepreneurs who have entered on a sustaining trajectory should turn around and sell out to one of the industry leaders behind them. If executed successfully, getting ahead of the leaders on the sustaining curve and then selling out quickly can be a straightforward way to make an attractive financial return. This is common practice in the health care industry, and was the well-chronicled mechanism by which Cisco Systems "outsourced" (and financed with equity capital, rather than expense money) much of its sustaining-product development in the 1990s.

A sustaining-technology strategy is *not* a viable way to build new-growth businesses, however. If you create and attempt to sell a better product into an established market to capture established competitors' best customers, the competitors will be motivated to fight rather than to flee.[9] This advice holds even when the entrant is a huge corporation with ostensibly deeper pockets than the incumbent.

For example, electronic cash registers were a radical but sustaining innovation relative to electromechanical cash registers, whose market was dominated by National Cash Register (NCR). NCR *totally* missed the advent of the new technology in the 1970s—so badly, in fact, that NCR's product sales literally went to zero. Electronic registers were so superior that there was no reason to buy an electromechanical product except as an antique. Yet NCR survived on service revenues for over a year, and when it finally introduced its own electronic cash register, its extensive sales organization quickly captured the same share of the market as the company had enjoyed in the electro-mechanical realm.[10] The attempts that IBM and Kodak made in the 1970s and 1980s to beat Xerox in the high-speed photocopier business are another example. These companies were *far* bigger, and yet they failed to outmuscle Xerox in a sustaining-technology competition. The firm that beat Xerox was Canon—and that victory started with a disruptive tabletop copier strategy.

Similarly, corporate giants RCA, General Electric, and AT&T failed to outmuscle IBM on the sustaining-technology trajectory in mainframe computers. Despite the massive resources they threw at IBM, they couldn't make a dent in IBM's position. In the end, it was the disruptive personal computer makers, not the major corporations who picked a direct, sustaining-innovation fight, who bested IBM in computers. Airbus entered the commercial airframe industry head-on against Boeing, but doing so required massive subsidies from European governments. In the future, the most profitable growth in the airframe industry will probably come from firms with disruptive strategies, such as Embraer and Bombardier's Canadair, whose regional jets are aggressively stretching up-market from below.[11]

Disruption Is a *Relative* Term

An idea that is disruptive to one business may be sustaining to another. Given the stark odds that favor the incumbents in the sustaining race but entrants in disruptive ones, we recommend a strict rule: If your idea for a product or business appears disruptive to some established companies but might represent a *sustaining* improvement for others, then you should go back to the drawing board. You need to define an opportunity that is disruptive relative to *all* the established players in the targeted market, or you should not invest in the idea. If it is a sustaining innovation relative to the business model of a significant incumbent, you are picking a fight you are very unlikely to win.

Take the Internet, for example. Throughout the late 1990s, investors poured billions into Internet-based companies, convinced of their "disruptive" potential. An important reason why many of them failed was that the Internet was a sustaining innovation relative to the business models of a host of companies. Prior to the advent of the Internet, Dell Computer, for example, sold computers directly to customers by mail and over the telephone. This business was already a low-end disruptor, moving up its trajectory. Dell's banks of telephone salespeople had to be highly trained in order to walk their customers through the various configurations of components that were and were not feasible. They then manually entered the information into Dell's order fulfillment systems.

For Dell, the Internet was a sustaining technology. It made Dell's core business processes work better, and it helped Dell make more money in the way it was structured to make money. But the identical strategy of selling directly to customers over the Internet was very disruptive relative to Compaq's business model, because that company's cost structure and business processes were targeted at in-store retail distribution.

The theory of disruption would conclude that if Dell (and Gateway) had not existed, then start-up Internet-based computer retailers might have succeeded in disrupting competitors such as Compaq. But because the Internet was sustaining to powerful incumbents, entrant Internet computer retailers have not prospered.

A Disruptive Business Model Is a Valuable Corporate Asset

A disruptive business model that can generate attractive profits at the discount prices required to win business at the low end is an extraordinarily valuable growth asset. When its executives carry the business model up-market to make higher-performance products that sell at higher price points, much of the increment in pricing falls to the bottom line—and it continues to fall there as long as the disruptor can keep moving up, competing at the margin against the higher-cost disruptee. When a company tries to take a higher-cost business model down-market to sell products at lower price points, almost none of the incremental revenue will fall to its bottom line. It gets absorbed into overheads. This is why, as we discuss in chapter 7, established firms that hope to capture the growth created by disruption need to do so from within an autonomous business with a cost structure that offers as much headroom as possible for subsequent profitable migration up-market.

Moving up the trajectory into successively higher-margin tiers of the market and shedding less-profitable products at the low end is something that all good managers must do in order to keep their margins strong and their stock price healthy. Standing still is not an option, because firms that stop moving up find themselves in a rebaresque situation, slugging it out with hard-to-differentiate products against competitors whose costs are comparable.[12]

This ultimately means that in doing what they must do, every company prepares the way for its own disruption. This is the innovator's dilemma. But it also is the beginning of the innovator's solution. Disruption does not guarantee success, but it sure helps: *The Innovator's Dilemma* showed that following a strategy of disruption increased the odds of creating a successful growth business from 6 percent to 37 percent.[13] Because the established company's course of action is mandated so clearly, it is also clear what executives who seek to create new-growth businesses should do: Target products and markets that the established companies are motivated to ignore or run away from. Many of the most profitable growth trajectories in history have been initiated by disruptive innovations.

Two Types of Disruption

For the sake of simplicity, *The Innovator's Dilemma* presented the disruptive innovation diagram in only two dimensions. In reality, there are two different types of disruptions, which can best be visualized by adding a third axis to the disruption diagram, as shown in figure 2-3. The vertical and horizontal axes are as before: the performance of the product on the vertical axis, with time plotted on the horizontal dimension. The third axis represents new customers and new contexts for consumption.

Our original dimensions—time and performance—define a particular market application in which customers purchase and use a product or service. In geometric terms, this application and set of customers reside in a plane of competition and consumption, which

FIGURE 2-3

The Third Dimension of the Disruptive Innovation Model

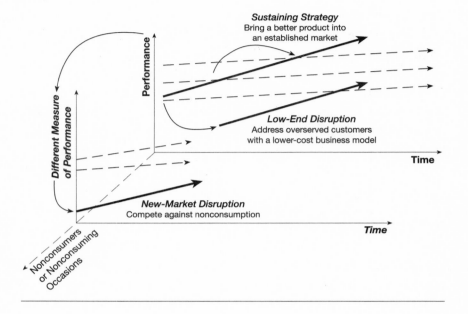

The *Innovator's Dilemma* called a *value network*. A value network is the context within which a firm establishes a cost structure and operating processes and works with suppliers and channel partners in order to respond profitably to the common needs of a class of customers. Within a value network, each firm's competitive strategy, and particularly its cost structure and its choices of markets and customers to serve, determines its perceptions of the economic value of an innovation. These perceptions, in turn, shape the rewards and threats that firms expect to experience through disruptive versus sustaining innovations.[14]

The third dimension that extends toward us in the diagram represents new contexts of consumption and competition, which are new value networks. These constitute either new customers who previously lacked the money or skills to buy and use the product, or different situations in which a product can be used—enabled by improvements in simplicity, portability, and product cost. For each of these new value networks, a vertical axis can be drawn representing a product's performance as it is defined in that context (which is a different measure from what is valued in the original value network).

Different value networks can emerge at differing distances from the original one along the third dimension of the disruption diagram. In the following discussion, we will refer to disruptions that create a new value network on the third axis as *new-market disruptions*. In contrast, *low-end disruptions* are those that attack the least-profitable and most overserved customers at the low end of the original value network.

New-Market Disruptions

We say that new-market disruptions compete with "nonconsumption" because new-market disruptive products are so much more affordable to own and simpler to use that they enable a whole new population of people to begin owning and using the product, and to do so in a more convenient setting. The personal computer and Sony's first battery-powered transistor pocket radio were new-market disruptions, in that their initial customers were new consumers—they had not owned or used the prior generation of products and services. Canon's desktop photocopiers were also a new-market disruption, in that they enabled people to begin conveniently making their own photocopies around the corner from their offices, rather than taking their originals to the corporate high-speed photocopy center where a technician had to run the job for them. When Canon made photocopying so convenient, people ended up making *a lot* more copies. New-market disruptors' challenge is to create a new value network, where it is nonconsumption, not the incumbent, that must be overcome.

Although new-market disruptions initially compete against nonconsumption in their unique value network, as their performance improves they ultimately become good enough to pull customers out of the original value network into the new one, starting with the least-demanding tier. The disruptive innovation doesn't invade the mainstream market; rather, it pulls customers out of the mainstream value network into the new one because these customers find it more convenient to use the new product.

Because new-market disruptions compete against nonconsumption, the incumbent leaders feel no pain and little threat until the disruption is in its final stages. In fact, when the disruptors begin pulling customers out of the low end of the original value network, it actually feels good to the leading firms, because as they move up-market in their own world, for a time they are replacing the low-margin revenues that disruptors steal, with higher-margin revenues from sustaining innovations.[15]

Low-End Disruptions

We call disruptions that take root at the low end of the original or mainstream value network *low-end* disruptions. Disruptions such as steel minimills, discount retailing, and the Korean automakers' entry into the North American market have been pure low-end disruptions in that they did not create new markets—they were simply low-cost business models that grew by picking off the least attractive of the established firms' customers. Although they are different, new-market and low-end disruptions both create the same vexing dilemma for incumbents. New-market disruptions induce incumbents to ignore the attackers, and low-end disruptions motivate the incumbents to flee the attack.

Low-end disruption has occurred several times in retailing.[16] For example, full-service department stores had a business model that enabled them to turn inventories three times per year. They needed to earn 40 percent gross margins to make money within their cost structure. They therefore earned 40 percent three times each year, for a 120 percent annual return on capital invested in inventory (ROCII). In the 1960s, discount retailers such as Wal-Mart and Kmart attacked the low end of the department stores' market—nationally branded hard goods such as paint, hardware, kitchen utensils, toys, and sporting goods—that were so familiar in use that they could sell themselves. Customers in this tier of the market were overserved by department stores, in that they did not need well-trained floor salespeople to help them get what they needed. The discounters' business model enabled them to make money at gross margins of about 23 percent, on average. Their stocking policies and operating processes enabled them to turn inventories more than five times annually, so that they also earned about 120 percent annual ROCII. The discounters did not accept lower levels of profitability—their business model simply earned acceptable profit through a different formula.[17]

It is very hard for established firms *not* to flee from a low-end disruptor. Consider, for example, the choice that executives of full-service department stores had to make when the discount retailers were attacking the branded hard goods at the low end of department stores' merchandise mix. Retailers' critical resource allocation decision is the use of floor or shelf space. One option for department store executives was to allocate more space to even higher-margin cosmetics and high-fashion apparel, where gross margins often exceeded 50 percent. Because their business model turned inventories three times annually, this option promised 150 percent ROCII.

The alternative was to defend the branded hard goods businesses, which the discounters were attacking with prices 20 percent below those of department stores. Competing against the discounters at those levels would send margins plummeting to 20 percent, which, given the three-times inventory turns that were on average inherent in their business model, entailed a ROCII of 60 percent. It thus made perfect sense for the full-service department stores to flee—to get out of the very tiers of the market that the discounters were motivated to enter.[18]

Many disruptions are hybrids, combining new-market and low-end approaches, as depicted by the continuum of the third axis in figure 2-3. Southwest Airlines is actually a hybrid disruptor, for example. It initially targeted customers who weren't flying—people who previously had used cars and buses. But Southwest pulled customers out of the low end of the major airlines' value network as well. Charles Schwab is a hybrid disruptor. It stole some customers from full-service brokers with its discounted trading fees, but it also created new markets by enabling people who historically were not equity investors—such as students—to begin owning and trading stocks.[19]

Figure 2-4 shows where some of history's more successful disruptors were positioned along the continuum of new-market to low-end disruption at their inception. The appendix to this chapter offers a brief historical explanation of each of the disruptive products or companies listed on the chart. This is not a complete census of disruptive companies, of course, and their position on the chart is only approximate. However, the array does convey our sense that disruption is a primary wellspring of growth. The prevalence of Japanese companies such as Sony, Nippon Steel, Toyota, Honda, and Canon in the period between 1960 and 1980 and the absence of disruptive Japanese companies in the 1990s, for example, explain a lot about why Japan's economy has stagnated. Many of its most influential companies grew dramatically by disrupting others; but the structure of Japan's economic system inhibits the creation of new waves of disruptive growth, in part because they might threaten those companies today.[20]

The chart also shows that disruption is an ongoing force that is always at work—meaning that disruptors in one generation become

FIGURE 2-4

Examples of Companies and Products Whose Roots Were in Disruption

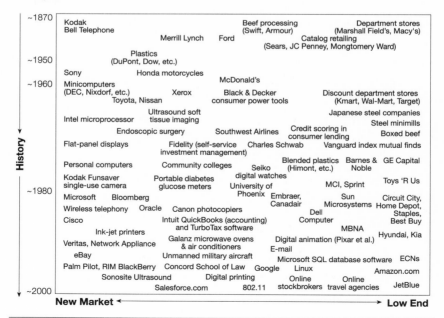

disruptees later. The Ford Model T, for example, created the first massive wave of disruptive growth in automobiles. Toyota, Nissan, and Honda then created the next wave, and Korean automakers Hyundai and Kia have now begun the third. AT&T's wireline long distance business, which disrupted Western Union, is being disrupted by wireless long distance. Plastics makers such as Dow, DuPont, and General Electric continue to disrupt steel, even as their low end is being eaten away by suppliers of blended polyolefin plastics such as Himont.

Shaping Ideas to Become Disruptive: Three Litmus Tests

At the beginning of this chapter, we mentioned that few technologies or product ideas are inherently sustaining or disruptive when they emerge from the innovator's mind. Instead, they go through a process of becoming fleshed out and shaped into a strategic plan in order to win funding. Many—but not all—of the initial ideas that get shaped into sustaining innovations could just as readily be shaped into disruptive business plans with far greater growth potential. The shaping process must be consciously managed, however, and not left to the dispersed and instinctive decisions of those who write business plans.

Executives must answer three sets of questions to determine whether an idea has disruptive potential. The first set explores whether the idea can become a new-market disruption. For this to happen, at least one and generally both of two questions must be answered affirmatively:

- Is there a large population of people who historically have not had the money, equipment, or skill to do this thing for themselves, and as a result have gone without it altogether or have needed to pay someone with more expertise to do it for them?
- To use the product or service, do customers need to go to an inconvenient, centralized location?

If the technology can be developed so that a large population of less skilled or less affluent people can begin owning and using, in a more convenient context, something that historically was available only to more skilled or more affluent people in a centralized, inconvenient location, then there is potential for shaping the idea into a new-market disruption.

The second set of questions explores the potential for a low-end disruption. This is possible if these two questions can be answered affirmatively:

- Are there customers at the low end of the market who would be happy to purchase a product with less (but good enough) performance if they could get it at a lower price?
- Can we create a business model that enables us to earn attractive profits at the discount prices required to win the business of these overserved customers at the low end?

Often, the innovations that enable low-end disruption are improvements that reduce overhead costs, enabling a company to earn attractive returns on lower gross margins, coupled with improvements in manufacturing or business processes that turn assets faster.

Once an innovation passes the new-market or low-end test, there is still a third critical question, or litmus test, to answer affirmatively:

- Is the innovation disruptive to *all* of the significant incumbent firms in the industry? If it appears to be sustaining to one or more significant players in the industry, then the odds will be stacked in that firm's favor, and the entrant is unlikely to win.

If an idea fails the litmus tests, then it cannot be shaped into a disruption. It may have promise as a sustaining technology, but in that case we would expect that it could not constitute the basis of a new-growth business for an entrant company.

For summary, table 2-1 summarizes and contrasts the characteristics of the three strategies that firms might pursue in creating new-growth businesses: sustaining innovations, low-end disruptions, and new-market disruptions. It compares the targeted product performance or features, the targeted customers or markets, and the business model implications that each route entails. We hope that managers can use this as a template so that they can categorize and see the implications of different plans that might be presented to them for approval.

TABLE 2-1

Three Approaches to Creating New-Growth Businesses

Dimension	Sustaining Innovations	Low-End Disruptions	New-Market Disruptions
Targeted performance of the product or service	Performance improvement *in attributes most valued by the industry's most demanding customers.* These improvements may be incremental or breakthrough in character.	Performance that is good enough along the traditional metrics of perform-ance at the low end of the mainstream market.	Lower performance in "traditional" attributes, but *improved performance in new attributes—typically simplicity and convenience.*
Targeted customers or market application	The *most attractive (i.e., profitable) customers* in the mainstream markets who are willing to pay for improved performance.	*Overserved customers* in the low end of the mainstream market.	Targets *non-consumption:* customers who historically lacked the money or skill to buy and use the product.
Impact on the required business model (processes and cost structure)	Improves or maintains profit margins by exploiting the *existing processes and cost structure* and making better use of current competitive advantages.	Utilizes a *new operating or financial approach or both*—a different combination of lower gross profit margins and higher asset utilization that can earn attractive returns at the discount prices required to win business at the low end of the market.	Business model must make money at lower price per unit sold, and at unit production volumes that initially will be small. Gross margin dollars per unit sold will be signifi-cantly lower.

Executives can use this categorization and the litmus tests to fore-see the competitive consequences of alternative strategies as they shape an idea. To illustrate, we'll examine three questions: whether Xerox could disrupt Hewlett-Packard's ink-jet printing business, how to create growth in air conditioning, and whether online banking had (or has) the potential to create a disruptive new-growth business.

Could Xerox Disrupt Hewlett-Packard?

We don't actually know if Xerox has considered the possibility of cre-ating a new business of the sort we will examine here, and we use the companies' names only to make the example more vivid. We've based this scenario solely on information from public sources. Xerox reportedly has developed outstanding ink-jet printing technology. What can it do with it? It could attempt to leapfrog Hewlett-Packard by making the best ink-jet printer on the market. Even if it could make a better printer, however, Xerox would be fighting a battle of sustaining technology against a company with superior resources and more at stake. HP would win that fight. But could Xerox craft a disruptive strategy for this technology? We'll test the conditions for a low-end strategy first.

To determine whether this strategy is viable, Xerox's managers should test whether customers in the lowest market tiers might be willing to buy a "good enough" printer that is cheaper than prevailing products.[21] At the highest tier of the market, customers seem willing to pay significantly more for a faster printer that produces sharper images. However, consumers in the less-demanding tiers are becoming increasingly indifferent to improvements. It is likely they would be interested in lower-cost alternatives. So the first question gets an affirmative answer.

The next question is whether Xerox could define a business model that could generate attractive returns at the discounted prices required to win business at the low end. The possibilities here don't look good. HP and other printer companies already outsource the fabrication and assembly of components to the lowest-cost sources in the world. HP makes its money selling ink cartridges—whose fabrication also is outsourced to low-cost suppliers. Xerox could enter the market by selling ink cartridges at lower prices, but unless it could define an overhead cost structure and business processes that would allow it to turn assets faster, Xerox could not sustain a product strategy of low-end disruption.[22]

This means we'll need to evaluate the potential for a new-market disruption—competing against nonconsumption. Is there a large, untapped population of computer owners who don't have the money or skill to buy and use a printer? Probably not. Hewlett-Packard already competed successfully against nonconsumption when it launched its easy-to-use, inexpensive ink-jet printers.

What about enticing existing printer owners to buy more printers, by enabling consumption in a new, more convenient context? Now, this might be achievable. Documents created on notebook computers are not easy to print. Notebook users have to find a stationary printer and connect to it either over a network or a printer cable, or they must transfer the file via removable media to a computer that is connected to a printer. If Xerox incorporated a lightweight, inexpensive printer into the base or spine of a notebook computer so that people on the go could get hard copies when and where they needed them, the company could probably win customers even if the printer wasn't as good as a stationary ink-jet printer. Only Xerox's engineers could determine whether the idea is technologically feasible. But as a strategy, this would pass the litmus tests.[23]

If Xerox attempted this, we would expect HP to ignore this new-market disruption at the outset because the market would be much smaller than the stationary printer market. HP's printer business is huge, and the company needs large sources of new revenue to sustain its growth. To trap Hewlett-Packard in an innovator's dilemma, Xerox should develop a business model that's attractive to Xerox but unattractive to the managers of HP and other leading established printer companies. This might entail pricing ink cartridges for embedded notebook printers low enough that the executives of HP's ink jet printer business would find the market unattractive relative to investments they might make to move up-market in search of the higher profits they could find by competing against higher-cost stationary laser printers.

Conditions for Growth in Air Conditioners

The window-mounted air conditioner market is widely known to be mature, dominated by giants such as Carrier and Whirlpool. Could a company like Hitachi wallop them? We would predict defeat if Hitachi tried to enter this market with a quieter product that offered more features and better energy efficiency.[24] Is a low-end disruption viable? Our sense is that there are overserved customers at the low end of the existing market. They signal their overservedness by opting for the least-expensive models they can find, unwilling to pay premium prices for the alternative products that are available to them. Hitachi might expand its already substantial manufacturing operations in China, making air conditioners for export to developed economies. This might bring modest but temporary success, because after the established companies respond by setting up their own manufacturing operations in China, Hitachi would find itself locked in a battle with competitors whose costs are comparable and whose distribution and service infrastructure are strong, and where the targeted customers already have manifested an unwillingness to pay premium prices for better products. Employing low-cost labor constitutes a low-cost business model only until competitors avail themselves of the same option.

How about a new-market disruption, however? There are hundreds of millions of nonconsumers of residential air conditioning in China, who have been blocked from that market because the power-hungry, expensive machines that historically have been available don't fit in the average family's pocketbook or apartment. If Hitachi could design a $49.95 product that would easily slip into the window of a cramped Shanghai apartment and reduce the temperature and humidity in a ten-foot by ten-foot room with ten amps of current, things might get interesting—because once Hitachi had a business model that could make money at that price point, taking on the rest of the up-market world would be easy. Parenthetically, while Western executives are understandably concerned about the threat that low-cost manufacturing in China poses to them, our guess is that China's greatest competitive asset is the unfathomable amount of nonconsumption in its markets, which makes them fertile ground for new-market disruptive companies of many sorts.

The Potential for Internet Banking

When we ask the test questions about Internet banking, we conclude that disruption using this technology is not possible. In the first place, there is not a large population of people who have been unable to open and maintain a bank account because they have lacked the money or skill. Existing banks' penetration of this market is high. This rules out a new-market disruption for Internet banking.

Second, are there current bank customers at the low end who would be happy to accept a bank account with fewer privileges and features in order to get the service at a lower price? The prevalence of advertisements featuring no-fee accounts is a testament that such customers exist. But is it possible to design a business model that would afford a disruptive online bank attractive profits at the discount prices required to win business at the low end? This is problematic. The cost of money is similar for all banks. E*Trade Bank and Sony Bank are seeking answers to the low-cost business model question.

Because the idea likely does not satisfy the conditions for either a new-market or a low-end disruption, Internet banking is likely to be implemented as a sustaining innovation by established banks. As for the third test, there already are many banks and credit unions, with only a limited number of office locations, that transact much of their business by mail. Internet banking would have a sustaining impact on their business models.

Disruption is a theory: a conceptual model of cause and effect that makes it possible to better predict the outcomes of competitive battles in different circumstances. The asymmetries of motivation chronicled in this chapter are natural economic forces that act on all businesspeople, all the time. Historically, these forces almost always have toppled the industry leaders when an attacker has harnessed them, because disruptive strategies are predicated upon competitors doing what is in their best and most urgent interest: satisfying their most important customers and investing where profits are most attractive. In a profit-seeking world, this is a pretty good bet.

Not all innovative ideas can be shaped into disruptive strategies, however, because the necessary preconditions do not exist; in such situations, the opportunity is best licensed or left to the firms that are already established in the market. On occasion, entrant companies have simply caught the leaders asleep at the switch and have succeeded with a strategy of sustaining innovation. But this is rare. Disruption does not guarantee success: It just helps with an important element in the total formula. Those who create new-growth businesses need to get on the right side of a number of other challenges, to which we will now turn.

Appendix: A Brief Description of the Disruptive Strategies of the Firms in Figure 2-4

Table 2-2 briefly summarizes our understanding of the disruptive roots of the success of the companies that are arrayed in figure 2-4. Because of space limitations, much important detail has been omitted. The companies are listed in alphabetical, rather than chronological, order. We do not pretend to be strong business historians, and as a consequence can only present here a partial listing of disruptive companies. Furthermore, it is often difficult to identify a specific year in which each firm's disruptive strategy was launched. Some firms existed for a considerable period, often in other lines of business, before the disruptive strategy that led to their ultimate success was implemented. In some cases it seems easier to visualize the disruption in terms of a product category, rather than by listing the name of one company. Hence, we ask our readers to regard this information as only suggestive, rather than definitive.

TABLE 2-2

Disruptive Strategies and Companies

Company or Product	Description
802.11	This is a protocol for high-bandwidth wireless transfer of data. It has begun disrupting local-area wireline networks. Its present limitations are that the signals can't travel long distances.
Amazon.com	A low-end disruption relative to traditional bookstores.
Barnes & Noble	Began as a local seller of mostly overstocked, surplus books. Evolved to become the dominant discount retailer of in-print books.
Beef processing	In the 1880s, Swift and Armour began huge, centralized beef slaughtering operations that transported large sides of beef by refrigerated railcar to local meat cutters. This disrupted local slaughtering operations.
Bell Telephone	Bell's original telephone could only carry a signal for three miles and therefore was rejected by Western Union, whose business was long-distance telegraphy, because Western Union couldn't use it. Bell started a new-market disruption, offering local communication, and as the technology improved, it pulled customers from telegraphy's long-distance value network into telephony.
Black & Decker	Prior to 1960, handheld electric tools were heavy and rugged, designed for professionals—and very expensive. B&D introduced a line of plastic-encased tools with universal motors that would only last twenty-five to thirty hours of operation—which actually was more than adequate for most do-it-yourselfers who drill a few holes per month. In today's dollars, B&D brought the cost of these tools down from $150 to $20, enabling a whole new population to own and use their own tools.

TABLE 2-2

Disruptive Strategies and Companies

Company or Product	Description
Blended plastics	These blends of inexpensive polyolefin plastics such as polypropylene, sold by firms such as Himont, create composite materials that in many ways share the best properties of their constituent materials. They are getting better at a stunning rate, disrupting markets that historically had been the province of engineering plastics made by firms such as GE Plastics.
Bloomberg L.P.	Bloomberg began by providing basic financial data to investment analysts and brokers. It has gradually improved its data offerings and analysis and subsequently moved into the financial news business. It has substantially disrupted Dow Jones and Reuters as a result. More recently it has created its own elecronic clearing network to disrupt stock exchanges. Issuers of government securities can auction their initial offerings over the Bloomberg system, disrupting investment banks.
Boxed beef	The "boxed beef" model of Iowa Beef Packers completed the disruption of local butchering operations. Instead of shipping large sides of beef to local meat cutters for further cutting, IBP cut the beef into finished or nearly finished cuts for placement directly in supermarket cases.
Canon photocopiers	Until the early 1980s, when people needed photocopies, they had to take their originals to the corporate photocopy center, where a technician ran the job for them. He *had* to be a technician, because the high-speed Xerox machine there was very complicated and needed servicing frequently. When Canon and Ricoh introduced their countertop photocopiers, they were slow, produced poor-resolution copies, and didn't enlarge or reduce or collate. But they were so inexpensive and simple to use that people could afford to put one right around the corner from their office. At the beginning people still took their high-volume jobs to the copy center. But little by little Canon improved its machines to the point that immediate, convenient access to high-quality, full-featured copying is almost a constitutional right in most workplaces today.
Catalog retailing	Sears, Roebuck and Montgomery Ward took root as catalog retailers— enabling people in rural America to buy things that historically had not been accessible. Their business model, entailing annual inventory turns of four times and gross margins of 30 percent, was disruptive relative to the model of full-service department stores, which required 40 percent gross margins because they turned inventories only three times annually. Sears and Montgomery Ward later moved up-market, building retail stores.
Charles Schwab	Started in 1975 as one of the first discount brokers. In the late 1990s Schwab created a separate organization to build an online trading business. It was so successful that the company folded its original organization into the disruptive one.
Circuit City, Best Buy	Disrupted the consumer electronics departments of full-service and discount department stores, which has sent them up-market into higher-margin clothing.

TABLE 2-2

Disruptive Strategies and Companies

Company or Product	Description
Cisco	Cisco's router uses packet-switching technology to direct the flow of information over the telecommunications system, rather than the circuit-switching technology of the established industry leaders such as Lucent, Siemens, and Nortel. The technology divides information into virtual "envelopes" called packets and sends them out over the Internet. Each packet might take a different route to the addressed destination; when they arrive, the packets are put in the right order and "opened" for the recipient to see. Because this process entailed a few seconds' latency delay, packet switching could not be used for voice telecommunications. But it was good enough to enable a new market to emerge—data networks. The technology has improved to the point that today, the latency delay of a packet-switched voice call is almost imperceptibly slower than that of a circuit-switched call, enabling VOIP, or voice-over-Internet-protocol telephony.
Community colleges	In some states, up to 80 percent of the graduates of reputable four-year state universities take some or all of their required general education courses at much less expensive community colleges, and then transfer those credits to the university—which (unconsciously) is becoming a provider of upper-division courses. Some community colleges have begun offering four-year degrees. Their enrollment is booming, often with nontraditional students who otherwise would not have taken these courses.
Concord School of Law	Founded by Kaplan, a unit of the Washington Post Company, this online law school has attracted a host of (primarily) nontraditional students. The school's accreditation allows its graduates to take the California Bar exam, and its graduates' success rate is comparable to those of many other law schools. Many of its students don't enroll to become lawyers, however. They want to understand law to help them succeed in other careers.
Credit scoring	A formulaic method of determining creditworthiness, substituting for the subjective judgments of bank loan officers. Developed by a Minneapolis firm, Fair Isaac. Used initially to extend Sears and Penney's in-store credit cards. As the technology improved, it was used for general credit cards, and then auto, mortgage, and now small-business loans.
Dell Computer	Dell's direct-to-customer retailing model and its fast-throughput, high asset-turns manufacturing model allowed it to come underneath Compaq, IBM, and Hewlett-Packard as a low-end disruptor in personal computers. Clayton Christensen, the quintessential low-end consumer, wrote his doctoral thesis on a Dell notebook computer purchased in 1991 because it was the cheapest portable computer on the market. Because of Dell's reputation for marginal quality, students needed special permission from Harvard to use doctoral stipend money to buy a Dell rather than a computer with a more reputable brand. Today Dell supplies most of the Harvard Business School's computers.
Department stores	Department stores such as Z.C.M.I. in Salt Lake City, Marshall Field's in Chicago, and Macy's in New York disrupted small shopkeepers. The department stores made money by accelerating inventory turns to three times per year, which enabled them to earn attractive profit with 40 percent gross margins. Because their salespeople were much less knowledgeable about products, at the outset department stores had to start at the simplest end of the merchandise mix, with products that were so familiar in use that they sold themselves.

TABLE 2-2

Disruptive Strategies and Companies

Company or Product	Description
Digital animation	The fixed cost and skill required to make a full-length animated movie historically was so high that almost nobody could do it except Disney. Digital animation technology now enables far more companies (such as Pixar) to compete against Disney.
Digital printing	Offset printing is being disrupted by the ability of local ink- and laser-jet printers to print custom, on-demand color documents at ever-improving speeds and quality. It has initially taken root in applications such as sales brochures.
Discount department stores	Department stores such as Korvette's in New York, and later Kmart, Wal-Mart, and Target, disrupted full-service department stores. The discount stores made money by accelerating inventory turns to five times per year, which enabled them to earn attractive profit with 23 percent gross margins. Because their salespeople were much less knowledgeable about products, at the outset the discount department stores had to start at the simplest end of the merchandise mix, with branded hard goods that were so familiar in use that they sold themselves. They subsequently have moved up-market into soft goods such as clothing.
eBay	Most of the Internet start-ups of the late 1990s attempted to use the Internet as a sustaining innovation relative to the business models of established companies. eBay was a notable exception because it pursued a new-market disruptive strategy—enabling owners of collectibles that could never turn the heads of auction house executives to sell off things that they no longer needed.
ECNs	Electronic clearing networks (ECNs) allow buyers and sellers of equities to exchange them over a computer, at a fraction of the cost of doing it on a formal stock exchange. Island, one of the leading ECNs, can handle on one workstation volume amounting to 20 percent of the NASDAQ's volume.
E-mail	E-mail is disrupting postal services. The volume of personal communication that is done by letter is dropping precipitously, leaving postal services with magazines, bills, and junk mail.
Embraer and Canadair regional jets	The regional passenger jet business is booming, as the capacity of their jets over the past fifteen years has stretched from 30 to 50, 70, and now 106. As Boeing and Airbus struggle to make bigger, faster jets for transcontinental and transoceanic travel, their growth has stagnated; the industry has consolidated (Lockheed and McDonnell Douglas have been folded in); and the growth is at the bottom of the market.
Endoscopic surgery	Minimally invasive surgery was actively disregarded by leading surgeons because the technique could only address the simplest procedures. But it has improved to the point that even certain relatively complicated heart procedures are done through a small port. The disruptive impact has primarily been on equipment makers and hospitals.
Fidelity Management	Created "self-service" personal financial management through its easy-to-buy families of mutual funds, 401k accounts, insurance products, and so forth. Fidelity was founded a few years after World War II, but began its disruptive movements in the 1970s, as best we can tell.

TABLE 2-2

Disruptive Strategies and Companies

Company or Product	Description
Flat-panel displays (Sharp et al.)	We normally think of disruptive technologies as being inexpensive, and many people are puzzled at how we could call flat-panel displays disruptive. Haven't they come from the high end? Actually, no. Flat-panel LCD displays took root in digital watches and then moved to calculators, notebook computers, and small portable televisions. These were applications that historically had no electronic displays at all, and LCD displays were *much* cheaper than alternative means of bringing imaging to those applications. Flat screens have now begun invading the mainstream market of computer monitors and in-home television screens, disrupting the cathode ray tube. They are able to sustain substantial premium prices because of their two-dimensional character.
Ford	Henry Ford's Model T was so inexpensive that he enabled a much larger population of people who historically could not afford cars to own one.
Galanz	China's Galanz captured nearly 40 percent of the world microwave oven market in the 1990s. Although the company could have followed a strategy of low-end disruption—using low-cost Chinese labor to make appliances for export—it instead chose to be a new-market disruptor, making ovens that were small enough and consumed little-enough power to be used in cramped Chinese apartments and were cheap enough for non-microwave-oven owners to afford. Once they had built a business model that could make profits at market-enabling price points for the domestic Chinese market, taking on the rest of the world was as easy as egg-drop soup.
GE Capital	Has disrupted major portions of the commercial banks' historical markets, primarily through low-end disruptive strategies.
Google	Google and its competing Internet search engines are disrupting directories of many sorts, including the Yellow Pages.
Honda motorcycles	Honda's Supercub, introduced in the late 1950s, disrupted makers of big, thunderous motorcycles such as Harley-Davidson, Triumph, BMW, and others. It took root as an off-road recreational motorized bicycle, and then improved. Honda was joined by Yamaha, Kawasaki, and Suzuki.
Ink-jet printers	These were a disruption to the laser jet printer and a sustaining technology relative to the dot-matrix printer. We put ink-jet printers toward the "new-market" end of the disruption spectrum because their compact size, light weight, and low initial cost enabled a whole new population of computer owners—primarily students—to individually own and use a printer. Although they were slow and produced fuzzy images at the outset, ink-jet printers are now the mainstream printer of choice, having pushed laser jets to the high end. Hewlett-Packard stayed atop this industry by setting up an autonomous ink-jet business unit to compete against its laser jet printer business.
Intel microprocessor	Intel's earliest microprocessor in 1971 could only constitute the brain of a four-function calculator. Makers of computers whose logic circuitry is based on microprocessors have disrupted firms that made mainframes and minicomputers, whose logic circuitry was based on printed wiring boards.

TABLE 2-2

Disruptive Strategies and Companies

Company or Product	Description
Intuit's QuickBooks accounting software	Whereas the established industry leaders in accounting software enabled small-business managers to run all sorts of sophisticated reports for analytical purposes, QuickBooks, which was a derivative of Intuit's personal finance software product Quicken, basically helped them keep track of their cash. It created a huge new market among very small business owners (most with fewer than five employees) who historically did not keep their books on computer. Within two years of launch, Intuit had seized 85 percent of the small-business accounting software market—mainly by creating new growth. The stealing of the established companies' customers came later, as QuickBooks' functionality improved.
Intuit's TurboTax	PC-based accounting software is disrupting personal tax preparation services such as H&R Block.
Japanese steel makers	Firms such as Nippon Steel, Nippon Kokkan, and Kobe and Kawasaki Steel began their growth by exporting very low quality steel to Western markets starting in the late 1950s. As their customers (including disruptive Japanese automakers like Toyota) grew, the Japanese steel industry had to increase capacity dramatically, enabling it to incorporate the latest steelmaking technology such as continuous casting and basic oxygen furnaces in the new mills. This accelerated their up-market trajectory dramatically.
JetBlue	Whereas Southwest Airlines initially followed a strategy of new-market disruption, JetBlue's approach is low-end disruption. Its long-range viability depends on the major airlines' motivation to run away from the attack, as integrated steel mills and full-service department stores did.
Kodak	Until the late 1800s, photography was extremely complicated. Only professionals could own and operate the expensive equipment. George Eastman's simple "point and shoot" Brownie camera allowed consumers to take their own pictures. They could then mail the roll of film to Kodak, which would develop it and return the photos by mail.
Kodak Funsaver	Kodak's Funsaver brand single-use camera was born after painful labor within Kodak, because its profit model and gross margins were lower than Kodak could earn by selling roll film, and the quality of the images was not as good as those taken in high-quality 35mm cameras. But Kodak commercialized it through a different division, and it sold almost exclusively to people who would not have bought film anyway because they didn't have a camera. Although it has potential to move up-market and take share against traditional cameras with a new brand, Maxx, we worry that Kodak might have stopped driving it in this direction.
Korean auto manufacturers (Hyundai and Kia)	Korean automakers, including Hyundai and Kia, gained more points of world-wide market share in the 1990s than any other country's automakers. And yet few of the established firms are concerned, because their gains have come in what is, to the established firms, the lowest-profit portion of the market.
Linux	The disruptiveness of the Linux operating system can only be expressed relative to the alternatives now in the market. Its most successful deployment thus far is within the market for server operating systems—sandwiched between high-end UNIX systems and the Microsoft Windows NT operating system (which has been moving disruptively up-market against UNIX for some time). From its initial foothold in Internet servers, it has gained significant share against UNIX operating systems such as Sun's Solaris. The position of Linux may actually block the further up-market movement of Microsoft NT. Linux has begun to disrupt the market for operating system software on handheld devices as well.

TABLE 2-2

Disruptive Strategies and Companies

Company or Product	Description
MBNA	We noted earlier that credit scoring is a formulaic method of determining the creditworthiness of a loan applicant. It was originally implemented in commercial banks as a sustaining technology, to reduce the costs of credit evaluation. In the 1990s, however, it was deployed in high-volume, low-cost "monoline" business models by firms such as MBNA, Capital One, and First USA, which have substantially disrupted commercial banks' credit card business. At the time of this writing, in fact, Citibank is the only remaining major commercial bank with a substantial and profitable credit card business.
McDonald's	The fast food industry has been a hybrid disruptor, making it so inexpensive and convenient to eat out that they created a massive wave of growth in the "eating out" industry. Their earliest victims were mom-and-pop diners. In the last decade the advent of food courts has taken fast food up-market. Expensive, romantic restaurants still thrive at the high end, of course.
MCI, Sprint	These firms were low-end disruptors relative to AT&T's long-distance telephone business. They enjoyed a unique opportunity to do this, because AT&T's long-distance rates were set by regulation at artificially high levels in order to subsidize local residential telephone service.
Merrill Lynch	Charles Merrill's mantra in 1912 was to "Bring Wall Street to Main Street." By employing salaried rather than commissioned brokers, he made it inexpensive enough to trade stocks that middle-income Americans could become equity investors. Merrill Lynch moved up-market over the next 90 years toward investors of higher net worth. Most of the brokerage firms that held seats on the New York Stock Exchange in the 1950s and 1960s have been merged out of existence because Merrill Lynch disrupted them.
Microsoft	Its operating system was inadequate versus those of mainframe and mini-computer makers, versus UNIX, and versus Apple's system. But its migration from DOS to Windows to Windows NT is taking the firm up-market, to the point that the UNIX world is seriously threatened. Microsoft, in turn, faces a threat from Linux. See also SQL.
Minicomputers	Companies such as Digital Equipment, Prime, Wang, Data General, and Nixdorf were new-market disruptors relative to mainframe computer makers. Their relative simplicity and low price enabled departments (particularly engineering) in organizations to have their own computers, instead of having to rely on inconvenient, centralized mainframe computers that typically were optimized for generating financial reports.
Online stock-brokers	Online trading of equities is a sustaining technology relative to the business models of discount brokers such as Ameritrade and is disruptive relative to full-service brokers such as Merrill Lynch. For Schwab, which started as a bare-bones discount broker but had moved up toward the mainstream market by the mid-1990s, Internet-based trading was disruptive enough that the company had to set up a separate division.
Online travel agencies	Enabled by electronic ticketing, online travel agencies such as Expedia and Travelocity have so badly disrupted full-service, bricks-and-mortar agencies such as American Express that many airlines have dramatically cut the substantial commissions that historically they had paid to travel agencies.

TABLE 2-2

Disruptive Strategies and Companies

Company or Product	Description
Oracle	Oracle's relational database software was disruptive relative to that of the prior leaders, Cullinet and IBM, whose hierarchical or transactional database software ran on mainframe computers and was used to generate standard financial reports. Relational databases ran on minicomputers (and then microprocessor-based computers). Users without deep programming expertise could readily create their own custom reports and analyses using Oracle's modular, relational architecture.
Palm Pilot, RIM BlackBerry	Handheld devices are new-market disruptions relative to notebook computers.
Personal computers	Microprocessor-based computers made by firms such as Apple, IBM, and Compaq were true new-market disruptions in that for years they were sold and used in their unique value network before they began to capture sales from higher-end professional computers.
Plastics	Plastics as a category have disrupted steel and wood, in that the "quality" of plastic parts often was inferior to those of wood and steel along the metrics by which performance was measured in traditional applications. But their low cost and ease of shaping created many new applications, and plastics have pulled many applications out of the original metal and wood value networks into the plastic network. The disruption is particularly obvious if you look at where plastics were used in automobiles thirty years ago versus today.
Portable diabetes blood glucose meters	Disrupted makers of large blood glucose testing machines in hospital laboratories, enabling patients with diabetes to monitor their own glucose levels.
Salesforce.com	This company, with its inexpensive, simple, Internet-based system, is disrupting the leading providers of customer relationship management software, such as Siebel Systems.
Seiko watches	Remember when Seiko watches were those cheap, throw-away black plastic watches? Seiko, Citizen, and Texas Instruments (which subsequently exited) disrupted the American and European watch industries.
Sonosite	This firm makes a handheld ultrasound device that now enables health care professionals who historically needed the assistance of highly trained technicians with expensive equipment to look inside the bodies of patients in their care, and thereby to provide more accurate and timely diagnoses. The company floundered for a time attempting to implement its product as a sustaining innovation. But as of the time this book was being written, it seemed to have caught its disruptive stride in an impressive way.
Sony	Sony pioneered the use of transistors in consumer electronics. Its portable radios and portable televisions disrupted firms such as RCA that made large TVs and radios using vacuum tube technology. During the 1960s and 1970s, Sony launched a series of new-market disruptions, with products such as videotape players, handheld consumer video recorders, cassette tape players, the Walkman, and the 3.5-inch floppy disk drive.
Southwest Airlines	It was a hybrid disruptor because its original strategy was to compete against driving and buses and to fly in and out of nonmainstream airports. In addition, because its prices were so low, it also took business from established airlines. Just as Wal-Mart enjoys profit protection from being in small towns whose market can support only one discount store, many of Southwest's routes offer the same protection.

TABLE 2-2

Disruptive Strategies and Companies

Company or Product	Description
SQL database software	Microsoft's SQL database software product is disrupting Oracle, which has moved up-market into expensive, integrated enterprise systems. Microsoft's Access product, in turn, is disrupting SQL.
Staples	With its direct competitors Office Max and Office Depot, Staples disrupted small stationery stores as well as commercial office supplies distributors.
Steel minimills	Have been disrupting integrated mills around the world since the mid-1960s, as recounted in the text.
Sun Microsystems	Sun, Apollo (HP), and Silicon Graphics, which built their systems around RISC microprocessors, took root in essentially the same value network as mini-computers, and disrupted them. These firms, in turn, are now being disrupted by CISC microprocessor-based computer makers such as Compaq and Dell.
Toyota	Entered the U.S. market with cheap subcompact cars like the Corona. These were so inexpensive that people who historically couldn't afford a new car now could buy one, or families could acquire a second car. Toyota now makes Lexuses, you may have noticed. Nissan has migrated from its Datsun to Infiniti, and Honda has progressed from its miniature CVCC to the Acura.
Toys 'R Us	Disrupted the toy departments of full-service and discount department stores, which has sent them up-market into higher-margin clothing.
Ultrasound	Ultrasound technology is disruptive relative to X-ray imaging. Hewlett-Packard, Accuson, and ATL created a multibillion-dollar industry by imaging soft tissues. The leading X-ray equipment makers, including General Electric, Siemens, and Philips, became leaders in the two major radical sustaining technology revolutions in imaging: CT scanning and magnetic resonance imaging (MRI). Because ultrasound was a new-market disruption, none of the X-ray companies participated in ultrasound until very recently, when they acquired major ultrasound equipment companies.
University of Phoenix	A unit of Apollo, the University of Phoenix is disrupting four-year colleges and certain professional graduate programs. It began by providing employee training courses for businesses, often de facto, but sometimes by formal contract. Its programs have expanded into a variety of open-enrollment, degree-granting programs. Today it is one of the largest educational institutions in the United States and is one of the leading providers of online education.
Unmanned aircraft	These machines took root initially as drone targets to uncover hidden anti-aircraft emplacements. They then moved up-market into surveillance roles, and in the 2001–2002 war in Afghanistan, moved for the first time into limited weapons-carrying roles.
Vanguard	Index mutual funds have been a low-end disruption relative to managed mutual funds. At the time of this writing, Vanguard's assets had grown to rival closely those of the former undisputed mutual fund leader, Fidelity Management.
Veritas and Network Appliance	Network-attached storage and IP storage area networks are disruptive approaches to enterprise data storage, relative to the centralized storage systems supplied by companies such as EMC. Some of these distributed networked storage systems are so simple to augment that an office assistant can simply "snap" an additional storage server onto a network.

TABLE 2-2

Disruptive Strategies and Companies

Company or Product	Description
Wireless telephony	Cellular and digital wireless phones have been on a disruptive path against wireline phones for twenty-five years. Initially they were large, power-hungry car phones with spotty efficacy, but gradually they have improved to the point where, by some estimates, nearly one-fifth of mobile telephone users have chosen to "cut the cord" and do without wireline telephone service. The viability of the wireline long-distance business is now in jeopardy.
Xerox	Photocopying has been a new-market disruption relative to offset printing, enabling nonprinters to make copies in the convenience of their workplace. Xerox's initial machines were so expensive and complicated that they were housed in corporate photocopy centers manned by technicians.

Notes

1. We mentioned in chapter 1 that in early stages of theory building, the best that scholars can do is suggest categories that are defined by the attributes of the phenomena. Such studies are important stepping stones in the path of progress. One such important book is Richard Foster, *Innovation: The Attacker's Advantage* (New York: Summit Books, 1986). Another study predicted that the leaders will fail when an innovation entails development of completely new technological competencies. See Michael L. Tushman and Philip Anderson, "Technological Discontinuities and Organizational Environments," *Administrative Science Quarterly* 31 (1986). The research of MIT Professor James M. Utterback and his colleagues on dominant designs has been particularly instrumental in moving this body of theory toward circumstance-based categorization. See, for example, James M. Utterback and William J. Abernathy, "A Dynamic Model of Process and Product Innovation" *Omega* 33, no. 6 (1975): 639–656; and Clayton M. Christensen, Fernando F. Suarez, and James M. Utterback, "Strategies for Survival in Fast-Changing Industries," *Management Science* 44, no. 12 (2001): 207–220.

2. Demanding customers are those customers who are willing to pay for increases on some dimension of performance—faster speeds, smaller sizes, better reliability, and so on. Less-demanding or undemanding customers are those customers who would rather make a different trade-off, accepting less performance (slower speeds, larger sizes, less reliability, and so on) in exchange for commensurately lower prices. We depict these trajectories as straight lines because empirically, when charted on semi-long graph paper, they in fact are straight, suggesting that our ability to utilize improvement

increases at an exponential pace—though a pace that is shallower than the trajectory of technological progress.

3. After watching students and managers read, interpret, and talk about this distinction between sustaining and disruptive technologies, we have observed a stunningly common human tendency to take a new concept, new data, or new way of thinking and morph it so that it fits one's existing mental models. Hence, many people have equated our use of the term *sustaining innovation* with their preexisting frame of "incremental" innovation, and they have equated the term *disruptive technology* with the words *radical, breakthrough, out-of-the-box,* or *different.* They then conclude that disruptive ideas (as they define the term) are good and merit investment. We regret that this happens, because our findings relate to a very specific definition of disruptiveness, as stated in our text here. It is for this reason that in this book we have substituted the term *disruptive innovation* for the term *disruptive technology*—to minimize the chance that readers will twist the concept to fit into what we believe is an incorrect way of categorizing the circumstances.

4. *The Innovator's Dilemma* notes that the only times that established companies succeeded in staying atop their industries when confronted by disruptive technologies were when the established firms created a completely separate organization and gave it an unfettered charter to build a completely new business with a completely new business model. Hence, IBM was able to remain atop its industry when minicomputers disrupted mainframes because it competed in the minicomputer market with a different business unit. And when the personal computer emerged, IBM addressed that disruption by creating an autonomous business unit in Florida. Hewlett-Packard remained the leader in printers for personal computing because it created a division to make and sell ink-jet printers that was completely independent from its printer division in Boise, which made and sold laser jet printers. Since publication of *The Innovator's Dilemma,* a number of companies that were faced with disruption have succeeded in becoming leaders in the wave of disruption coming at them by setting up separate organizational units to address the disruption. Charles Schwab became the leading online broker; Teradyne, the maker of semiconductor test equipment, became the leader in PC-based testers; and Intel introduced its Celeron chip, which reclaimed the low end of the microprocessor market. We hope that as more established companies learn to address disruptions through independent business units when faced with disruptive opportunities, the odds that historically were overwhelmingly favorable to entrant firms and their venture capital backers will become more favorable to established leaders who seek to create new-growth opportunities.

5. An exception to this statement is found in Japan, where a couple of integrated mills have subsequently acquired existing minimill companies.

6. The economists' simple notion that price is determined at the intersection of supply and demand curves explains this phenomenon. Price gravitates to the cash cost of the marginal, or highest-cost, producer whose capacity is required for supply to meet the quantity demanded. When the marginal producers were high-cost integrated mills, minimills could make money in rebar. When the marginal, highest-cost producers were minimills, then the price of rebar collapsed. The same mechanism destroyed the temporary profitability to the minimills of each subsequent tier of the market, as described in the text that follows.

7. That cost reduction rarely creates competitive advantage is argued persuasively in Michael Porter, "What Is Strategy?" *Harvard Business Review,* November–December 1996, 61–78.

8. We recommend in particular Steven C. Wheelwright and Kim B. Clark, *Revolutionizing New Product Development* (New York: The Free Press, 1992); Stefan Thomke, *Experimentation Matters: Unlocking the Potential of New Technologies for Innovation* (Boston: Harvard Business School Press, 2003); Stefan Thomke and Eric von Hippel, "Customers as Innovators: A New Way to Create Value," *Harvard Business Review,* April 2002, 74–81; and Eric von Hippel, *The Sources of Innovation* (New York: Oxford University Press, 1988).

9. This model explains quite clearly why the major airline companies in the United States are so chronically unprofitable. Southwest Airlines entered as a new-market disruptor (a concept defined in chapter 3), competing within Texas for customers who otherwise would not have flown at all, but would have used automobiles and buses. The airline has grown carefully into nonmajor airports, staying away from head-on competition against the majors. It is the low-end disruptors to this industry—airlines with names such as Jet-Blue, AirTran, People Express, Florida Air, Reno Air, Midway, Spirit, Presidential, and many others—that create the chronic unprofitability.

When leaders in most other industries get attacked by low-end disruptors, they can run away up-market and remain profitable (and often improve profitability) for some time. The integrated steel companies fled up-market away from the minimills. The full-service department stores fled up-market into clothing, home furnishings, and cosmetics when the discount department stores attacked branded hard goods such as hardware, paint, toys, sporting goods, and kitchen utensils at the low-margin end of the merchandise mix. Today, the discount department stores such as Target and Wal-Mart are fleeing up-market into clothing, home furnishings, and cosmetics as hard goods discounters such as Circuit City, Toys 'R Us, Staples, Home Depot, and Kitchens Etc. attack the low end; and so on.

The problem in airlines is that the majors cannot flee up-market. Their high fixed-cost structure makes it impossible to abandon the low end. Hence, low-end disruptors easily enter and attack; once one of them gets big enough, however, the major airlines declare that enough is enough, and they turn around and fight. This is why no low-end disruptor to date has survived for longer than a few years. But because low-end disruption by new companies is so easy to start, the majors can never raise low-end pricing up to levels of attractive profitability.

10. This history is recounted in a marvelous paper by Richard S. Rosenbloom, "From Gears to Chips: The Transformation of NCR and Harris in the Digital Era," working paper, Harvard Business School Business History Seminar, Boston, 1988.

11. We would be foolish to claim that it is impossible to create new-growth companies with a sustaining, leap-beyond-the-competition strategy. It is more accurate to say that the odds of success are very, very low. But some sustaining entrants have succeeded. For example, EMC Corporation took the high-end data storage business away from IBM in the 1990s with a different product architecture than IBM's. But as best we can tell, EMC's products were *better* than IBM's in the very applications that IBM served. Hewlett-Packard's laser jet printer business was a sustaining technology relative to the dot-matrix printer, a market dominated by Epson. Yet Epson missed it. The jet engine was a radical but sustaining innovation relative to the piston aircraft engine. Two of the piston engine manufacturers, Rolls-Royce and Pratt & Whitney, navigated the transition to jets successfully. Others, such as Ford, did not. General Electric was an entrant in the jet revolution, and became very successful. These are anomalies that the theory of disruption cannot explain. Although our bias is to assume that most managers most of the time are on top of their businesses and manage them in competent ways, it is also true that sometimes managers simply fall asleep at the switch.

12. This partially explains, for example, why Dell Computer has been such a successful disruptor—because it has raced up-market in order to compete against higher-cost makers of workstations and servers such as Sun Microsystems. Gateway, in contrast, has not prospered to the same extent even though it had a similar initial business model, because it has not moved up-market as aggressively and is stuck with undifferentiable costs selling undifferentiable computers. We believe that this insight represents a useful addendum to Professor Michael Porter's initial notion that there are two viable types of strategy—differentiation and low cost (Michael Porter, *Competitive Strategy* [New York: Free Press, 1980]). The research of disruption adds a dynamic dimension to Porter's work. Essentially, a low-cost strategy yields attractive profitability only until the higher-cost competitors have been

driven from a tier in the market. Then, the low-cost competitor needs to move up so that it can compete once again against higher-cost opponents. Without the ability to move up, a low-cost strategy becomes an equal-cost strategy.

13. See Clayton M. Christensen, *The Innovator's Dilemma* (Boston: Harvard Business School Press, 1997), 130.

14. The concept of value networks was introduced in Clayton M. Christensen, "Value Networks and the Impetus to Innovate," chapter 2 in *The Innovator's Dilemma*. Professor Richard S. Rosenbloom of the Harvard Business School originally identified the existence of value networks when he advised Christensen's early research. In many ways, the situation in a value network corresponds to a "Nash equilibrium," developed by Nobel laureate John Nash (who became even more renowned through the movie *A Beautiful Mind*). In a Nash equilibrium, given Company A's understanding of the optimal, self-interested (maximum-profit) strategy of each of the other companies in the system, Company A cannot see any better strategy for itself than the one it presently is pursuing. The same holds true for all other companies in the system. Hence, none of the companies is motivated to change course, and the entire system therefore is relatively inert to change. Insofar as the companies within a value network are in a Nash equilibrium, it creates a drag that constrains how fast customers can begin utilizing new innovations. This application of Nash equilibriums to the uptake of innovations was recently introduced in Bhaskar Chakravorti, *The Slow Pace of Fast Change* (Boston: Harvard Business School Press, 2003). Although Chakravorti did not make the linkage himself, his concept is a good way to visualize two things about the disruptive innovation model. It explains why the pace of technological progress outstrips the abilities of customers to utilize the progress. It also explains why competing against nonconsumption, creating a completely new value network, is often in the long run an easier way to attack an established market.

15. Some people have concluded on occasion that when the incumbent leader doesn't instantly get killed by a disruption, the forces of disruption somehow have ceased to operate, and that the attackers are being held at bay. (See, for example, Constantinos Charitou and Constantinos Markides, "Responses to Disruptive Strategic Innovation," *MIT Sloan Management Review,* Winter 2003, 55.) These conclusions reflect a shallow understanding of the phenomenon, because disruption is a process and not an event. The forces are operating all of the time in every industry. In some industries it might take decades for the forces to work their way through an industry. In other instances it might take a few years. But the forces—which really

are the pursuit of the profit that is associated with competitive advantage—are always at work. Similarly, other writers on occasion have noticed that the leader in an industry actually did not get killed by a disruption, but skillfully caught the wave. They then conclude that the theory of disruption is false. This is erroneous logic as well. When we see an airplane fly, it does not disprove the law of gravity. Gravity continues to exert force on the flying plane—it's just that engineers figured out how to deal with the force. When we see a company succeed at disruption, it is because the management team figured out how to harness the forces to facilitate success.

16. See Clayton M. Christensen and Richard S. Tedlow, "Patterns of Disruption in Retailing," *Harvard Business Review,* January–February 2000, 42–45.

17. Ultimately, Wal-Mart was able to create processes that turned assets faster than Kmart. This allowed it to earn higher returns at comparable gross profit margins, giving Wal-Mart a higher sustainable growth rate.

18. The reason it is so much easier for firms in the position of the full-service department stores to flee from the disruption rather than stand to fight it is that in the near term, inventory and asset turns are hard to change. The full-service department stores offered to customers a much broader product selection (more SKUs per category), which inevitably depressed inventory turns. Discounters not only offered a narrower range of products that focused only on the fastest-turning items, but also their physical infrastructure typically put all merchandise on the sales floor. Department stores, in contrast, often had to maintain stockrooms to provide back-up for the limited quantities of any given item that could be placed on their SKU-laden shelves. Hence, when disruptive discounters invaded a tier of their merchandise mix from below, the department stores could not readily drop margins and accelerate turns. Moving up-market where margins still were adequate was always the more feasible and attractive alternative.

19. Low-end disruptions are a direct example of what economist Joseph Schumpeter termed "creative destruction." Low-end disruptions create a step-change cost reduction within an industry—but it is achieved by entrant firms destroying the incumbents. New-market disruption, in contrast, entails a period of substantial creative creation—new consumption—before the destruction of the old occurs

20. For a deeper exploration of the macroeconomic impact of disruption, see Clayton M. Christensen, Stuart L. Hart, and Thomas Craig, "The Great Disruption," Foreign Affairs 80, no. 2 (March–April 2001): 80–95; and Stuart L. Hart and Clayton M. Christensen, "The Great Leap: Driving Innovation from the Base of the Pyramid," *MIT Sloan Management Review,* Fall 2002, 51–56. The *Foreign Affairs* paper asserts that disruption was the fundamental engine of Japan's economic miracle of the 1960s, 1970s, and 1980s. Like

other companies, these disruptors—Sony, Toyota, Nippon Steel, Canon, Seiko, Honda, and others—have soared to the high end, now producing some of the world's highest-quality products in their respective markets. Like the American and European companies that they disrupted, Japan's giants are now stuck at the high end of their markets, where there is no growth. The reason America's economy did not stagnate for an extended period after its leading companies got pinned to the high end was that people could leave those companies, pick up venture capital on the way down, and start new waves of disruptive growth. Japan's economy, in contrast, lacks the labor market mobility and the venture capital infrastructure to enable this. Hence, Japan played the disruptive game once and profited handsomely. But it is stuck. There truly seem to be microeconomic roots to the country's macroeconomic malaise. The *Sloan* paper builds upon the *Foreign Affairs* piece, asserting that today's developing nations are an ideal initial market for many disruptive innovations, and that disruption is a viable economic development policy.

21. Our choice of wording in this paragraph is important. When customers cannot differentiate products from each other on any dimension that they can value, then price is often the customer's basis of choice. We would not say, however, that when a consumer buys the lowest-priced alternative, the axis of competition is cost based. The right question to ask is whether customers will be willing to pay higher prices for further improvements in functionality, reliability, or convenience. As long as customers reward improvements with commensurately higher prices, we take it as evidence that the pace of performance improvement has not yet overshot what customers can use. When the marginal utility that customers receive from additional improvements on any of these dimensions approaches zero, then cost is truly the basis of competition.

22. We emphasize the term *product* strategy in this sentence because there certainly seems to be scope for two other low-end disruptive plays in this market. One would be a private-label strategy to disrupt the Hewlett-Packard brand. The other would be a low-cost distribution strategy through an online retailer such as Dell Computer.

23. There actually is a fourth strategy to be evaluated here—making components for sale to Hewlett-Packard and its subsystem suppliers. We will discuss this strategy at greater length in chapters 4 and 5.

24. Matsushita, in fact, attempted entry with a sustaining strategy of exactly this sort in the 1990s. Despite its strong Panasonic brand and its world-class capabilities in assembling electromechanical products, the company has been bloodied and has captured minimal market share.

CHAPTER THREE

WHAT PRODUCTS WILL CUSTOMERS WANT TO BUY?

What products should we develop as we execute our disruptive strategy? Which market segments should we focus upon? How can we know for sure, in advance, what product features and functions the customers in those segments will and will not value? How should we communicate the benefits of our products to our customers, and what brand-building strategy can best create enduring value?

All companies face the continual challenge of defining and developing products that customers will scramble to buy. But despite the best efforts of remarkably talented people, most attempts to create successful new products fail. Over 60 percent of all new-product development efforts are scuttled before they ever reach the market. Of the 40 percent that do see the light of day, 40 percent fail to become profitable and are withdrawn from the market. By the time you add it all up, three-quarters of the money spent in product development investments results in products that do not succeed commercially.[1] These development efforts are all launched with the expectation of success, but they seem to flourish or flop in unexpected ways. Once again, we argue that the failures are really not random at all: They are predictable—and avoidable—if managers get the categorization stage of theory right. Of the many dimensions of business building, the challenge of creating products that large numbers of customers will buy at profitable prices screams out for accurately predictive theory.

The process that marketers call market segmentation is, in our parlance, the categorization stage of theory building. Only if managers define market segments that correspond to the circumstances in which customers find themselves when making purchasing decisions can they accurately theorize which products will connect with their customers. When managers segment markets in ways that are misaligned with those circumstances, market segmentation can actually *cause* them to fail—essentially because it leads managers to aim their new products at phantom targets.

We begin this chapter by describing a way to think about market segmentation that might differ from what you've seen before. We believe that this approach, based on the notion that customers "hire" products to do specific "jobs," can help managers segment their markets to mirror the way their customers experience life. In so doing, this approach can also uncover opportunities for disruptive innovation.

We will then crawl beneath this concept of segmentation and explore the forces that cause even the best managers to segment their markets erroneously. A lot of marketers actually know how to do what we urge in this chapter. The problem is that predictable forces in operating companies cause companies to segment markets in counterproductive ways. Finally, we show how segmenting markets according to the jobs that customers are trying to get done addresses other important marketing challenges—such as brand management and product positioning—to help disruptive businesses grow. Taken together, this set of insights constitutes a theory of how to connect disruptive innovations with the right customers in order first to create a foothold in a market and then to grow profitably along the sustaining trajectory into market-dominating products and services.

Pomp and Circumstances in Segmenting Markets

Much of the art of marketing focuses on segmentation: identifying groups of customers that are similar enough that the same product or service will appeal to all of them.[2] Marketers often segment markets by product type, by price point, or by the demographics and psychographics of the individuals or companies who are their customers. With all the effort expended on segmentation, why do the innovation strategies based on these categorization or segmentation schemes fail so frequently? The reason, in our view, is that these delineations are defined by the *attributes* of products and customers. As we see over and over in this book, theories based on attribute-based categorizations can reveal *correlations* between attributes and outcomes. But it is only when marketing theory offers a plausible statement of causality and is built upon circumstance-based categorization (segmentation) schemes that managers can confidently assert what features, functions, and positioning will *cause* customers to buy a product.

Predictable marketing requires an understanding of the circumstances in which customers buy or use things. Specifically, customers—people and companies—have "jobs" that arise regularly and need to get done. When customers become aware of a job that they need to get done in their lives, they look around for a product or service that they can "hire" to get the job done. This is how customers experience life. Their thought processes originate with an awareness of needing to get something done, and then they set out to hire something or someone to do the job as effectively, conveniently, and inexpensively as possible. The functional, emotional, and social dimensions of the jobs that customers need to get done constitute the circumstances in which they buy. In other words, the jobs that customers are trying to get done or the outcomes that they are trying to achieve constitute a circumstance-based categorization of markets.[3] Companies that target their products at the *circumstances* in which customers find themselves, rather than at the *customers* themselves, are those that can launch predictably successful products. Put another way, the critical unit of analysis is the *circumstance* and *not the customer*.

To see why this is so, consider a quick-service restaurant chain's effort to improve its milkshake sales and profits.[4] This chain's marketers segmented its customers along a variety of psychobehavioral dimensions in order to define a profile of the customer most likely to buy milkshakes. In other words, it first structured its market by product—

milkshakes—and then segmented it by the characteristics of existing milkshake customers. These are both attribute-based categorization schemes. It then assembled panels of people with these attributes, and explored whether making the shakes thicker, chocolatier, cheaper, or chunkier would satisfy them better. The chain got clear inputs on what the customers wanted, but none of the improvements to the product significantly altered sales or profits.

A new set of researchers then came in to understand what customers were trying to get done for themselves when they "hired" a milkshake, and this approach helped the chain's managers see things that traditional market research had missed. To learn what customers sought when they hired a milkshake, the researchers spent an eighteen-hour day in a restaurant carefully chronicling who bought milkshakes. They recorded the time of each milkshake purchase, what other products the customer purchased, whether the customer was alone or with a group, whether he or she consumed it on the premises or drove off with it, and so on. The most surprising insight from this work was that nearly half of all milkshakes were bought in the early morning. Most often, the milkshake was the only item these customers purchased, and it was rarely consumed in the restaurant.

The researchers returned to interview customers who purchased a morning milkshake to understand what they were trying to get done when they bought it, and they asked what other products they hired instead of a milkshake on other days when they had to get the same job done. Most of these morning milkshake customers had hired it to achieve a similar set of outcomes. They faced a long, boring commute and needed something to make the commute more interesting! They were "multitasking"—they weren't yet hungry, but knew that if they did not eat something now, they would be hungry by 10:00. They also faced constraints. They were in a hurry, were often wearing their work clothes, and at most had only one free hand.

When these customers looked around for something to hire to get this job done, sometimes they bought bagels. But bagels got crumbs all over their clothes and the car. If the bagels were topped with cream cheese or jam, their fingers and the steering wheel got sticky. Sometimes they hired a banana to do the job, but it got eaten too fast and did not solve the boring commute problem. The sorts of sausage, ham, or egg sandwiches that the restaurant also sold for breakfast made their hands and the steering wheel greasy, and if customers tried to drag out the time they took to eat the sandwich, it got cold. Doughnuts didn't last through the 10:00 hunger attack. It turned out that the milkshake did the job better than almost any available alternative. If managed competently, it could take as long as twenty minutes to suck the viscous milkshake through the thin straw, addressing the boring commute problem. It could be eaten cleanly with one hand with little risk of spillage, and the customers felt less hungry after consuming the shake than after using most of the alternatives. Customers were not satisfied that the shake was healthy food, but it didn't matter because becoming healthy wasn't the job for which they were hiring the product.[5]

The researchers observed that at other times of the day, it was often parents who purchased milkshakes, in addition to a complete meal, for their children. What job were they trying to get done? They were emotionally exhausted from repeatedly having to say "No" to their kids all day, and they just needed to feel like they were reasonable parents. They hired milkshakes as an innocuous way to placate their children and to feel like they were loving parents. The researchers observed that the milkshakes didn't do this job very well, though. They saw parents waiting impatiently after they had finished their own meal while their children struggled to suck the thick milkshake up the thin straw. Many were discarded half-full when the parents declared that time had run out.

Segmenting the market along demographic or psychographic lines indeed provides information on individual customers.[6] But the same busy father who needs a viscous, time-consuming milkshake in the morning needs something very different later in the day for his child. When researchers asked customers who have multiple jobs in their lives what attributes of the milkshake they should improve upon, and when the researchers then averaged each consumer's response with those of others in the same demographic or psychographic segment, it led to a one-size-fits-none product that didn't do well any of the jobs that customers were trying to get done.[7]

Who is the quick-service chain really competing against in the morning? Its statistics compare its sales with the milkshake sales of competing chains. But in the customers' minds, the morning milkshake competes against boredom, bagels, bananas, doughnuts, instant breakfast drinks, and possibly coffee. In the evening, milkshakes compete against cookies, ice cream, and promised purchases in the future that parents hope their children won't remember.

Knowing what job a product gets hired to do (and knowing what jobs are out there that aren't getting done very well) can give innovators a much clearer road map for improving their products to beat the *true* competition from the customer's perspective—in every dimension of the job. To tackle the boring commute job, for example, the chain's managers could swirl in tiny chunks of real fruit. This would nail the boring commute job even better, because the drivers would at random suck crisp, flavorful chunks into their mouths, adding a dimension of unpredictability and anticipation to a monotonous morning routine. (Remember, fruit might make it healthier, but improving health is not the primary job that the shake gets hired to do.) The chain could make the shake even thicker, so it would last longer. And they could set up a self-service machine in each restaurant that customers could operate with a prepaid card, to get in and out fast.

Addressing the evening job-to-be-done would entail a very different product—one with lower viscosity for quicker consumption, and served in a small, entertainingly designed container. It would be an inexpensive add-on to the bundled children's meal, so that when a child begged the parent for it, the parent could readily say "OK" with little forethought.

If the restaurant chain implemented innovations such as these that really helped get the jobs done and discarded improvements that were irrelevant to the jobs that the product is hired to do, it would succeed—but not by capturing milkshake sales from competing quick-service chains or by cannibalizing other products on its menu. Rather, the growth would come by taking share from products in other categories that customers sometimes employed, with limited satisfaction, to get their particular jobs done. And perhaps more important, the products would find new growth among "nonconsumers." Competing against nonconsumption often offers the biggest source of growth in a world of one-size-fits-all products that do no jobs satisfactorily. We will return to this topic in chapter 4.

Using Circumstance-Based Segmentation
to Gain a Disruptive Foothold

The first time that builders of a new-growth business need to assess what the target customers really are trying to get done is when they are searching for the disruptive foothold—the initial product or service that is the point of entry for a new-market disruption. When managers position a disruptive product squarely on a job that has been poorly addressed in the past that a lot of people are trying to get done, they create a launch pad for subsequent growth through sustaining innovations that build on the initial platform.[8]

How can managers identify these foothold opportunities? It may never be possible to get every dimension of a product introduction in a new-market disruption right at the outset, which makes it very important to use the methods of strategy discovery we outline in chapter 8. We believe, however, that a jobs-to-be-done lens can help innovators come to market with an initial product that is much closer to what customers ultimately will discover that they value. The way to get as close as possible to this target is to develop hypotheses by carefully *observing* what people seem to be trying to achieve for themselves, and then to ask them about it.[9]

Sony's founder, Akio Morita, was a master at watching what consumers were trying to get done and at marrying those insights with solutions that helped them do the job better. Between 1950 and 1982, Sony successfully built twelve different new-market disruptive growth businesses. These included the original battery-powered pocket transistor radio, launched in 1955, and the first portable solid-state black-and-white television, in 1959. They also included videocassette players; portable video recorders; the now-ubiquitous Walkman, introduced in 1979; and 3.5-inch floppy disk drives, launched in 1981. How did Sony find these foothold applications that yielded such tremendous up-side fruit?

Every new-product launch decision during this era was made personally by Morita and a trusted group of about five associates. They searched for disruptive footholds by observing and questioning what people really were trying to get done. They looked for ways that miniaturized, solid-state electronics technology might help a larger population of less-skilled and less-affluent people to accomplish, more conveniently and at less expense, the jobs they were already trying to get done through awkward, unsatisfactory means. Morita and his team had an extraordinary track record in finding these footholds for disruption.

Interestingly, 1981 signaled the end of Sony's disruptive odyssey, and for the next eighteen years the company did not launch a single new disruptive growth business. The company continued to be innovative, but its innovations were *sustaining* in character—they were better products targeted at existing markets. Sony's PlayStation, for example, is a great product, but it was a late entrant into a well-established market. Likewise, its Vaio notebook computers are great products, but they too were late entrants into a well-established market.

What caused this abrupt shift in Sony's innovation strategy? In the early 1980s Morita began to withdraw from active management of the company in order to involve himself in Japanese politics.[10] To take his place, Sony began to employ marketers with MBA's to help identify new-growth opportunities. The MBA's brought with them sophisticated, quantitative, attribute-based techniques for segmenting markets and assessing market potential. Although these methods uncovered some underserved opportunities on trajectories of sustaining improvement in established markets, they were weak at synthesizing insights from intuitive observation. In searching for an initial product foothold in new-market disruption, observation and questioning to determine what customers are trying to do, coupled with strategies of rapid development and fast feedback, can greatly improve the probability that a company's products will converge quickly upon a job that people are trying to get done.

Innovations That Will Sustain the Disruption

Gaining a foothold is just the first battle in the war. The exciting growth happens when an innovation *improves* in ways that allow it to displace incumbent offerings. These are sustaining improvements, relative to the initial innovation: improvements that stretch to meet the needs of more and more profitable customers.

With low-end disruptions, it can be easy to determine the right sequence of product improvements in the up-market march. After the
steel minimills established their foothold in the rebar market, for example, the next logical step was fairly obvious: Tackle angle iron and
thicker bars and rods—the grades of steel that were just above rebar.
For Target Stores, the goal was to replicate the product line, brands,
and ambiance that previously were only available in expensive, full-
service department stores. The low-end disruptor's marketing task is
to extend the lower-cost business model up toward products that do
the jobs that more profitable customers are trying to get done.

With new-market disruptions, in contrast, the challenge is to *in-
vent* the upward path, because nobody has been up that trajectory before. Choosing the right improvements is critical to the disruptive
march up-market. Here again, job-based segmentation logic can help.

Let's examine one of the hottest markets of the last decade—handheld wireless electronic devices. The BlackBerry, a handheld wireless
e-mail device made by the Canadian company Research in Motion
(RIM), is an important competitor in this field. RIM found the Black-
Berry's disruptive foothold at a new spot on the third axis in the disruption diagram, competing against nonconsumption by bringing the
ability to receive and send e-mail to new contexts such as waiting
lines, public transit, and conference rooms. So what's next? How does
RIM sustain the product improvement and growth trajectory for its
BlackBerry? Surely, dozens of new ideas are pouring into RIM executives' offices every month for improvements that might be introduced
in the next-generation BlackBerry. Which of these ideas should RIM
invest in, and which should it ignore? These are crucial decisions,
with hundreds of millions of dollars in profits at stake in a rapidly
growing market.

RIM's executives could believe that their market is structured by
product categories characterized by some moniker such as "We compete in handheld wireless devices." If so, they will see the BlackBerry
as competing against products such as the Palm Pilot, Handspring's
Treo, Sony's Clié, mobile telephone handsets made by Nokia, Motorola, and Samsung, and Microsoft Pocket-PC-based devices such as
Compaq's I-Paq and Hewlett-Packard's Jordana. In order to get ahead
of these competitors, RIM would need to develop better products

faster than the competition. Sony's Clié, for example, has a digital camera. Nokia's phones offer not just live conversation and voice messages, but short text messaging as well. The Palm Pilot's consummately convenient calendaring, rolodexing, and note-keeping features have almost become industry standards. And does the fact that Compaq and Hewlett-Packard offer stripped-down versions of Word and Excel software mean that RIM will be left behind if it does not follow suit?

Defining the market by the characteristics of the product *causes* managers to think that in order to beat the competition, RIM would need to build some number of these features into its next-generation BlackBerry device. RIM's competitors, of course, would be thinking the same thing—all trying to cram their competitors' superior features into their products in a race to get ahead of the pack. As suggested in table 3-1, our worry is that defining market segments in a product-based way actually *causes* a headlong, arms race–like rush toward undifferentiable, one-size-fits-all products that perform poorly any specific jobs that customers might hire them to do.

Alternatively, RIM's executives might segment their market in demographic terms—targeting the business traveler, for example—and then add to the BlackBerry those product improvements that would meet those customers' needs. This framing would lead RIM to consider a very different set of innovations. Stripped-down customer relationship management (CRM) software might be considered essential, because it would allow salespeople to review account histories and order status quickly before contacting customers. Downloadable electronic books and magazines would obviate customers' having to carry bulky reading material in their briefcases. Wireless Internet access, with the attendant capabilities to alter travel reservations, trade stocks, and find restaurants via global positioning satellites, could be very appealing. Expense-reporting software coupled with the ability to transmit reports to headquarters wirelessly might be a must.

Every executive who has participated in decisions to define and fund innovation projects will empathize with the tortured difficulty of answering questions such as these. No wonder that many have come to regard innovation as a random crap shoot—or worse, a game of Russian roulette.

TABLE 3-1

How You View the Market for Handheld Devices Will Determine What Product Features You Consider to Be Relevant

Product View	Demographic View	Job-to-Be-Done View
Market Definition The handheld wireless device market	**Market Definition** The traveling salesperson	**Market Definition** Use small snippets of time productively
Competitors Palm Pilot, Handspring Treo, Sony Clié, HP Jordana, Compaq I-Paq, wireless phones	**Competitors** Notebook computers, wireline Internet access, wireless and wireline telephones	**Competitors** Wireless telephones, *Wall Street Journal*, CNN Airport News, listening to boring presentations, doing nothing
Features to consider Digital camera Word Excel Outlook Voice phone Organizer Handwriting recognition	**Features to consider** Wireless Internet access; bandwidth for data Downloadable CRM data/functionality Wireless access to online travel agencies Online stock trading E-books and e-technical manuals E-mail Voice	**Features to consider** E-mail Voice mail Voice phone Headline news, frequent updates Simple, single-player games Entertaining "top ten" lists Always on

But what if RIM structured the segments of this market according to the jobs that people are trying to get done? We've not conducted serious research on this, but just from watching people who pull out their Black-Berries, it seems to us that most of them are hiring it to help them be productive in small snippets of time that otherwise would be wasted. You see BlackBerry owners reading e-mails while waiting in line at airports. When an executive puts an always-on BlackBerry on the table in a meeting, what is she trying to do? Just in case the meeting gets a little slow or boring, she wants to be able to glance through a few messages unobtrusively, just to be a bit more productive. When the pace of the meeting picks up, she can slide the BlackBerry aside and pay attention again.

What is the BlackBerry competing against? What gets hired when people need to be productive in small snippets of time and they don't pick up a BlackBerry? They often pick up a wireless phone. Sometimes they pick up the *Wall Street Journal*. Sometimes they make notes to themselves. Sometimes they stare mindlessly at the CNN Airport Network, or sit with glazed eyes in a boring meeting. From the *customer's* point of view, *these* are the BlackBerry's most direct competitors.

What improvements on the basic BlackBerry wireless e-mail platform does this framing of the market imply? Word, Excel, and CRM software are probably out—it's just really hard to boot up, shift mental gears, be productive, and gear down these activities within a five-minute snippet of time. Snap-on digital cameras likewise aren't likely to be hired to get this job done.

However, wireless telephony is a no-brainer for RIM, because leaving and returning voice messages is another way to be productive in small snippets of time. Financial news headlines and stock quotes would help the BlackBerry compete more effectively against the *Wall Street Journal*. And mindless, single-player games or automatically downloaded Letterman-like lists of ten might help the BlackBerry gain share against boredom. Viewing the market in terms of the jobs that its customers are trying to get done would define for RIM an innovation agenda that is grounded in the way its customers live their lives. The good news for RIM shareholders is that this appears to be the trajectory the BlackBerry is on.[11]

Doing this make-me-productive-in-small-snippets-of-time job perfectly is not trivial, of course. Adding voice telephony to the BlackBerry would increase power consumption. This, however, is the type of challenge classically associated with sustaining innovation. RIM's biggest issue is probably not a lack of engineering talent; it is deciding which problems it should deploy that talent against.[12]

What should Palm do? In the context of the job that the BlackBerry is hired to do, a camera makes no sense. But might it make sense on a product like the Palm Pilot that is used to keep track of people? In addition to just displaying a name card, a camera would enable users to store the person's image as well—helping Palm Pilot users be better organized by remembering not just people's names but their faces, too.[13]

In the Japanese mobile phone market, the strategies of mobile telephony providers J-Phone and NTT DoCoMo to add a camera and photo viewer to the mobile phone and to provide the data services required to send and receive low-quality digital photos met with instant success in the early 2000s. Why? A few years earlier these firms had created a booming new-market disruption selling wireless Internet access through services like DoCoMo's I-Mode. Their customers were primarily teenagers, who had hired mobile access to the Internet in order to have fun with their friends downloading wallpaper and ring tones. The popularity of limited-functionality cameras and photo viewers on these teenagers' phones makes sense when viewed through the lens of jobs to be done: Mobile phones that send and receive photos offer these young people more and newer kinds of fun.

Should European and North American service and handset providers attempt to emulate this success by incorporating this functionality in *their* phones? At this writing, we expect camera-equipped phones to take off much more slowly in these markets, because many mobile phone users in these markets are adults who seem to have hired mobile phones to get work done or exchange important information in small snippets of time. Cameras and viewers rarely help get these jobs done better. If these companies were to market phones and these services to teenagers and children as a new way to have fun by taking and transmitting images, this product feature could create *substantial* growth. But if they follow their demonstrated propensity to deploy the functionality as a high-priced feature on phones that serious multitasking adults have hired to get down to business rather than play, our bet is that little growth will result.

If RIM evolved the BlackBerry to help people be ever more productive in small snippets of time, if Palm evolved its Pilot to help people be ever better organized, and if J-Phone's handsets were optimized to help teenagers have fun, the products would become quite differentiated in consumers' minds—and each could grow to own a large market share of its respective job. And because these different jobs arise at different points in time and space in consumers' lives, we'd bet that for a very long time most consumers would opt to own each product individually rather than having a single, Swiss army knife–like device—that is, until a one-size-fits-all device can do all these jobs without compromising functionality, simplicity, and convenience.

Unfortunately, it appears that many manufacturers in this space are now on a collision course. Each seems bent on packing every other competitor's functionality into a single, all-purpose device. Unchecked, this will lead to commoditized, undifferentiated products that don't do really well any of the jobs that they once got hired to do. This need not be so. The suicidal trajectory results from framing the market in terms of the attributes of products and the attributes of customers, rather than in terms of jobs to be done.

Why Do Executives Segment Markets Counterproductively?

In many ways, what we have said to this point is not news—or at least it shouldn't be. Good researchers have written persuasively, using their own vocabulary, that a jobs-to-be-done perspective is the only way to see accurately what products and services customers will value in the future, and why.[14] Indeed, all executives would *say* that they dream of dominating their market with a highly differentiated product. And most marketers will claim that the very purpose of their work is to understand what customers *do* with their products.

In the face of such desires and beliefs, why do so many managers instead seem to rush headlong in the *other* direction, basing product improvement trajectories on attribute-based segmentation schemes that lead to undifferentiated, one-size-fits-all products? There are at least four reasons or countervailing forces in established companies that *cause* managers to target innovations at attribute-based market segments that are not aligned with the way that customers live their lives. The first two reasons—the fear of focus and the demand for crisp quantification—reside in companies' resource allocation processes. The third reason is that the structure of many retail channels is attribute focused, and the fourth is that advertising economics influence companies to target products at customers rather than circumstances.

Fear of Focus

One reason why it is difficult to create packages of products and services that do particular jobs well is that the more clearly a product is focused on getting a specific job done perfectly, the less appealing it might become when hired for other jobs. Clarifying what job a product should be hired to do, unfortunately, often clarifies what it should *not* be hired to do. Focus helps and it hurts—and it is easier to quantify the hurt than the help.

This is an especially vexing issue for companies such as RIM, Palm, Nokia, and HP as they chart course into a seemingly uncertain future. Each company is more or less positioned, for now, on a specific job: RIM's BlackBerry and Nokia in killing time productively, Palm's Pilot in keeping folks organized, and HP in stripped-down access to computer-based tasks.

If they define their market in terms of the product category, the most tangible growth opportunities are customers and applications that already have been captured by the other companies. So RIM looks to organizer software to help it steal Palm's customers, even as Palm wrestles with ways to make its Pilot a mobile e-mail device.[15] If these companies frame the market as a product category, then *not* to pack all these features into the product indeed seems to sacrifice growth potential.

In contrast, a theory of growth that is grounded on circumstance-based categories—jobs to be done—would lead RIM *not* to copy most features in other handheld devices. This is because the real competition comes from newspapers, mobile phones, CNN Airport Network, and plain old boredom. There is exciting growth potential *within* this job, if RIM can improve its product so that it does the job better than the real competition. It would grow the size of the product category by stealing share from competitors that are outside the category. Furthermore, pursuing this trajectory of improvement would *enhance,* rather than destroy, RIM's product differentiation and its consequent ability to sustain profit margins.

Focus is scary—until you realize that it only means turning your back on markets you could never have anyway. Sharp focus on jobs that customers are trying to get done holds the promise of *greatly* improving the odds of success in new-product development.

Senior Executives' Demand for Quantification of Opportunities

The job that line executives often hire market research to do in the resource allocation process is to define the size of the opportunity, not to understand how customers and markets work.

The information technology (IT) systems in most companies collect, aggregate, and summarize data in various ways to help managers make better decisions. The reports are undoubtedly helpful, but they also lead companies to develop new products and services destined to fail in the marketplace. Almost all corporate IT reports are structured around one of three constructs: products, customers, and organizational units. The data show managers how much of each product is being sold, how profitable each is, which customers are buying which products, and what costs and revenues are associated with servicing each customer. IT systems also report revenues and costs by business units, so that managers can measure the success of the organizations for which they have responsibility.

The odds of developing successful new products begin to tumble when managers collectively begin to assume that the *customer's* world is structured in the same way that the data are aggregated. When managers define market segments along the lines for which data are available rather than the jobs that customers need to get done, it becomes impossible to predict whether a product idea will connect with an important customer job. Using these data to define market segments causes managers to aim innovation at phantom targets. When they frame the customer's world in terms of products, innovators start racing against competitors by proliferating features, functions, and flavors of products that mean little to customers.[16] Framing markets in terms of customer demographics, they average across several different jobs that arise in customers' lives and develop one-size-fits-all products that rarely leave most customers fully satisfied. And framing markets in terms of an organization's boundaries further restricts innovators' abilities to develop products that will truly help their customers get the job done perfectly.

Like it or not, although market researchers often develop a solid understanding of the jobs that customers are trying to do, the primary language through which the nature of the opportunity must be described in the resource allocation process is the language of market size. Asking marketers to understand this concept is not the solution to the problem—because whether it is called "marketing myopia" or jobs-to-be-done, this concept has been taught before.[17] It is a process problem. Because senior managers typically hire market research to quantify the size of opportunities rather than to understand the customer, the resource allocation process systematically and predictably perverts companies' concept of the structure of their market so that it ultimately conforms to the lines along which data are available.

As a result, corporate IT systems and the CIOs who administer them figure among the most important contributors to failure in innovation. Data purchased from external sources have the same impact, because they are structured by product attributes, not by job. The readily available data actually obfuscate the paths to growth.

The solution is not to use data that are collected for historical performance measurement purposes in the processes of new-product development. Keep such data quarantined: They are the wrong data for the job. The size and nature of job-based or circumstance-based market categories actually can be quantified, but this entails a different research process and statistical methodology than is typically employed in most market quantification efforts.[18]

The Structure of Channels

Many retail and distribution channels are organized by product categories rather than according to the jobs that customers need to get done.[19] This channel structure limits innovators' flexibility in focusing their products on jobs that need to be done, because products need to be slotted into the product categories to which shelf space has been allocated.

As an illustration of this challenge, a manufacturer of power tools observed that when hanging a door, tradesmen used at least seven different tools, none of which were job specific, and wasted a lot of time picking up these tools and putting them down. The company developed a new tool concept positioned on the job that made it *much* easier to hang doors accurately. However, it could not be categorized as a plane, a chisel, a screwdriver, a drill, a level, or a hammer. When the company presented the product to the tool buyer of a major retail chain, the buyer responded, "Look. I have a job to do. Here's the plan-o-gram for my shelf space. I buy drills, sanders, and saws. The vendor that offers the most horsepower at a price point gets the space. Your product doesn't help me."

This phenomenon leads many new-market disruptors to seek new channels to the customer—a topic we address in chapter 4. If the product is disruptive to the established retail or wholesale channels because it doesn't help those institutions make more money in the way they are structured to make money, they won't sell it. Consequently, successful disruptive innovators often find that their product must enable a new class of retailers, distributors, or value-added resellers to move up-market and disrupt established channels.[20]

Solving this problem by devising a new channel that is structured and motivated to sell the disruptive, job-positioned product seems ludicrous to executives who need innovations to grow very big, very fast. Doesn't a big established channel promise a much faster ramp to volume? Ironically, it often does not. Finding or building new channels often means turning your back on profits that probably would not have materialized in existing channels anyway.

Advertising Economics and Brand Strategies

The fourth reason why marketing executives tend to segment markets by product or customer attributes is to facilitate communication with customers. It seems easier to devise a communications strategy and to choose the most cost-effective marketing media buys if consumer markets are sliced along dimensions such as age, sex, lifestyle, or product category. The same seems true if marketers slice commercial markets by geography, industry, or size of business. But when communication strategies drive segmentation schemes, the attributes of the targeted customers can confuse the product development process, causing companies to develop products that do several jobs poorly, and none perfectly.

Think back to our example of the quick-service food restaurant's milkshakes, and consider a member of a demographic segment—a forty-year-old married man with two young sweet-toothed children, who also has a long, boring commute to work and gets hungry at lunchtime. What and how should the chain communicate to this customer? If it tells him that he can quickly buy a viscous, interest-ingly chunky milkshake from a self-serve machine when he needs some-thing to keep his hands busy during his boring commute, how can the chain also tell him that he should come back to hire a small liquid shake when he needs to capitulate to his children? Or drop by to hire a hamburger when feed-me-fast-at-lunchtime is the job? Sending sep-arate communications about each of these jobs to the same customer is prohibitively expensive, and yet communicating all of them to the customer at once would be confusing. So what's the chain to do?

The answer is that just as it needs to develop products for the cir-cumstance and not the customer, the chain needs to *communicate to the circumstance,* and not necessarily to the consumer. It can commu-nicate to the circumstance with a *brand,* if it employs the right brand-ing strategy. If it does this, then when customers find themselves in the circumstance, they will think instinctively of the brand and know what product to buy in order to get that job done.

Brands are, at the beginning, hollow words into which marketers stuff meaning. If a brand's meaning is positioned on a job to be done, then when the job arises in a customer's life, he or she will remember the brand and hire the product. Customers pay significant premiums for brands that do a job well.

Some executives worry that a low-end disruptive product might harm their established brand. They can escape this problem by append-ing a second word to their corporate brand. We call this word a *purpose* brand because it communicates to a circumstance—to a *job* that the dis-ruptive product should be hired to do. If customers hire a disruptive product to do the wrong job, it will disappoint and thereby tarnish the corporation's brand.[21] If the disruptive product is hired for the job that it was designed to do, it will delight the customer and thereby strengthen the corporate brand—even though the disruptive product's functional-ity may not be as good as that of mainstream products. This is because customers define quality within the context of the job to be done.

Let's examine Kodak's experience when it launched single-use cameras, which were a classic new-market disruption. Because of their inexpensive plastic lenses, the quality of photographs taken with single-use cameras was not as good as the photos taken by good

35mm cameras. As a result, the proposition to launch a single-use camera business encountered vigorous opposition within Kodak's film division. The corporation finally gave responsibility for the opportunity to a completely different organizational unit, which launched single-use cameras with a purpose brand—the Kodak Funsaver. This was a product to be hired when customers needed to save memories of fun occasions but had forgotten to bring a camera. The Funsaver camera competed against nonconsumption. Customers whose basis of comparison was to have no photos at all were delighted with the quality of this solution to saving their fun. Creating a purpose brand for a disruptive job differentiated the product, clarified its intended use, delighted the customers, and thereby *strengthened* the Kodak brand.

Marriott Corporation has done the same thing by developing a brand architecture that is consistent with several different jobs its customers experience in life. This architecture has facilitated the creation of new disruptive businesses, while strengthening the Marriott brand at the same time. Under the endorsement of the Marriott brand, we have been taught to hire a Marriott Hotel when the job is to convene a major business meeting, and to choose a Courtyard by Marriott ("The hotel designed by business travelers for business travelers") when the job is to get a clean, quiet place to work into the evening. We learned to hire Fairfield Inn by Marriott when the job is finding an inexpensive place to stay as a family, and Residence Inn by Marriott to find a home away from home. The Marriott brand remains unsullied by all of this, because the purpose brands make the job clear.

In contrast, if Marriott marketers had positioned Courtyard hotels in a segment defined by a lower price point—a cheaper, lower-quality solution to the same job that the top-tier Marriott-brand hotels are hired to do—then the disruption could indeed have damaged the Marriott brand. But if a crisply defined purpose brand guides customers to hire the various hotels to do very different jobs, and if the hotel chains each are designed to do their respective jobs perfectly, then they *all* will be viewed as high-quality hotels, thereby strengthening the endorsing power of the Marriott brand. Brand strategies that make it easy for customers to make the connection between a job that arises and the product they can hire to do the job perfectly can make disruption all the easier.

The Dangers of Asking Customers to Change Jobs

At a fundamental level, the things that people want to accomplish in their lives don't change quickly. This is why in our disruptive innovation research, the trajectories of improvement that customers can utilize in any given application or tier of the market tend to be quite flat. Given this stability, an idea stands little chance of success if it requires customers to prioritize jobs they haven't cared about in the past. Customers don't just "change jobs" because a new product becomes available. Rather, the new product will succeed to the extent it helps customers accomplish more effectively and conveniently what they're already trying to do.

Let's test the viability of a new-product idea by exploring the potential for digital imaging to create growth by disrupting photographic film. How did most of us use photographic film prior to digital photography? We wanted good shots, so we often took multiple pictures of the same pose, in case somebody blinked at the wrong instant. When we dropped our film off at the developer's, most of us ordered double prints. If one of the pictures turned out well, we wanted a spare easily available to send to a friend or relative. We brought the photos home, flipped through them, put them back into the envelope, and put them into a box or drawer. About 98 percent of all images were looked at only once. Only rare, conscientious people went back and mounted the best photos in an album. Most of us wanted to maintain good photo albums and intended to do so, but the fact was that we just had higher priorities.

Some digital imaging companies then came along with interesting propositions. "If you'll just take the time to learn how to use this software, you can edit out the red-eye in all those flash pictures that you only look at once" was one. "You can now keep all your pictures neatly arranged and sortable in online photo albums" was another. It turns out that the vast majority of digital camera owners do neither of these things. Why? Because they weren't prioritizing those things before. Innovations that make it easier for customers to do what they weren't already trying to get done must compete against customers' priorities. This is very hard to do.

Digital camera owners use their cameras for jobs they already had been trying to get done. For example, most of us use such a camera to verify on the spot that the image is good, and if it isn't, we delete it and try again—the same job as taking multiple shots on film of the same pose. And we send digital images much less expensively and conveniently to far more people over the Internet than we ever had been able to do when we ordered double prints. (Interestingly, have you noticed what we do after we've looked at an image that has been e-mailed to us? We click "close," putting it back in some "envelope" on our hard drive.) The things we prioritize in our lives are remarkably stable.

Another example: Hundreds of millions have been spent to apply new technologies—the Internet and e-book displays, specifically—to reshape the college textbook industry. Innovators have attempted to develop and sell tablets that can display downloaded e-books. And with many textbooks, you can click on a URL to obtain far more information about the topic than could possibly be included within the limits of a book. Would we expect these investments to generate significant growth? Our guess is that they will not. Although we would like to believe that all undergraduate students are rigorous seekers of knowledge, the job that many college students are really trying to get done, from our observation, is to pass their courses without having to read the textbook at all.

These companies have spent *a lot* of money helping students to do more easily something that they have been trying *not* to do. It would probably take far less money to create from the same technology a service called "Cram.com"—a utility that would make it easier and cheaper for students to cram more effectively for their exams. This would likely work because cramming is something that students already are trying to do, but with marginal efficacy. There are *a lot* of textbook-avoiders on campuses—a huge market of nonconsumption.

After logging on, Cram.com would ask subscribers what course they need to cram for—say, College Algebra. Then it would ask which of this list of textbooks the professor expected them to have read by now. It would ask them to click on the type of problem that they are having trouble with, and it would walk them through a tutorial.

The next year, Cram.com would need to offer a new and improved service, one that made it even easier and faster to cram better—inching up from the least-conscientious to the sporadically diligent tiers of the student population. After a few years, two students might be overheard in the college bookstore anguishing over the exorbitant price of a textbook: "You know, my brother took that course last year. He's a good student, but he never even bought the book. He just used Cram.com from the beginning of the semester, and he did great." Bingo. A new-market disruption that helped customers achieve what they already had been trying to do.

Identifying disruptive footholds means connecting with specific jobs that people—your future customers—are trying to get done in their lives. The problem is that in an attempt to build convincing business cases for new products, managers are compelled to quantify the opportunities they perceive, and the data available to do this are typically cast in terms of product attributes or the demographic and psychographic profiles of a given population of potential consumers. This mismatch between the true needs of consumers and the data that shape most product development efforts leads most companies to aim their innovations at nonexistent targets. The importance of identifying these jobs to be done goes beyond simply finding a foothold. Only by staying connected with a given job as improvements are made, and by creating a purpose brand so that customers know what to hire, can a disruptive product stay on its growth trajectory.

Notes

1. See, for example, chapter 7 in Dorothy Leonard, *Wellsprings of Knowledge* (Boston: Harvard Business School Press, 1996).
2. Some researchers (for example, Joe Pine, in his classic work *Mass Customization* [Boston: Harvard Business School Press, 1992]) argues that ultimately

segmentation may be unimportant because individual customers' needs might be addressed individually. Although this is conceivable, getting there will take some time. We will show in chapters 5 and 6 that in many circumstances it is not possible. Segmentation, in other words, will always be important.

3. We are deeply indebted to two of our colleagues who originally introduced us to this way of thinking about the structure of markets. The first is Richard Pedi, CEO of Gage Foods in Bensenville, Illinois. Rick coined for us the language "jobs to be done." Independently, Anthony Ulwick of Lansana, Florida–based Strategyn, Inc., has developed and used a very similar concept in his consulting work, using the phrase "outcomes that customers are seeking." Tony has published a number of pieces on these concepts, including "Turn Customer Input into Innovation," *Harvard Business Review,* January 2002, 91–98. Tony uses these concepts to help his firm's clients develop products that connect with what their customers are trying to get done. We are also indebted to David Sundahl, who as Professor Christensen's research associate helped formulate many of the initial ideas upon which this chapter was built.

4. Many of the details in this account have been changed to protect the proprietary interests of the company while preserving the fundamental character of the study and its conclusions.

5. The language in this paragraph reveals a nested system. Within the overarching job to be done are many unique outcomes that need to be achieved in order for the job to be done perfectly. Hence, when we use the term *outcome* in our work on segmentation, we refer to the individual things that need to be done right, such as lasting a long time, not creating a mess, and so on, in order for the job to get done right.

6. One can see this problem even in the recent marketing trend toward so-called markets of one. Markets of one drive companies to provide customization options that meet all the needs of individual customers. But customization comes at a price. What is more, it often does not provide an understanding of the underlying outcomes-driven logic of customer purchasing decisions. Because market research tools as sophisticated as geocoding pay attention to the attributes of people, they cannot yield market segmentation schemes that make sense to customers—each of whom has many jobs that he or she is trying to get done. There actually is a lot of commonality in jobs to be done within a population of people and companies, suggesting that targeting markets of one may often not be a viable or desirable marketing objective.

7. The observation that customers search across product categories to find ways to achieve needed outcomes is grounded in psychological research,

which demonstrates that our perceptual systems are geared toward understanding what we can use objects to do and whether they are optimal for
such purposes. For example, psychologist James J. Gibson, widely respected
for his research on theories of perception, has written about "affordances,"
a concept that mirrors what we term "jobs" or "outcomes." According to
Gibson, "The affordances of the environment are what it offers . . . , what it
provides or furnishes, either for good or ill." Gibson asserts that we see the
world not in terms of primary qualities, like being yellow or being twenty-
four ounces by volume, but in terms of outcomes: "What we perceive when
we look at objects are their [outcomes], not their qualities. We can discrimi-
nate the dimensions of difference if required to do so in an experiment, but
what the object affords us is what we normally pay attention to." What matters about the ground, for example, is that it provides us a platform on
which to stand, walk, build, and so forth. We don't "hire" the ground for its
color or moisture content per se. The affordances of products, in Gibson's
terms, are the outcomes that those products enable their users to achieve. See
James J. Gibson, *The Ecological Approach to Visual Perception* (Boston:
Houghton Mifflin, 1979), 127.

8. Finding a "killer app" has been a holy grail of innovators ever since Larry
   Downes and Chunka Mui popularized the term in *Unleashing the Killer App*
   (Boston: Harvard Business School Press, 1998). Unfortunately, much of
   what has been written on this search has simply comprised accounts of historically successful killer apps. We think that a rigorous study of such applications would show that they were killers because the product or service was
   squarely positioned on a job that a lot of people already were trying to get
   done—the innovation in question simply helped them get it done better, and
   more conveniently.

9. The firm headed by Mr. Ulwick that we mentioned in note 3 has proprietary
   methods for categorizing job-defined markets and measuring their size.

10. This information was recounted to us in a July 2000 interview with Mickey
    Schulhoff, who worked for over twenty years as CEO of Sony America and
    served for much of this time as a member of Sony Corporation's board of
    directors.

11. We must emphasize here that we have absolutely no inside information
    about any of the companies or products mentioned in this section, nor have
    we conducted any formal market research on these products or jobs.
    Rather, we have written this material simply to illustrate how theories that
    are constructed on circumstance-based categories about what products will
    connect with customers can bring clarity and predictability to what histori-
    cally has been a hit-and-miss task in innovation. It may very well be, for ex-
    ample, that given RIM's strategy of emphasizing sales to enterprises rather

than individual customers, it is the corporate CIO manager who has the job to do: being sure that the firm's knowledge workers are able to communicate and be contacted on a real-time, no-excuses basis. The same exercise would be useful if applied to this job.

12. As this book was being written, in fact, RIM and Nokia announced a partnership through which Nokia will license RIM's software to enable wireless e-mail on Nokia's phones—a deal that makes sense for both firms because in many ways their products are hired to do the same job. Whether one would prefer to produce the BlackBerry that ultimately will compete against wireless phones to do this job, or whether it would be better to provide the software inside others' wireless phones, as the new Nokia-RIM arrangement provides, is a question that the theory in chapters 5 and 6 will address.

13. We have gone out on the end of a very long limb in making these statements, because the future has not yet happened. We have presented this analysis provocatively in order to illustrate the fundamental principle. In all probability, the makers of wireless hand-held devices will engage in a headlong rush to incorporate every competitor's latest features on their products, leading the industry very prematurely to a situation in which products are undifferentiated, commoditized, one-size-fits-all solutions. When this happens, we urge our readers *not* to conclude that "Christensen and Raynor were wrong." We would assert that although some blurring and copying of features will inevitably occur, the longer each manufacturer focuses on incorporating those features and functions that do a unique job well and the longer they position their marketing message on that unique job, the faster the suppliers of these devices will grow because they will gain share not against each other, but against other products and services that get hired to do those jobs. We would also argue that these firms will preserve their differentiability and profitability longer if they focus their improvement trajectory on a unique job. The fact that they are unlikely to do this does not disprove the principle.

14. See, for example, Leonard, *Wellsprings of Knowledge;* Eric von Hippel, *The Sources of Innovation* (New York: Oxford University Press, 1988); and Stefan Thomke, *Experimentation Matters: Unlocking the Potential of New Technologies for Innovation* (Boston: Harvard Business School Press, 2003).

15. In concept, of course, being able to carry one small device that does everything in a briefcase or purse is something that all customers would say they want. But it is rare that there are no technological trade-offs to adding diverse functionality to a product. Software makes it less expensive to tailor a single physical platform to do a range of focused jobs. Our proposition, however, is that even in this situation, a company would do better by using

one single hardware platform to market different software-defined, optimized products that are positioned on different jobs. It is likely that for a long time electronic devices that combine such a wide range of functionality in the interests of doing many jobs simultaneously—organize me, connect me, help me have fun, and so forth—are likely to end up more like a Swiss army knife: a pretty good knife, terrible scissors, a marginal bottle opener, and a crummy screwdriver. As long as the jobs that customers need to get done arise at independent points in time and space, we would expect that most customers will continue to carry multiple devices until a one-size-fits-all omnibus device can do all jobs as well as its focused competitors.

16. The experience that Intuit had in disrupting the small business accounting software market with its QuickBooks product typifies this situation. Until the early 1990s the only available small business software had been written by accountants for accountants. Because they defined their market in terms of the product, they framed their competitors as other makers of accounting software. The vision that this framing gave them about how to get ahead of their competitors, therefore, was to engage in an arms race of sorts: Be faster adding features and functionality in the form of new reports and analyses that could be run. The industry gradually converged upon undifferentiated, one-size-fits-all products, into which everybody had appended everybody else's features.

    Intuit's marketers were wont to watch what jobs the customers of Intuit's Quicken personal financial management software were trying to get done for themselves when using the product. In the course of doing this, they observed to their surprise that a large proportion of Quicken users were employing it to keep track of their small business's finances. The job, they learned, was basically to keep track of cash. These small business owners had their fingers in every dimension of their business and did not need all of the financial reports and analyses that the prevailing software providers had cobbled into their products. Intuit launched QuickBooks at this job that small business owners needed to get done—"Just help me be sure I don't run out of cash"—and succeeded spectacularly. Within two years the company had seized 85 percent of the market with a disruptive product that lacked most of the functionality of the competing products.

17. Theodore Levitt has been a leading proponent of this view among those who research and write about issues in marketing. Christensen remembers that when he was an M.B.A. student he heard Ted Levitt declare, "People don't want to buy a quarter-inch *drill*. They want a quarter-inch *hole*." In our words, they have a job to do, and they hire something to do the job. Levitt's best-known explanation of these principles is found in Theodore Levitt,

"Marketing Myopia," *Harvard Business Review,* September 1975, reprint 75507.

18. For suggestions on how the magnitude of job-defined market segments can be measured, see Anthony W. Ulwick, "Turn Customer Input into Innovation," *Harvard Business Review*, January 2002, 91–98.

19. We are grateful to Mike Collins, founder and CEO of the Big Idea Group, for his comments that led to many of the ideas in this section. Mike reviewed an early draft of this chapter, and his thoughts were extraordinarily helpful.

20. One reason that some (but not all) "category killer" retail formats—companies such as Home Depot and Lowe's—have been able to disrupt established retailers so successfully is that they are organized around jobs to be done.

21. Because many marketers inadvertently and over time tend to segment their markets along attribute-based categorizations of products and people, it is unfortunate, but not surprising, that they often do to their brands the same thing that they have done to their products. Brands often have become omnibus words that don't do well any of the jobs that customers need to get done when they hire the brand. Because most advertisers want a brand's meaning to be flexible enough for a range of products to be housed under its umbrella, many brands have lost their association with a job. When this happens, customers remain confused about what product to buy to get the job done when they find themselves in a particular circumstance.

CHAPTER FOUR

WHO ARE THE BEST CUSTOMERS FOR OUR PRODUCTS?

Which customers should we target? Which customer base will be the most valuable foundation for future growth? Is our growth potential greatest if we pursue the largest markets? How can we predict which competitors will target which sets of customers? What sales and distribution channels will most capably embrace our product and devote the resources required to grow the market as fast as possible?

The message of chapter 2 was that although sustaining innovations are critical to the growth of existing businesses, a disruptive strategy offers a much higher probability of success in building new-growth businesses. Chapter 3's message was that managers often segment markets along the lines for which data are available, rather than in ways that reflect the things that customers are trying to get done. Using flawed segmentation schemes, they often introduce products that customers don't want, because they aim at a target that is irrelevant to what customers are trying to get done. This chapter addresses two questions that are closely tied to the last: Which initial customers are most likely to become the solid foundation upon which we can build a successful growth business? And how should we reach them?

It's relatively straightforward to find the ideal customers for a low-end disruption. They are current users of a mainstream product who seem disinterested in offers to sell them improved-performance products. They may be willing to accept improved products, but they are unwilling to pay premium prices to get them.[1] The key to success with low-end disruptions is to devise a business model that can earn attractive returns at the discount prices required to win business at the low end.

It is much trickier to find the new-market customers (or "nonconsumers") on the third axis of the disruptive innovation model. How can you know whether current nonconsumers can be enticed to begin consuming? When only a fraction of a population is using a product, of course, some of the nonconsumption may simply reflect the fact that there just isn't a job needing to be done in the lives of those nonconsumers. That is why the "jobs question" is a critical early test for a viable new-market disruption. A product that purports to help nonconsumers do something that they weren't already prioritizing in their lives is unlikely to succeed.

For example, throughout the 1990s a number of companies thought they saw a growth opportunity in the significant proportion of American households that did not yet own a computer. Reasoning that the cause of nonconsumption was that computers cost too much, they decided that they could create growth by developing an "appliance" that could access the Internet and perform the basic functions of a computer at a price around $200. A number of capable companies, including Oracle, tried to open this market, but failed. We suspect that there just weren't any jobs needing to get done in those nonconsuming households for which less-expensive computers were a solution. Chapter 3 taught us that circumstances like this are *not* good growth opportunities.

Another kind of nonconsumption occurs, however, when people are trying to get a job done but are unable to accomplish it themselves because the available products are too expensive or too complicated. Hence, they put up with getting it done in an inconvenient, expensive, or unsatisfying way. This type of nonconsumption is a growth opportunity. A new-market disruption is an innovation that enables a larger population of people who previously lacked the money or skill now to begin buying and using a product and doing the job for themselves. From this point onward, we will use the terms *nonconsumers* and *nonconsumption* to refer to this type of situation, where the job needs to get done but a good solution historically has been beyond reach. We sometimes say that innovators who target these new markets are *competing against nonconsumption.*

We'll begin with three short case studies of new-market disruption, and then synthesize across these histories a common pattern that typifies the customers, applications, and channels where new-market disruptions tend to find their foothold. We'll explore why so few companies historically have sought nonconsumers as the foundation for growth, and then close by suggesting what to do about it.

New-Market Disruptions: Three Case Histories

New-market disruptions follow a remarkably consistent pattern, regardless of the type of industry or the era in history when the disruption occurred. In this section we'll synthesize this pattern from three disruptions: one from the 1950s, one that began in the 1980s and continues in the present, and a third that is still in its nascent stage. In these and scores of other cases we've studied, it is stunning to see the sins of the past so regularly visited upon the later generations of disruptees. Today we can see dozens of companies making the same predictable mistakes, and the disruptors capitalizing on them.

The Disruption of Vacuum Tubes by Transistors

Scientists at AT&T's Bell Laboratories invented the transistor in 1947. It was disruptive relative to the prior technology, vacuum tubes. The early transistors could not handle the power required for the electronic products of the 1950s—tabletop radios, floor-standing televisions, early digital computers, and products for military and commercial telecommunications. As depicted in the original value network of figure 4-1, the vacuum tube makers, such as RCA, licensed the transistor from Bell Laboratories and brought it into their own laboratories, framing it as a technology problem. As a group they aggressively invested hundreds of millions of dollars trying to make solid-state technology good enough that it could be used in the market.

FIGURE 4-1

Value Networks for Vacuum Tubes and Transistors

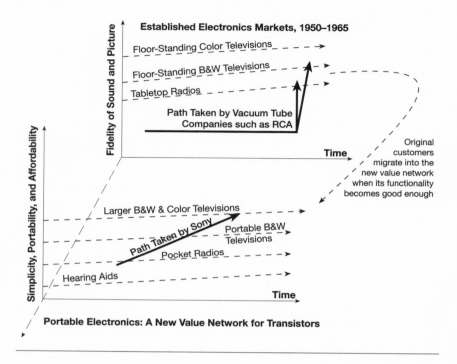

Portable Electronics: A New Value Network for Transistors

While the vacuum tube makers worked feverishly in their laboratories targeting the existing market, the first application emerged in a new value network on the third axis of the disruption diagram: a germanium transistor hearing aid, an application that *valued* the low power consumption that made transistors worthless in the mainstream market. Then in 1955 Sony introduced the world's first battery-powered, pocket transistor radio—an application that again valued transistors for attributes that were irrelevant in mainstream markets, such as low power consumption, ruggedness, and compactness.

Compared with the tabletop radios made by RCA, the sound from the Sony pocket radio was tinny and static-laced. But Sony thrived because it chose to *compete against nonconsumption* in a new value network. Rather than marketing its radio to consumers who owned tabletop devices, Sony instead targeted the rebar of humanity—teenagers, few of whom could afford big vacuum tube radios. The portable transistor radio offered them a rare treat: the chance to listen to rock and roll music with their friends in new places out of the earshot of their parents. The teenagers were thrilled to buy a product that wasn't very good, because their alternative was no radio at all.

The next application emerged in 1959, with the introduction of Sony's twelve-inch black-and-white portable television. Again, Sony's strategy was to compete against nonconsumption, as it made televisions available to people who previously couldn't afford them, many of whom lived in small apartments that lacked the space for floor-standing televisions. These customers were delighted to own products that weren't nearly as good as the large TVs in the established market, because the alternative was no television at all.

As these major new disruptive markets for transistor-based products emerged, the traditional makers of vacuum tube–based appliances felt no pain because Sony wasn't competing for their customers. Furthermore, the vacuum tube makers' aggressive efforts to develop solid-state electronics in their own laboratories gave them comfort that they were doing what they should about the future.

When solid-state electronics finally became good enough to handle the power required in large televisions and radios, Sony and its retailers simply vacuumed out the customers from the original plane, as depicted in figure 4-1. Within a few years the vacuum tube–based companies, including the venerable RCA, had vaporized.

Targeting customers who had been nonconsumers worked magic for Sony in two ways. First, because its customers' reference point was having no television or radio at all, they were delighted with simple, crummy products. The performance hurdle that Sony had to clear therefore was relatively easy. This entailed a much lower R&D investment prior to commercialization than the vacuum tube makers had to make to commercialize the identical technology. The established market presented a *much* higher performance barrier to surmount, because customers there would only embrace solid-state electronics when they became superior to vacuum tubes in those applications.[2]

Second, Sony's sales grew to significant levels before RCA and its competitors felt any threat. The painlessness of Sony's attack persisted even after its products improved to become performance-competitive with low-end vacuum tube–based products. When Sony started to pull the least-attractive customers from the original value network into its new one, losing those who bought their lowest-margin products actually felt good to makers of vacuum tube–based appliances. They were immersed in an aggressive up-market foray of their own into color television. These were large, complicated machines that sold for very attractive margins in their original value network. As a result, the vacuum tube companies' profit margins actually improved as they were being disrupted. There simply was no crisis to prompt them to counterattack Sony.

When the crisis became clear, the manufacturers of vacuum tube products couldn't just switch to the new technology and pull customers back into their old business model, because the cost structure of that model and of their distribution and sales channels was not competitive. The only way they could have retained or recaptured their customers would have been to reposition their companies in the new value network. That would have entailed, among other restructurings, shifting to a completely different channel of distribution.

Vacuum tube–based appliances were sold through appliance stores that made most of their profits replacing burned-out vacuum tubes in the products they had sold. Appliance stores couldn't make money selling solid-state televisions and radios because they didn't have vacuum tubes that would burn out. Sony and the other vendors of transistor-based products therefore had to create a new channel in their new value network. These were chain stores such as F. W. Woolworth and discount retailers such as Korvette's and Kmart, which themselves had been "nonvendors"—they hadn't been able to sell radios and televisions because they had lacked the ability to service burned-out vacuum tubes. When RCA and its vacuum tube cohort finally started making solid-state products and turned to the discount channel for distribution, they found that the shelf space had already been claimed.

The punishing thing about this outcome, of course, is that RCA and its colleagues didn't fail because they didn't invest aggressively in the new technology. They failed because they tried to cram the disruption into the largest and most obvious market, which was filled with customers whose business could only be won by selling them a product that was better in performance or cost than they already were using.

Angioplasty: A Disruption of Heart-Stopping Proportions

Balloon angioplasty is an ongoing example of a new-market disruption. Prior to the early 1980s, the only people with heart disease who could receive interventional therapy were those who were at high and immediate risk of death. There was *a lot* of nonconsumption in this market: Most people who suffered from heart disease simply went untreated. Angioplasty enabled a new group of providers—cardiologists—to treat coronary artery disease by threading a catheter into a partially clogged artery of these previously untreated patients and puffing up a balloon. It was often ineffective: Half of the patients suffered restenosis, or a reclogging of the artery, within a year. But because the procedure was simple and inexpensive, more patients with partially occluded arteries could begin receiving treatment. The cardiologists benefited too, because even without being trained in surgery they could keep the fees for themselves, and had to refer fewer patients to the heart surgeons, who earned the most handsome fees. Angioplasty thereby created a huge new growth market in cardiac care.

If its inventors had attempted to market angioplasty as a sustaining technology—a better alternative than cardiac bypass surgery—it would not have worked. Angioplasty *couldn't* solve difficult blockage problems at the outset. Any attempt to improve it enough so that heart surgeons would choose angioplasty over bypass surgery would have entailed extraordinary time and expense.

Could the inventors have commercialized angioplasty as a low-end disruption—a less-expensive way for heart surgeons to treat their least-sick patients? No. Patients and surgeons weren't yet overserved by the efficacy of bypass surgery.

The successful disruptive innovators chose a third approach: enabling less-seriously ill patients to receive therapy that was better than the alternative (nothing), and enabling cardiologists profitably to pull into their own practices patients who previously had to wait until they were sick enough to be referred to more expensive experts. Under these circumstances a booming new market emerged.

Figure 4-2 shows the growth that resulted from this disruption. Interestingly, for a very long time cardiac bypass surgery continued to grow, even as angioplasty began thriving and improving in its new value network. The reason was that in their efforts to treat patients with partially occluded arteries, cardiologists discovered many more patients whose arteries were too clogged to be opened with angioplasty—patients whose disease previously was not diagnosed. So heart surgeons felt no threat—in fact, they felt *healthy*, for a long time—just like the large steel mills and the makers of vacuum tubes.[3]

As cardiologists and their device suppliers pursued the higher profits that came from better products and premium services, they discovered that they could insert stents to prop open even difficult-to-open arteries. (Stents caused the up-kink in angioplasty growth that began in 1995.) Customers who otherwise would have needed bypass

FIGURE 4-2

Number of Angioplasty and Cardiac Bypass Surgery Procedures

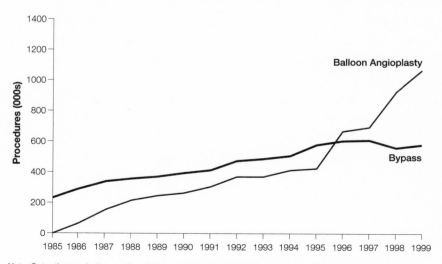

Note: Outpatient and other nonhospital procedures not included (angioplasty numbers are underestimated).

Source: American Heart Association National Center.

surgery are now being pulled into the new value network, and the cardiologists have done this without having to be trained as heart surgeons. This disruption has been underway for two decades, but the surgeons only recently have sensed the threat as the number of open-heart cardiac surgeries has begun to decline. In the most complex tiers of the market, there will be demand for open-heart surgery for a long time. But that market will shrink—and now that the disruption is apparent, there is little that the heart surgeons can do.

Like pocket radios and portable TVs, the "channels"—the venues in which interventional cardiac care is delivered—are also being disrupted. Bypass surgery is a hospital-based procedure because of the risks it entails. But little by little, as technology has improved cardiologists' ability to diagnose and prevent complications, more and more angioplasty procedures are being performed in cardiac care clinics, whose costs make them disruptive relative to full-service hospitals.

Solar Versus Conventional Electrical Energy

Consider solar energy as a third example. It defies profitable commercialization despite billions of dollars invested to make the technology viable. This is indeed daunting when the business plan is to compete against conventional sources of electricity in developed countries. About two-thirds of the world's population has access to electric power transmitted from central generating stations. In advanced economies this power is available almost all the time, is a very cost-effective means of getting work done, and is available essentially twenty-four hours per day, cloudy and sunny weather alike. This is a tough standard for solar energy to compete against.

Yet if developers of this technology instead targeted nonconsumers—the two billion people in South Asia and Africa who have no access to conventionally generated electricity—the prospects for solar energy might look quite different. The standard of comparison for those potential customers is no electricity at all. Their homes aren't filled with power-hungry appliances, either, so it would be a vast improvement over the present state of affairs for these customers if they could store enough energy during daylight to power an electric light at night. Solar energy would be *much* less expensive, and would probably entail fewer headaches from governmental approvals and corruption, than would building a conventional generation and distribution infrastructure in those areas.

Some might protest that photovoltaic cells are simply too expensive ever to be made and sold profitably to impoverished populations. Maybe. But many of the technical paradigms in present photovoltaic technology were developed in attempts at *sustaining* innovation—to push the bleeding edge of performance as far as possible in the quest to compete against consumption in North America and Europe. Targeting new unserved markets would lower the performance hurdle, allowing some to conclude, for example, that instead of building the cells on silicon wafers they can deposit the required materials onto a sheet of plastic in a continuous, roll-to-roll process.

If history is any guide, the commercially viable innovations in clean energy will not come from government-financed research projects designed to make solar energy a preferred source of power in developed markets. Rather, the successful innovations will emerge from companies who carve disruptive footholds by targeting nonconsumption and moving up-market with better products only after they have started simple and small.

Extracting Growth from Nonconsumption: A Synthesis

We distill from these histories four elements of a pattern of new-market disruption. Managers can use this pattern as a template to find ideal customers and market applications for disruptive innovations, or they can use it to shape nascent ideas into business plans that match this proven pattern for generating new-market growth. These elements are as follows:

1. The target customers are trying to get a job done, but because they lack the money or skill, a simple, inexpensive solution has been beyond reach.

2. These customers will compare the disruptive product to having nothing at all. As a result, they are delighted to buy it even though it may not be as good as other products available at high prices

to current users with deeper expertise in the original value network. The performance hurdle required to delight such new-market customers is quite modest.

3. The technology that enables the disruption might be quite sophisticated, but disruptors deploy it to make the purchase and use of the product simple, convenient, and foolproof. It is the "foolproofedness" that creates new growth by enabling people with less money and training to begin consuming.

4. The disruptive innovation creates a whole new value network. The new consumers typically purchase the product through new channels and use the product in new venues.

The history of each new-market disruptor in figure 2-4 mirrors this pattern. From Black & Decker to Intel, from Microsoft to Bloomberg, from Oracle to Cisco, from Toyota to Southwest Airlines, and from Intuit's QuickBooks to Salesforce.com, new-market disruptions fit this pattern. In so doing, they have been a dominant engine of growth not just for shareholder value but for the world economy.

Disruptions that fit this pattern succeed because while all of this is happening, the established competitors view the entrants in the emerging market as irrelevant to their well-being.[4] The growth in the new value network does not affect demand in the mainstream market for some time—in fact, incumbents sometimes prosper for a time *because* of the disruption. What is more, the incumbents are comfortable that they have sensed the threat and are responding. But it is the wrong response. They invest massive sums trying to advance the technology enough to please the customers in the existing value network. In so doing, they force the disruptive technology to compete on a sustaining basis—and nearly always, they fail.

It's quite stunning, when you think about it. This pattern would strike most managers as a dream come true. What more could you want than a situation where customers are easily delighted, powerful competitors ignore you, and you're locked arm-in-arm with channel partners in a win-win race toward exciting growth? We will explore next why this dream so often becomes a nightmare instead, and then suggest what to do about it.

What Makes Competing Against Nonconsumption So Hard?

The logic of competing against nonconsumption as the means for creating new-growth markets seems obvious. Despite this, established companies repeatedly do just the opposite. They choose to compete at the outset against consumption, trying to stretch the disruptive innovation to compete against—and ultimately supplant—established products, sold by well-entrenched competitors in large, obvious market applications. Doing this requires enormous amounts of money, and such attempts almost always fail. Established firms *almost always* do this, rather than shaping their ideas to fit the pattern of successful disruption noted earlier. Why?

In a very insightful stream of research, Harvard Business School Professor Clark Gilbert has helped us understand the fundamental mechanism that causes the established competitors in an industry to consistently cram the disruptive technology into the mainstream market. With that understanding, Gilbert also provides guidance to established company executives on how to avoid this trap, and capture the growth created by disruption instead.[5]

Threats Versus Opportunities

Gilbert has borrowed insights from the fields of cognitive and social psychology, as exemplified in the work of Nobel Prize winners Daniel Kahneman and Amos Tversky, to study disruption.[6] Kahneman and Tversky examined how individuals and groups perceive risk and noted that if you frame a phenomenon to an individual or a group as a threat, it elicits a far more intense and energetic response than if you frame the same phenomenon as an opportunity. Furthermore, other researchers have observed that when people encounter a significant threat, a response called "threat rigidity" sets in. The instinct of threat rigidity is to cease being flexible and to become "command and control" oriented—to focus everything on countering the threat in order to survive.[7]

You can see exactly this behavior among the established firms that experience new-market disruptions. Because the disruptions emerge at a time when the established firms' core business is robust, framing the new-market disruption as an opportunity simply does not get people's attention: It makes little sense to invest in new-growth businesses when the present ones are doing well.

When visionary executives and technologists *do* see the disruption coming, they frame it as a threat, seeing that their companies could be imperiled if these technologies succeed. This framing as a threat rather than an opportunity is what elicits a resource commitment from the established firms to address the technology. But because they instinctively define the disruption as a threat, they focus on being able to protect their customers and their current business. They want to be there with the new technology ready when they must switch to it in order to protect their current customers. This causes the organization to pursue a strategy that not only misses the growth opportunity but also leads to its eventual destruction—because the disruptors who take root in nonconsumption eventually kill them. This just means, however, that established firms must reposition themselves on the other side of the dilemma, at the appropriate time.

How to Get Commitment *and* Flexibility

Gilbert's work, fortunately, not only defines an innovator's dilemma but suggests a way out. The solution is twofold: First, get top-level commitment by framing an innovation as a threat during the resource allocation process. Later, shift responsibility for the project to an autonomous organization that can frame it as an opportunity.

In his study of how major metropolitan newspapers responded to the threat or opportunity of going online, Gilbert showed that in the initial period of threat framing, the project to address the disruption was *always* housed within the budgetary and strategic responsibility of the mainstream organization—because it had to be. In the case of newspapers, this entailed putting the newspaper online. The advertisers and readers of the online version were the same as those of the paper version. The newspapers did *exactly* what the vacuum tube and solar energy companies did: try to make the disruptive technology good enough that existing customers would use it instead of the existing physical newspaper.

At first blush, this market targeting seems senseless: Concerns about cannibalism become self-fulfilling prophecies. But threat framing makes sense of the paradox. Because current customers are the lifeblood of the company, they must be protected at all costs: "If the technology ever does in fact become good enough to begin to steal away our customers, we will be there with the new technology, ready to defend ourselves."

In contrast to the dilemma facing the incumbents, threat framing isn't a vexing issue for entrant firms. For them, the disruption is pure opportunity. This asymmetry of perceptions explains why incumbents so consistently try to cram the disruptive technology into mainstream markets, whereas the entrants pursue the new-market opportunity. Understanding this asymmetry, however, points to a solution. After senior managers have made a resolute commitment to address the disruption, responsibility to commercialize the disruption needs to be placed in an independent organizational unit for which the innovation represents *pure opportunity*.

This is what Gilbert noted in his newspaper study. After the initial period of threat framing that elicited resource commitment, Gilbert noted that a number of newspaper organizations spun off their online groups to become independently managed, stand-alone profit centers. When this happened, members of the newly independent groups switched their orientation, seeing themselves as involved in an *opportunity* with significant growth potential. When this happened, quite rapidly those organizations evolved significantly *away* from being just online replications of the newspaper. They implemented different services, found different suppliers, and earned their revenue from a different set of advertisers than the mainstream paper. Those newspapers that continued to house responsibility for their online effort within the mainstream news organization, in contrast, have continued on the self-destructive course of cannibalism, offering an online newspaper in defense of the core business.

Gilbert's recommendations are summarized in figure 4-3. The disruption is best framed as a threat within the resource allocation process in order to garner adequate resources. But once the investment commitment has been made, those engaged in venture building must see only upside opportunity to create new growth. Otherwise, they will find themselves with a dangerous lack of flexibility or commitment.

An initial decision to fund a disruptive growth business is not the end of the resource allocation process or of the conflict between threat and opportunity framing. For several years in each annual budgeting cycle, the disruptive opportunity will seem insignificant. The way that many corporate entrepreneurs deal with these annual challenges to the value of new-growth ventures is by promising big numbers in the future in exchange for resources in the present. This is suicidal for two reasons. First, the biggest markets whose size can be substantiated are those that exist. The very effort to articulate a convincing case for resources actually forces the entrepreneurs to cram the innovation as a sustaining technology in the existing market. Second, if results fall short of projected numbers, senior managers often conclude that the

FIGURE 4-3

How to Garner Resource Commitments and Target Them at Disruptive Growth Opportunities

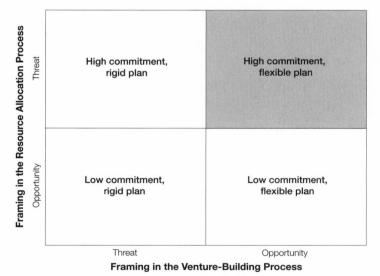

Source: Clark Gilbert, "Can Competing Frames Coexist? The Paradox of Threatened Response," Working paper 02-056, Harvard Business School, Boston, 2002.

potential market size is disappointingly small—and they cut resources as a result.

How do you deal with the rational need of the executives who manage resource allocation to focus investments where the risk/reward opportunity is most attractive? The answer is not to change the rules of evidence in the resource allocation process, because in successful companies, the well-honed operation of this process is critical to success on the sustaining trajectory. Decisions in that process can be rules based, because the environment is clear.

But companies that hope to create growth through new-market disruption need *another,* parallel process into which they can channel potentially disruptive opportunities. Ideas will enter this parallel process only partially formed. Those who manage this process then need to shape them into business plans that conform to the four elements of the pattern noted previously. Executives who allocate resources in this process should approve or kill project budgets based on fit with the pattern, not numerical rules. Fit constitutes a much more reliable predictor of success than do numbers in the uncertain environment of new-market disruption. If a project fits the pattern, executives can approve it with confidence that the *initial conditions* are conducive to successful growth.[8] Ultimate success, of course, depends on aligning all the related actions and decisions that we discuss in later chapters.

Reaching New-Market Customers Often Requires Disruptive Channels

In the final pages of this chapter, we hope to amplify the fourth element of the pattern of successful new-market disruption: going to market through a disruptive channel. The term *channel* as it is commonly used in business refers to the wholesale and retail companies that distribute and sell products. We assign a broader meaning to this word, however: A company's channel includes not just wholesale distributors and retail stores, but *any* entity that adds value to or creates value around the company's product as it wends its way toward the hands of the end user. For example, we will consider computer makers such as IBM and Compaq as the *channels* that Intel's microprocessors and Microsoft's operating system use to reach the end-use customer. A physician's practice is the channel through which many health care products provide the needed care to patients. A company's salesforce is an important channel through which all products must pass.

We use this broader definition of channel because there needs to be *symmetry* of motivation across the entire chain of entities that add value to the product on its way to the end customer. If your product does not help all of these entities do their fundamental job better—which is to move up-market along their own sustaining trajectory toward higher-margin business—then you will struggle to succeed. If your product provides the fuel that entities in the channel need to move toward improved margins, however, then the energy of the channel will help your new venture succeed.

Disruption causes others to be disinterested in what you are doing. This is exactly what you want with competitors: You want them to ignore you. But offering something that is disruptively unattractive to your *customers*—which includes all of the downstream entities that compose your channel—spells disaster. Companies in your channel are customers with a job to get done, which is to grow profitably.

Retailers and Distributors Need to Grow Through Disruption, Too

Retailers and distributors face competitive economics similar to those of the minimills we described in chapter 2. They need to keep moving up. If they don't, and just sell the same mix of merchandise against competitors whose costs and business models are similar, margins will erode to the minimum sustainable levels. This need to move up-market is a powerful, persistent disruptive energy in the channel. Harnessing it is crucial to success.

If a retailer or distributor can carry its business model up-market into higher-margin tiers, the incremental gross margin falls almost directly to the bottom line. Hence, innovating managers should find channels that will see the new product as a fuel to propel the channel up-market. When disruptive products enable the channel to disrupt *its* competitors, then the innovators harness the energies of the channel in building the disruption.

When Honda began its disruption of the North American motorcycle market with its small, cheap Super Cub motorized bicycle, the fact that it could not get Harley-Davidson motorcycle dealers to carry Honda products was *good* news, not bad—because the salespeople in the dealerships always would have been able to make higher commissions by choosing to sell Harleys instead of Hondas. Honda's business took off when it began to distribute through power equipment and sporting goods retailers, because it gave those retailers a chance to migrate toward higher-margin product lines. In each of the most successful disruptions we have studied, the product and its channel to the customer formed this sort of mutually beneficial relationship.

This is an important reason why Sony became such a successful disruptor. Discount retailers such as Kmart, which had no after-sale capability to repair vacuum tube–based electronic products, were emerging at the same time as Sony's disruptive products. Solid-state radios and televisions constituted the fuel that enabled the discounters to disrupt appliance stores. By selecting a channel that had up-market disruptive potential itself, Sony harnessed the energies of its channel to promote and position its products.

The fuel that a disruptive company provides to its channel will become spent, meaning that getting your products in the channels that stand to benefit the most is a perpetual challenge. This happened to Sony. After the discounters had driven the appliance stores out of the consumer electronics market and the products were being sold by equal-cost discount retailers, margins on those products eroded to subsistence levels. Consumer electronics no longer provided the fuel that the discounters needed to move up-market. Consequently, they de-emphasized electronics, gradually leaving them to be sold in even lower-cost retailers such as Circuit City and Best Buy. The discount department stores had to then look to clothing, which was the next fuel that would enable them to move up and compete against higher-margin retailers again.

Value-added distributors or resellers face the same motivations as retailers. As an example, Intel and SAP established a joint venture called Pandesic in 1997 to develop and sell a simpler, less-expensive version of SAP's enterprise resource planning (ERP) software to small and medium-sized businesses—a new-market disruption.[9] SAP's products historically had been targeted at huge enterprises, which would ante up several million dollars to purchase the software, and another $10 million to $200 million to implement it. The sale and implementation of SAP's products was largely done by its channel partners—implementation consultants such as Accenture, which experienced tremendous growth riding the ERP wave.

Pandesic's managers decided to take their lower-priced, easier-to-implement ERP package to market through the same channel partners. But when the IT implementation consultants had to choose whether to spend their time selling huge multimillion-dollar SAP implementation projects to global corporations or selling lower-ticket Pandesic software and straightforward implementation projects to small businesses, how would you expect them to expend their energy? Naturally, they pushed big-ticket SAP product implementations that helped them make the most money given their size and cost structure. There was no energy for Pandesic's disruptive product in the channel that Pandesic chose, and the venture failed.

A company's own salesforce will react the same way, especially if they work on commission. Every day salespeople need to decide which customers to call on, and which they will not call on. When they are with customers, they must decide which products they will promote and sell, and which they will not mention. The fact that they are your own employees doesn't matter much: Salespeople can only prioritize those things that it makes sense for them to prioritize, given the way they make money. Rarely will people who sell a company's mainstream products on the sustaining trajectory be successful in pushing the disruptive ones. It is foolish to give them a special financial incentive to push the disruptive products, because that would take their eye off their critical responsibility of selling the most profitable products on the sustaining trajectory. Disruptive products require disruptive channels.

Customers as Channels

For materials and components manufacturers, the end-use products constitute an important entity in their channel. In a similar way, service providers who use a product in order to deliver their service are the product's channel to the end-use customer. For example, computer makers such as Compaq and Dell Computer constitute the "channel" by which Intel's microprocessors reach an important market. The improvements in Intel's microprocessor have been the fuel propelling makers of desktop machines up-market so that they can continue to compete against higher-cost computer makers such as Sun.

The same situation exists in service businesses. Just as lower-performing products can take root in simple applications and then get disruptively better, so too technological progress often enables less-skilled service providers to disrupt more highly trained and expensive providers above them. In a way that is analogous to Intel's relationship with Dell, it is the potentially disruptive service providers that constitute the channel for the companies providing the enabling disruptive technology.

Let us illustrate the importance of fueling a disruptive channel by visiting health care again. In this industry today, many physicians are in a dogfight similar to that of the steel minimills. They are locked in a price-driven struggle against other physicians' practices and the companies that reimburse for the cost of care, working ever harder to make attractive income. A major health care equipment company has begun launching a series of disruptive products that will help office-based caregivers to move disruptively upward—to pull into their own practices procedures that historically had to be referred to more expensive outpatient clinics.

One example is in diagnosing and resolving colon disorders. To date, if a patient appeared to have a possible lesion or tumor in the colon, the physician would perform a colonoscopy in a relatively expensive clinic or hospital. Threading the flexible scope through a serpentine colon requires the skill of a very capable specialist. If the colonoscopy revealed a problem, then the patient would be referred to an even higher-cost surgeon, who would operate to correct the problem in an even higher-cost hospital. This company is introducing a technology that is *much* easier to use and that will enable the less-specialized diagnosing physicians to perform these procedures safely and effectively right in their offices—and thereby to pull into the cost structure of their office value-added procedures that historically could only be done in more expensive channels.

This device could be marketed as a sustaining innovation to the specialists who already have mastered the difficult-to-use traditional scopes. You can imagine what the physician would ask the salesperson: "Why do I need this? Does it allow me to see better or do more than what I have right now? Is the scope cheaper? Won't this thing here break?" This is a sustaining-technology conversation.

If the company marketed this as a disruptive technology enabling less-specialized physicians to do this procedure in their offices, however, the physician would likely ask, "What will it take to get trained on this thing?" This is a disruptive conversation.

What kinds of customers will provide the most solid foundation for future growth? You want customers who have long wanted your product but were not able to get one until you arrived on the scene. You want to be able to easily delight these customers, and you want them to need you. You want customers whom you can have all to yourself, protected from the advances of competitors. And you want your customers to be so attractive to those you work with that everyone in your value network is motivated to cooperate in pursuing the opportunity.

The search for customers like this is not a quixotic quest. These are the kinds of customers that you find when you shape innovative ideas to fit the four elements of the pattern of competing against nonconsumption.

Despite how appealing these kinds of customers appear to be on paper, the resource allocation process forces most companies, when faced with an opportunity like this, to pursue exactly the opposite kinds of customers: They target customers who already are using a product to which they have become accustomed. To escape this dilemma, managers need to frame the disruption as a threat in order to secure resource commitments, and then switch the framing for the team charged with building the business to be one of a search for growth opportunities. Carefully managing this process in order to focus on these ideal customers can give new-growth ventures a solid foundation for future growth.

Notes

1. Economists have great language for this phenomenon. As the performance of a product overshoots what customers are able to utilize, the customers experience diminishing marginal utility with each increment in product performance. Over time the marginal price that customers are willing to pay for an improvement comes to equal the marginal utility that they receive from consuming the improvement. When the marginal increase in price that a company can sustain in the market for an improved product approaches zero, it suggests that the marginal utility that customers derive from using the product also is approaching zero.

2. We stated earlier that few technologies are intrinsically sustaining or disruptive in character. These are extremes in a continuum, and the disruptiveness of an innovation can only be described relative to various companies' business models, to customers, and to other technologies. What the transistor case illustrates is that attempting to commercialize some technologies as sustaining innovations in large and obvious markets is *very* costly.

3. Figure 4-2 was constructed from data provided by the American Heart Association National Center. Because these data measure only those procedures performed in hospitals, angioplasty procedures that were performed in outpatient and other nonhospital settings are not included. This means that the angioplasty numbers in the chart are underestimated, and that the underestimation becomes more significant over time.

4. There are many other examples of this, in addition to those cited in the text. For example, full-service stock brokers such as Merrill Lynch continue to move up-market in their original value network toward clients of even larger net worth, and their top and bottom lines improve as they do so. They do not yet feel the pain that they ultimately will experience as the online discount brokers find ways to provide ever-better service.

5. See Clark Gilbert and Joseph L. Bower, "Disruptive Change: When Trying Harder Is Part of the Problem," *Harvard Business Review,* May 2002, 94–101; and Clark Gilbert, "Can Competing Frames Co-exist? The Paradox of Threatened Response," working paper 02-056, Boston, Harvard Business School, 2002.

6. Daniel Kahneman and Amos Tversky, "Choice, Values, and Frames," *American Psychologist* 39 (1984): 341–350. Kahneman and Tversky published prodigiously on these issues. This reference is simply an example of their work.

7. The phenomenon of threat rigidity has been examined by a number of scholars, notably Jane Dutton and her colleagues. See, for example, Jane E. Dutton and Susan E. Jackson, "Categorizing Strategic Issues: Links to Organizational Action," *Academy of Management Review* 12 (1987): 76–90;

and Jane E. Dutton, "The Making of Organizational Opportunities—An Interpretive Pathway to Organizational Change," *Research in Organizational Behavior* 15 (1992): 195–226.

8. Arthur Stinchcombe has written eloquently on the proposition that getting the initial conditions right is key to causing subsequent events to happen as desired. See Arthur Stinchcombe, "Social Structure and Organizations," in *Handbook of Organizations,* ed. James March (Chicago: McNally, 1965), 142–193.

9. Clark Gilbert, "Pandesic—The Challenges of a New Business Venture," case 9-399-129 (Boston: Harvard Business School, 2000).

CHAPTER FIVE

GETTING THE SCOPE OF THE BUSINESS RIGHT

Which activities should a new-growth venture do internally in order to be as successful as possible as fast as possible, and which should it outsource to a supplier or a partner? Will success be best built around a proprietary product architecture, or should the venture embrace modular, open industry standards? What causes the evolution from closed and proprietary product architectures to open ones? Might companies need to adopt proprietary solutions again, once open standards have emerged?

Decisions about what to in-source and what to procure from suppliers and partners have a powerful impact on a new-growth venture's chances for success. A widely used theory to guide this decision is built on categories of core and competence. If something fits your core competence, you should do it inside. If it's not your core competence and another firm can do it better, the theory goes, you should rely on them to provide it.[1]

Right? Well, sometimes. The problem with the core-competence/not-your-core-competence categorization is that what might seem to be a noncore activity today might become an absolutely critical competence to have mastered in a proprietary way in the future, and vice versa.

Consider, for example, IBM's decision to outsource the microprocessor for its PC business to Intel, and its operating system to Microsoft. IBM made these decisions in the early 1980s in order to focus on what it did best—designing, assembling, and marketing computer systems. Given its history, these choices made perfect sense. Component suppliers to IBM historically had lived a miserable, profit-free existence, and the business press widely praised IBM's decision to outsource these components of its PC. It dramatically reduced the cost and time required for development and launch. And yet in the process of outsourcing what it did not perceive to be core to the new business, IBM put into business the two companies that subsequently captured most of the profit in the industry.

How could IBM have known in advance that such a sensible decision would prove so costly? More broadly, how can any executive who is launching a new-growth business, as IBM was doing with its PC division in the early 1980s, know which value-added activities are those in which future competence needs to be mastered and kept inside?[2]

Because evidence from the past can be such a misleading guide to the future, the only way to see accurately what the future will bring is to use theory. In this case, we need a circumstance-based theory to describe the mechanism by which activities become core or peripheral. Describing this mechanism and showing how managers can use the theory is the purpose of chapters 5 and 6.

Integrate or Outsource?

IBM and others have demonstrated—inadvertently, of course—that the core/noncore categorization can lead to serious and even fatal mistakes. Instead of asking what their company does best today, managers should ask, "What do we need to master today, and what will we need to master in the future, in order to excel on the trajectory of improvement that customers will define as important?"

The answer begins with the job-to-be-done approach: Customers will not buy your product unless it solves an important problem for them. But what constitutes a "solution" differs across the two circumstances in figure 5-1: whether products are not good enough or are more than good enough. The advantage, we have found, goes to

FIGURE 5-1

Product Architectures and Integration

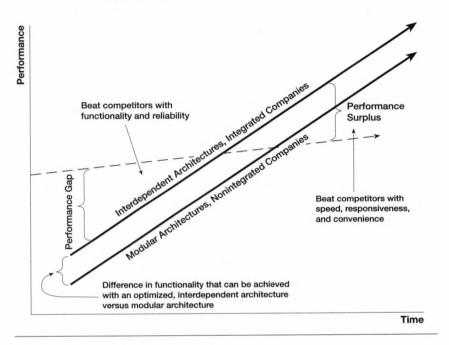

integration when products are not good enough, and to outsourcing —or specialization and dis-integration—when products are more than good enough.

To explain, we need to explore the engineering concepts of *inter-dependence* and *modularity* and their importance in shaping a product's design. We will then return to figure 5-1 to see these concepts at work in the disruption diagram.

Product Architecture and Interfaces

A product's *architecture* determines its constituent components and subsystems and defines how they must interact—fit and work together—in order to achieve the targeted functionality. The place where any two components fit together is called an *interface*. Interfaces exist within a product, as well as between stages in the value-added chain.

For example, there is an interface between design and manufacturing, and another between manufacturing and distribution.

An architecture is *interdependent* at an interface if one part cannot be created independently of the other part—if the way one is designed and made depends on the way the other is being designed and made. When there is an interface across which there are unpredictable interdependencies, then the same organization must simultaneously develop *both* of the components if it hopes to develop *either* component.

Interdependent architectures optimize *performance,* in terms of functionality and reliability. By definition, these architectures are proprietary because each company will develop its own interdependent design to optimize performance in a different way. When we use the term *interdependent architecture* in this chapter, readers can substitute as synonyms *optimized* and *proprietary* architecture.

In contrast, a *modular* interface is a *clean* one, in which there are no unpredictable interdependencies across components or stages of the value chain. Modular components fit and work together in well-understood and highly defined ways. A *modular architecture* specifies the fit and function of all elements so completely that it doesn't matter who makes the components or subsystems, as long as they meet the specifications. Modular components can be developed in independent work groups or by different companies working at arm's length.

Modular architectures optimize *flexibility,* but because they require tight specification, they give engineers fewer degrees of freedom in design. As a result, modular flexibility comes at the sacrifice of performance.[3]

Pure modularity and interdependence are the ends of a spectrum: Most products fall somewhere between these extremes. As we shall see, companies are more likely to succeed when they match product architecture to their competitive circumstances.

Competing with Interdependent Architecture in a Not-Good-Enough World

The left side of figure 5-1 indicates that when there is a performance gap—when product functionality and reliability are not yet good enough to address the needs of customers in a given tier of the market—companies must compete by making the best possible products. In the race to do this, firms that build their products around proprietary, interdependent architectures enjoy an important competitive advantage against competitors whose product architectures are modular, because the standardization inherent in modularity takes too many degrees of design freedom away from engineers, and they cannot optimize performance.

To close the performance gap with each new product generation, competitive forces compel engineers to fit the pieces of their systems together in ever-more-efficient ways in order to wring the most performance possible out of the technology that is available. When firms must compete by making the best possible products, they cannot simply assemble standardized components, because from an engineering point of view, standardization of interfaces (meaning fewer degrees of design freedom) would force them to back away from the frontier of what is technologically possible. When the product is not good enough, backing off from the best that can be done means that you'll fall behind.

Companies that compete with proprietary, interdependent architectures *must* be integrated: They must control the design and manufacture of *every* critical component of the system in order to make *any* piece of the system. As an illustration, during the early days of the mainframe computer industry, when functionality and reliability were not yet good enough to satisfy the needs of mainstream customers, you could not have existed as an independent contract manufacturer of mainframe computers because the way the machines were designed depended on the art that would be used in manufacturing, and vice versa. There was no clean interface between design and manufacturing. Similarly, you could not have existed as an independent supplier of operating systems, core memory, or logic circuitry to the mainframe industry because these key subsystems had to be interdependently and iteratively designed, too.[4]

New, immature technologies are often drafted into use as sustaining improvements when functionality is not good enough. One reason why entrant companies rarely succeed in commercializing a radically new technology is that breakthrough sustaining technologies are rarely plug-compatible with existing systems of use.[5] There are almost always many unforseen interdependencies that mandate change in other elements of the system before a viable product that incorporates a radically new technology can be sold. This makes the new product development cycle tortuously long when breakthrough technology is expected to be the foundation for improved performance. The use of advanced ceramics materials in engines, the deployment of high-bandwidth DSL lines at the "last mile" of the telecommunications infrastructure, the building of superconducting electric motors for ship propulsion, and the transition from analog to digital to all-optical telecommunications networks could all only be accomplished by extensively integrated companies whose scope could encompass all of the interdependencies that needed to be managed. This is treacherous terrain for entrants.

For these reasons it wasn't just IBM that dominated the early computer industry by virtue of its integration. Ford and General Motors, as the most integrated companies, were the dominant competitors during the not-good-enough era of the automobile industry's history. For the same reasons, RCA, Xerox, AT&T, Standard Oil, and US Steel dominated their industries at similar stages. These firms enjoyed near-monopoly power. Their market dominance was the result of the not-good-enough circumstance, which mandated interdependent product or value chain architectures and vertical integration.[6] But their hegemony proved only temporary, because ultimately, companies that have excelled in the race to make the best possible products find themselves making products that are too good. When that happens, the intricate fabric of success of integrated companies like these begins to unravel.

Overshooting and Modularization

One symptom that these changes are afoot—that the functionality and reliability of a product have become too good—is that salespeople will return to the office cursing a customer: "Why can't they see that our product is better than the competition? They're treating it like a *commodity!*" This is evidence of overshooting. Such companies find themselves on the right side of figure 5-1, where there is a performance surplus. Customers are happy to *accept* improved products, but they're unwilling to pay a premium price to get them.[7]

Overshooting does not mean that customers will no longer pay for improvements. It just means that the *type* of improvement for which they will pay a premium price will change. Once their requirements for functionality and reliability have been met, customers begin to redefine what is not good enough. What becomes not good enough is that customers can't get exactly what they want exactly when they need it, as conveniently as possible. Customers become willing to pay premium prices for improved performance along this new trajectory of innovation in speed, convenience, and customization. When this happens, we say that the *basis of competition* in a tier of the market has changed.

The pressure of competing along this new trajectory of improvement forces a gradual evolution in product architecture, as depicted in figure 5-1—away from the interdependent, proprietary architectures that had the advantage in the not-good-enough era toward *modular* designs in the era of performance surplus. Modular architectures help companies to compete on the dimensions that matter in the lower-right portions of the disruption diagram. Companies can introduce new products faster because they can upgrade individual subsystems without having to redesign everything. Although standard interfaces invariably force compromise in system performance, firms have the slack to trade away some performance with these customers because functionality is more than good enough.

Modularity has a profound impact on industry structure because it enables independent, nonintegrated organizations to sell, buy, and assemble components and subsystems.[8] Whereas in the interdependent world you had to make all of the key elements of the system in order to make any of them, in a modular world you can prosper by outsourcing or by supplying just one element. Ultimately, the specifications for modular interfaces will coalesce as industry standards. When that happens, companies can mix and match components from best-of-breed suppliers in order to respond conveniently to the specific needs of individual customers.

As depicted in figure 5-1, these nonintegrated competitors disrupt the integrated leader. Although we have drawn this diagram in two dimensions for simplicity, technically speaking they are hybrid disruptors because they compete with a modified metric of performance on the vertical axis of the disruption diagram, in that they strive to deliver rapidly exactly what each customer needs. Yet, because their nonintegrated structure gives them lower overhead costs, they can profitably pick off low-end customers with discount prices.

From Interdependent to Modular Design—and Back

The progression from integration to modularization plays itself out over and over as products improve enough to overshoot customers' requirements.[9] When wave after wave of sequential disruptions sweep through an industry, this progression repeats itself within each wave. In the original mainframe value network of the computer industry, for example, IBM enjoyed unquestioned dominance in the first decade with its interdependent architectures and vertical integration. In 1964, however, it responded to cost, complexity, and time-to-market pressure by creating a more modular design starting with its System 360. Modularization forced IBM to back away from the frontier of functionality, shifting from the left to the right trajectory of performance improvement in figure 5-1. This created space at the high end for competitors such as Control Data and Cray Research, whose interdependent architectures continued to push the bleeding edge of what was possible.

Opening its architecture was not a mistake for IBM: The economics of competition forced it to take these steps. Indeed, modularity reduced development and production costs and enabled IBM to custom-configure systems for each customer. This created a major new wave of growth in the industry. Another effect of modularization, however, was that nonintegrated companies could begin to compete effectively. A population of nonintegrated suppliers of plug-compatible components and subsystems such as disk drives, printers, and data input devices enjoyed lower overhead costs and began disrupting IBM en masse.[10]

This cycle repeated itself when minicomputers began their new-market disruption of mainframes. Digital Equipment Corporation initially dominated that industry with its proprietary architecture when minicomputers really weren't very good, because its hardware and operating system software were interdependently designed to maximize performance. As functionality subsequently approached adequacy, however, other competitors such as Data General, Wang Laboratories, and Prime Computer that were far less integrated but much faster to market began taking significant share.[11] As happened in mainframes, the minicomputer market boomed because of the better and less-expensive products that this intensified competition created.

The same sequence occurred in the personal computer wave of disruption. During the early years, Apple Computer—the most integrated company with a proprietary architecture—made by far the best desktop computers. They were easier to use and crashed much less often than computers of modular construction. Ultimately, when the functionality of desktop machines became good enough, IBM's modular, open-standard architecture became dominant. Apple's proprietary architecture, which in the not-good-enough circumstance was a competitive strength, became a competitive liability in the more-than-good-enough circumstance. Apple as a consequence was relegated to niche-player status as the growth explosion in personal computers was captured by the nonintegrated providers of modular machines.

The same transition will have occurred before long in the next two waves of disruptive computer products—notebook computers and hand-held wireless devices. The companies that are most successful in the beginning are those with optimized, interdependent architectures. Companies whose strategy is prematurely modular will struggle to be performance-competitive during the early years when performance is the basis of competition. Later, architectures and industry structures will evolve toward openness and disintegration.

Figure 5-2 summarizes these transitions in the personal computer industry in a simplified way, showing how the proprietary systems and vertically integrated company that was strongest during the industry's initial not-good-enough years gave way to a nonintegrated, horizontally stratified population of companies in its later years. It almost looks like the industry got pushed through a bologna slicer. The chart would look similar for each of the value networks in the industry. In each instance, the driver of modularization and disintegration was not the passage of time or the "maturation" of the industry per se.[12] What drives this process is this predictable causal sequence:

1. The pace of technological improvement outstrips the ability of customers to utilize it, so that a product's functionality and reliability that were not good enough at one point overshoot what customers can utilize at a later point.

2. This forces companies to compete differently: The basis of competition changes. As customers become less and less willing to reward further improvements in functionality and reliability with premium prices, those suppliers that get better and better at conveniently giving customers exactly what they want when they need it are able to earn attractive margins.

3. As competitive pressures force companies to be as fast and responsive as possible, they solve this problem by evolving the architecture of their products from being proprietary and interdependent toward being modular.

4. Modularity enables the dis-integration of the industry. A population of nonintegrated firms can now outcompete the integrated firms that had dominated the industry. Whereas integration at one point was a competitive necessity, it later becomes a competitive disadvantage.[13]

FIGURE 5-2

The Transition from Vertical Integration to Horizontal Stratification in the Microprocessor-Based Computer Industry

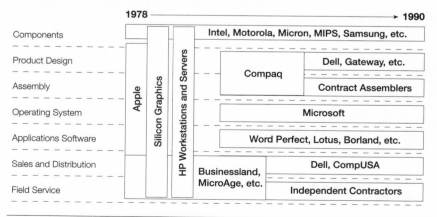

Figure 5-2 is simplified, in that the integrated business model did not disappear overnight—rather, it became less dominant as the trajectory of performance improvement passed through each tier of each market and the modular model gradually became more dominant.

We emphasize that the *circumstances* of performance gaps and performance surpluses drive the viability of these strategies of architecture and integration. This means, of course, that if the circumstances change again, the strategic approach must also change. Indeed, after 1990 there has been some reintegration in the computer industry. We describe one factor that drives reintegration in the next section, and return to it in chapter 6.

The Drivers of Reintegration

Because the trajectory of technological improvement typically outstrips the ability of customers in any given tier of the market to utilize it, the general current flows from interdependent architectures and integrated companies toward modular architectures and nonintegrated companies. But remember, customers' needs change too. Usually this happens at a relatively slower pace, as suggested by the dotted lines on the disruption diagram. On occasion there can be a discontinuous shift in the functionality that customers demand, essentially shifting the dotted line in figure 5-1 upward. This flips the industry back toward the left side of the diagram and resets the clock into an era in which integration once again is the source of competitive advantage.

For example, in the early 1980s Apple Computer's products employed a proprietary architecture involving extensive interdependence *within* the software *and* across the hardware–software interface. By the mid-1980s, however, a population of specialized firms such as WordPerfect and Lotus, whose products plugged into Microsoft's DOS operating system through a well-defined interface, had arisen to dethrone Apple's dominance in software. Then in the early 1990s, the dotted lines of functionality that customers needed in PC software seemed to shift up as customers began demanding to transfer graphics and spreadsheet files into word processing documents, and so on. This created a performance gap, flipping the industry to the not-good-enough side of the world where fitting interdependent pieces of the system together became competitively critical again.

In response, Microsoft interdependently knitted its Office suite of products (and later its Web browser) into its Windows operating system. This helped it stretch so much closer to what customers needed than could the population of focused firms that the nonintegrated software companies, including WordPerfect and Lotus's 123 spreadsheet, vaporized very quickly. Microsoft's dominance did not *arise* from monopolistic malfeasance. Rather, its integrated value chain under not-good-enough conditions enabled it to make products whose performance came closer to what customers needed than could nonintegrated competitors under those conditions.[14]

Today, however, things may be poised to flip again. As computing becomes more Internet-centric, operating systems with modular architectures (such as Linux), and modular programming languages (such as Java) constitute hybrid disruptions relative to Microsoft. This modularity is enabling a population of specialized firms to begin making incursions into this industry.

In a similar way, fifteen years ago in optical telecommunications the bandwidth available over a fiber was more than good enough for voice communication; as a consequence, the industry structure was horizontally stratified, not vertically integrated. Corning made the optical fiber, Siemens cabled it, and other companies made the multiplexers, the amplifiers, and so on. As the screams for more bandwidth intensified in the late 1990s, the dotted line in figure 5-1 shifted up, and the industry flipped into a not-good-enough situation. Corning found that it could not even design its next generation of fiber if it did not interdependently design the amplifier, for example. It *had* to integrate across this interface in order to compete, and it did so. Within a few years, there was more than enough bandwidth over a fiber, and the rationale for being vertically integrated disappeared again.

The general rule is that companies will prosper when they are integrated across interfaces in the value chain where performance, however it is defined at that point, is not good enough relative to what customers require at the next stage of value addition. There are often several of these points in the complete value-added chain of an industry. This means that an industry will rarely be completely nonintegrated or integrated. Rather, the points at which integration and nonintegration are competitively important will predictably shift over time.[15] We return to this notion in greater detail in chapter 6.

Aligning Your Architecture Strategy to Your Circumstances

In a modular world, supplying a component or assembling outsourced components are both appropriate "solutions." In the interdependent world of inadequate functionality, attempting to provide one piece of the system doesn't solve anybody's problem. Knowing this, we can predict the failure or success of a growth business based on managers' choices to compete with modular architectures when the circumstances mandate interdependence, and vice versa.

Attempting to Grow a Nonintegrated Business When Functionality Isn't Good Enough

It's tempting to think you can launch a new-growth business by providing one piece of a modular product's value. Managers often see specialization as a less daunting path to entry than providing an entire system solution. It costs less and allows the entrant to focus on what it does best, leaving the rest of the solution to other partners in the ecosystem. This works in the circumstances in the lower-right portions of the disruption diagram. But when functionality and reliability are inadequate, the seemingly lower hurdle that partnering or outsourcing seems to present usually proves illusory, and causes many growth ventures to fail. Modularity often is not technologically or competitively possible during the early stages of many disruptions.

To succeed with a nonintegrated, specialist strategy, you need to be certain you're competing in a modular world. Three conditions must be met in order for a firm to procure something from a supplier or partner, or to sell it to a customer. First, both suppliers and customers need to know what to specify—which attributes of the component are crucial to the operation of the product system, and which are not. Second, they must be able to measure those attributes so that they can verify that the specifications have been met. Third, there cannot be any poorly understood or unpredictable interdependencies across the customer–supplier interface. The customer needs to understand how the subsystem will interact with the performance of other pieces of the system so that it can be used with predictable effect. These three conditions—specifiability, verifiability, and predictability—constitute an effective modular interface.

When product performance is *not* good enough—when competition forces companies to use new technologies in nonstandard product architectures to stretch performance as far as possible—these three conditions often are *not* met. When there are complex, reciprocal, unpredictable interdependencies in the system, a single organization's boundaries must span those interfaces. People cannot efficiently resolve interdependent problems while working at arm's length across an organizational boundary.[16]

Modular Failures in Interdependent Circumstances

In 1996 the United States government passed legislation to stimulate competition in local telecommunication services. The law mandated that independent companies be allowed to sell services to residential and business customers and then to plug into the switching infrastructure of the incumbent telephone companies. In response, many nonintegrated competitive local exchange carriers (CLECs) such as Northpoint Communications attempted to offer high-speed DSL access to the Internet. Corporations and venture capitalists funneled billions of dollars into these companies.

The vast majority of CLECs failed. This is because DSL service was in the interdependent realm of figure 5-1. There were too many subtle and unpredictable interdependencies between what the CLECs did when they installed service on a customer's premises and what the telephone company had to do in response. It wasn't necessarily the *technical* interface that was the problem. The architecture of the telephone companies' billing system software, for example, was interdependent—making it very difficult to account and bill for the cost of a "plugged-in" CLEC customer. The fact that the telephone companies were integrated across these interdependent interfaces gave them a powerful advantage. They understood their own network and IT system architectures and could consequently deploy their offerings more quickly with fewer concerns about the unintended consequences of reconfiguring their own central office facilities.[17]

Similarly, in the eagerly anticipated wireless-access-to-data-over-the-Internet industry, most European and North American competitors tried to enter as nonintegrated specialists, providing one element of the system. They relied prematurely on industry standards such as Wireless Applications Protocol (WAP) to define the interfaces between the handset device, the network, and the new content being developed. Companies within each link in the value chain were left to their own devices to determine how best to exploit the wireless Internet. Almost no revenues and billions in losses have resulted. The "partnering" theology that had become de rigueur among telecommunications investors and entrepreneurs who had watched Cisco succeed by partnering turned out to be misapplied in a different circumstance in which it couldn't work—with tragic consequences.

Appropriate Integration

In contrast, Japan's NTT DoCoMo and J-Phone have approached the new-market disruptive opportunity of the wireless Internet with far greater integration across stages of the value chain. These growth ventures already claim tens of millions of customers and billions in revenue.[18] Although they do not own *every* upstream or downstream connection in the value chain, DoCoMo and J-Phone carefully manage the interfaces with their content providers and handset manufacturers. Their interdependent approach allows them to surmount the technological limitations of wireless data and to create user interfaces, a revenue model, and a billing infrastructure that make the customer experience as seamless as possible.[19]

The DoCoMo and J-Phone networks comprise competing, proprietary systems. Isn't this inefficient? Executives and investors indeed are often eager to hammer out the standards *before* they invest their money, to preempt wasteful duplication of competing standards and the possibility that a competitor's approach might emerge as the industry's standard. This works when functionality and reliability and the consequent competitive conditions permit it. But when they do not, then having competing proprietary systems is not wasteful.[20] Far more is wasted when huge sums are spent on an architectural approach that does not fit the basis of competition. True, one system ultimately may define the standard, and those whose standards do not prevail may fall by the wayside after their initial success, or they may become niche players. Competition of this sort inspired Adam Smith and Charles Darwin to write their books.

Parenthetically, we note that in some of its ventures abroad, such as in its partnership with AT&T Wireless in the United States, DoCoMo has followed its partners' strategy of adopting industry standards with less vertical integration and has stumbled badly, just like its American and European counterparts. It's not DoCoMo that makes the difference. It's employing the right strategy in the right circumstances that makes the difference.

Being in the Right Place at the Right Time

We noted earlier that the pure forms of interdependence and modularity are the extremes on a continuum, and companies may choose strategies anywhere along the spectrum at any point in time. A company may not necessarily fail if it starts with a prematurely modular architecture when the basis of competition is functionality and reliability. It will simply suffer from an important competitive disadvantage until the basis of competition shifts and modularity becomes the predominant architectural form. This was the experience of IBM and its clones in the personal computer industry. The superior performance of Apple's computers did not preclude IBM from succeeding. IBM just had to fight its performance disadvantage because it opted prematurely for a modular architecture.

What happens to the initial leaders when they overshoot, after having jumped ahead of the pack with performance and reliability advantages that were grounded in proprietary architecture? The answer is that they need to modularize and open up their architectures and begin aggressively to sell their subsystems as modules to other companies whose low-cost assembly capability can help grow the market. Had good theory been available to provide guidance, for example, there is no reason why the executives of Apple Computer could not have modularized their design and have begun selling their operating system with its interdependent applications to other computer assemblers, preempting Microsoft's development of Windows. Nokia appears today to be facing the same decision. We sense that adding even more features and functions to standard wireless handsets is overshooting what its less-demanding customers can utilize; and a disintegrated handset industry that utilizes Symbian's operating system is rapidly gaining traction. The next chapter will show that a company can begin with a proprietary architecture when disruptive circumstances mandate it, and then, when the basis of competition changes, open its architecture to become a supplier of key subsystems to low-cost assemblers. If it does this, it can avoid the traps of becoming a niche player on the one hand and the supplier of an undifferentiated commodity on the other. The company can become capitalism's equivalent of Wayne Gretzky, the hockey great. Gretzky had an instinct not to skate to where the puck presently was on the ice, but instead to skate to where the puck was going to be. Chapter 6 can help managers steer their companies not to the profitable businesses of the past, but to where the money *will be*.

> *There are few decisions in building and sustaining a new-growth business that scream more loudly for sound, circumstance-based theory than those addressed in this chapter. When the functionality and reliability of a product are not good enough to meet customers' needs, then the companies that will enjoy significant competitive advantage are those whose product architectures are proprietary and that are integrated across the performance-limiting interfaces in the value chain. When functionality and reliability become more than adequate, so that speed and responsiveness are the dimensions of competition that are not now good enough, then the opposite is true. A population of nonintegrated, specialized companies whose rules of interaction are defined by modular architectures and industry standards holds the upper hand.*
>
> *At the beginning of a wave of new-market disruption, the companies that initially will be the most successful will be integrated firms whose architectures are proprietary because the product*

isn't yet good enough. After a few years of success in performance improvement, those disruptive pioneers themselves become susceptible to hybrid disruption by a faster and more flexible population of nonintegrated companies whose focus gives them lower overhead costs.

For a company that serves customers in multiple tiers of the market, managing the transition is tricky, because the strategy and business model that are required to successfully reach unsatisfied customers in higher tiers are very different from those that are necessary to compete with speed, flexibility, and low cost in lower tiers of the market. Pursuing both ends at once and in the right way often requires multiple business units—a topic that we address in the next two chapters.

Notes

1. We are indebted to a host of thoughtful researchers who have framed the existence and the role of core and competence in making these decisions. These include C. K. Prahalad and Gary Hamel, "The Core Competence of the Corporation," *Harvard Business Review,* May–June 1990, 79–91; and Geoffrey Moore, *Living on the Fault Line* (New York: HarperBusiness, 2002). It is worth noting that "core competence," as the term was originally coined by C. K. Prahalad and Gary Hamel in their seminal article, was actually an apology for the diversified firm. They were developing a view of diversification based on the exploitation of established capabilities, broadly defined. We interpret their work as consistent with a well-respected stream of research and theoretical development that goes all the way back to Edith Penrose's 1959 book *The Theory of the Growth of the Firm* (New York: Wiley). This line of thinking is very powerful and useful. As it is used now, however, the term "core competence" has become synonymous with "focus"; that is, firms that seek to exploit their core competence do not diversify—if anything, they focus their business on those activities that they do particularly well. It is this "meaning in use" that we feel is misguided.

2. IBM arguably had much deeper technological capability in integrated circuit and operating system design and manufacturing than did Intel or Microsoft at the time IBM put these companies into business. It probably is more correct, therefore, to say that this decision was based more on what was *core* than what was *competence*. The sense that IBM needed to outsource was

based on the correct perception of the new venture's managers that they needed a far lower overhead cost structure to become acceptably profitable to the corporation and needed to be much faster in new-product development than the company's established internal development processes, which had been honed in a world of complicated interdependent products with longer development cycles, could handle.

3. In the past decade there has been a flowering of important studies on these concepts. We have found the following ones to be particularly helpful: Rebecca Henderson and Kim B. Clark, "Architectural Innovation: The Reconfiguration of Existing Product Technologies and the Failure of Established Firms," *Administrative Science Quarterly* 35 (1990): 9–30; K. Monteverde, "Technical Dialog as an Incentive for Vertical Integration in the Semiconductor Industry," *Management Science* 41 (1995): 1624–1638; Karl Ulrich, "The Role of Product Architecture in the Manufacturing Firm," *Research Policy* 24 (1995): 419–440; Ron Sanchez and J. T. Mahoney, "Modularity, Flexibility and Knowledge Management in Product and Organization Design," *Strategic Management Journal* 17 (1996): 63–76; and Carliss Baldwin and Kim B. Clark, *Design Rules: The Power of Modularity* (Cambridge, MA: MIT Press, 2000).

4. The language we have used here characterizes the extremes of interdependence, and we have chosen the extreme end of the spectrum simply to make the concept as clear as possible. In complex product systems, there are varying degrees of interdependence, which differ over time, component by component. The challenges of interdependence can also be dealt with to some degree through the nature of supplier relationships. See, for example, Jeffrey Dyer, *Collaborative Advantage: Winning Through Extended Enterprise Supplier Networks* (New York: Oxford University Press, 2000).

5. Many readers have equated in their minds the terms *disruptive* and *breakthrough*. It is extremely important, for purposes of prediction and understanding, not to confuse the terms. Almost invariably, what prior writers have termed "breakthrough" technologies have, in our parlance, a *sustaining* impact on the trajectory of technological progress. Some sustaining innovations are simple, incremental year-to-year improvements. Other sustaining innovations are dramatic, breakthrough leapfrogs ahead of the competition, up the sustaining trajectory. For predictive purposes, however, the distinction between incremental and breakthrough technologies rarely matters. Because both types have a sustaining impact, the established firms typically triumph. Disruptive innovations usually do not entail technological breakthroughs. Rather, they package available technologies in a disruptive business model. New breakthrough technologies that emerge from research

labs are almost always sustaining in character, and almost always entail unpredictable interdependencies with other subsystems in the product. Hence, there are two powerful reasons why the established firms have a strong advantage in commercializing these technologies.

6. Professor Alfred Chandler's *The Visible Hand* (Cambridge, MA: Belknap Press, 1977) is a classic study of how and why vertical integration is critical to the growth of many industries during their early period.

7. Economists' concept of utility, or the satisfaction that customers receive when they buy and use a product, is a good way to describe how competition in an industry changes when this happens. The marginal utility that customers receive is the incremental addition to satisfaction that they get from buying a better-performing product. The increased price that they are willing to pay for a better product will be proportional to the increased utility they receive from using it—in other words, the marginal price improvement will equal the improvement in marginal utility. When customers can no longer utilize further improvements in a product, marginal utility falls toward zero, and as a result customers become unwilling to pay higher prices for better-performing products.

8. Sanchez and Mahoney, in "Modularity, Flexibility and Knowledge Management in Product and Organization Design," were among the first to describe this phenomenon.

9. The landmark work of Professors Carliss Baldwin and Kim B. Clark, cited in note 3, describes the process of modularization in a cogent, useful way. We recommend it to those who are interested in studying the process in greater detail.

10. Many students of IBM's history will disagree with our statement that competition forced the opening of IBM's architecture, contending instead that the U.S. government's antitrust litigation forced IBM open. The antitrust action clearly influenced IBM, but we would argue that government action or not, competitive and disruptive forces would have brought an end to IBM's position of near-monopoly power.

11. Tracy Kidder's Pulitzer Prize–winning account of product development at Data General, *The Soul of a New Machine* (New York: Avon Books, 1981), describes what life was like as the basis of competition began to change in the minicomputer industry.

12. MIT Professor Charles Fine has written an important book on this topic as well: *Clockspeed* (Reading, MA: Perseus Books, 1998). Fine observed that industries go through cycles of integration and nonintegration in a sort of "double helix" cycle. We hope that the model outlined here and in chapter 6 both confirms and adds causal richness to Fine's findings.

13. The evolving structure of the lending industry offers a clear example of these forces at work. Integrated banks such as J.P. Morgan Chase have powerful competitive advantages in the most complex tiers of the lending market. Integration is key to their ability to knit together huge, complex financing packages for sophisticated and demanding global customers. Decisions about whether and how much to lend cannot be made according to fixed formulas and measures; they can only be made through the intuition of experienced lending officers.

    Credit scoring technology and asset securitization, however, are disrupting and dis-integrating the simpler tiers of the lending market. In these tiers, lenders know and can measure precisely those attributes that determine whether borrowers will repay a loan. Verifiable information about borrowers—such as how long they have lived where they live, how long they have worked where they work, what their income is, and whether they've paid other bills on time—is combined to make algorithm-based lending decisions. Credit scoring took root in the 1960s in the simplest tier of the lending market, in department stores' decisions to issue their own credit cards. Then, unfortunately for the big banks, the disruptive horde moved inexorably up-market in pursuit of profit—first to general consumer credit card loans, then to automobile loans and mortgage loans, and now to small business loans. The lending industry in these simpler tiers of the market has largely dis-integrated. Specialist nonbank companies have emerged to provide each slice of added value in these tiers of the lending industry. Whereas integration is a big advantage in the most complex tiers of the market, in overserved tiers it is a disadvantage.

14. Our conclusions support those of Stan J. Liebowitz and Stephen E. Margolis in *Winners, Losers & Microsoft: Competition and Antitrust in High Technology* (Oakland, CA: Independent Institute, 1999).

15. Another good illustration of this is the push being made by Apple Computer, at the time of this writing, to be the gateway to the consumer for multimedia entertainment. Apple's interdependent integration of the operating system and applications creates convenience, which customers value at this point because convenience is not yet good enough.

16. Specifiability, measurability, and predictability constitute what an economist would term "sufficient information" for an efficient market to emerge at an interface, allowing organizations to deal with each other at arm's length. A fundamental tenet of capitalism is that the invisible hand of market competition is superior to that of managerial oversight as a coordinating mechanism between actors in a market. This is why, when a modular interface becomes defined, an industry will dis-integrate at that interface. However, when specifiability, measurability, and predictability do *not* exist, efficient

markets cannot function. It is under these circumstances that managerial oversight and coordination perform better than market competition as a co-ordinating mechanism.

This is an important underpinning of the award-winning findings of Professor Tarun Khanna and his colleagues, which show that in developing economies, diversified business conglomerates outperform focused, independent companies, whereas the reverse is true in developed economies. See, for example, Tarun Khanna and Krishna G. Palepu, "Why Focused Strategies May Be Wrong for Emerging Markets," *Harvard Business Review,* July–August 1997, 41–51; and Tarun Khanna and Jan Rivkin, "Estimating the Performance Effects of Business Groups in Emerging Markets," *Strategic Management Journal* 22 (2001): 45–74.

A bedrock set of concepts in understanding why organizational integration is critical when the conditions of modularity are not met is developed in the transaction cost economics (TCE) school of thought, which traces its origins to the work of Ronald Coase (R. H. Coase, "The Nature of the Firm," *Econometrica* 4 [1937]: 386–405). Coase argued that firms were created when it got "too expensive" to negotiate and enforce contracts between otherwise "independent" parties. More recently, the work of Oliver Williamson has proven seminal in the exploration of transaction costs as a determinant of firm boundaries. See, for example, O. E. Williamson, *Markets and Hierarchies* (New York: Free Press, 1975); "Transaction Cost Economics," in *The Economic Institutions of Capitalism,* ed., O. E. Williamson (New York: Free Press, 1985), 15–42; and "Transaction-Cost Economics: The Governance of Contractual Relations," in *Organiational Economics,* ed., J. B. Barney and W. G. Ouichi (San Francisco: Jossey-Bass, 1986). In particular, TCE has been used to explain the various ways in which firms might expand their operating scope: either through unrelated diversification (C. W. L. Hill, et al., "Cooperative Versus Competitive Structures in Related and Unrelated Diversified Firms," *Organization Science* 3, no. 4 [1992]: 501–521); related diversification (D. J. Teece, "Economics of Scope and the Scope of the Enterprise," *Journal of Economic Behavior and Organization* 1 [1980]: 223–247); and D. J. Teece, "Toward an Economic Theory of the Multiproduct Firm," *Journal of Economic Behavior and Organization* 3 [1982], 39–63); or vertical integration (K. Arrow, The Limits of Organization [New York: W. W. Norton, 1974]; B. R. G. Klein, et al., "Vertical Integration, Appropriable Rents and Competitive Contracting Process," *Journal of Law and Economics* 21 [1978] 297–326; and K. R. Harrigan, "Vertical Integration and Corporate Strategy," *Academy of Management Journal* 28, no. 2 [1985]: 397–425). More generally, this line of research is known as the "market failures" paradigm for explaining changes in firm scope (K. N. M.

Dundas, and P. R. Richardson, "Corporate Strategy and the Concept of Market Failure," *Strategic Management Journal* 1, no. 2 [1980]: 177–188). Our hope is that we have advanced this line of thinking by elaborating more precisely the considerations that give rise to the contracting difficulties that lie at the heart of the TCE school.

17. Even if the incumbent local exchange carriers (ILECs) didn't understand all the complexities and unintended consequences better than CLEC engineers, organizationally they were much better positioned to resolve any difficulties, since they could appeal to organizational mechanisms rather than have to rely on cumbersome and likely incomplete *ex ante* contracts.

18. See Jeffrey Lee Funk, *The Mobile Internet: How Japan Dialed Up and the West Disconnected* (Hong Kong: ISI Publications, 2001). This really is an extraordinarily insightful study from which a host of insights can be gleaned. In his own language, Funk shows that another important reason why DoCoMo and J-Phone were so successful in Japan is that they followed the pattern that we describe in chapters 3 and 4 of this book. They initially targeted customers who were largely non-Internet users (teenaged girls) and helped them get done better a job that they had already been trying to do: have fun with their friends. Western entrants into this market, in contrast, envisioned sophisticated offerings to be sold to current customers of mobile phones (who primarily used them for business) and current users of the wireline Internet. An internal perspective on this development can be found in Mari Matsunaga, *The Birth of I-Mode: An Analogue Account of the Mobile Internet* (Singapore: Chuang Yi Publishing, 2001). Matsunaga was one of the key players in the development of i-mode at DoCoMo.

19. See "Integrate to Innovate," a Deloitte Research study by Michael E. Raynor and Clayton M. Christensen. Available at <http://www.dc.com/vcd>, or upon request from delresearch@dc.com.

20. Some readers who are familiar with the different experiences of the European and American mobile telephony industries may take issue with this paragraph. Very early on, the Europeans coalesced around a prenegotiated standard called GSM, which enabled mobile phone users to use their phones in any country. Mobile phone usage took off more rapidly and achieved higher penetration rates than in America, where several competing standards were battling it out. Many analysts have drawn the general conclusion from the Europeans' strategy of quickly coalescing around a standard that it is always advisable to avoid the wasteful duplication of competing mutually incompatible architectures. We believe that the benefits of a single standard have been largely exaggerated, and that other important differences between the United States and Europe which contributed significantly to the differential adoption rates have not been given their due.

First, the benefits of a single standard appear to have manifested themselves largely in terms of supply-side rather than demand-side benefits. That is, by stipulating a single standard, European manufacturers of network equipment and handsets were able to achieve greater scale economies than companies manufacturing for the North American markets. This might well have manifested itself in the form of lower prices to consumers; however, the relevant comparison is not the cost of mobile telephony in Europe versus North America—these services were not competing with each other. The relevant comparison is with wireline telephony in each respective market. And here it is worth noting that wireline local and long distance telephony services are much more expensive in Europe than in North America, and as a result, wireless telephony was a much more attractive substitute for wireline in Europe than in North America. The putative demand-side benefit of transnational usage has not, to our knowledge, been demonstrated in the usage patterns of European consumers. Consequently, we would be willing to suggest that a far more powerful cause of the relative success of mobile telephony in Europe was not that schoolgirls from Sweden could use their handset when on holiday in Spain, but rather the relative improvement in ease of use and cost provided by mobile telephony versus the wireline alternative.

Second, and perhaps even more important, European regulation mandated that "calling party pays" with respect to mobile phone usage, whereas North American regulators mandated that "mobile party pays." In other words, in Europe, if you call someone's mobile phone number, you pay the cost of the call; to the recipient, it's free. In North America, if someone calls you on your mobile phone, it's on your dime. As a result, Europeans were far freer in giving out their mobile phone numbers, hence increasing the likelihood of usage. For more on this topic, see Strategis Group, "Calling Party Pays Case Study Analysis; ITU-BDT Telecommunication Regulatory Database"; and ITU Web site: <http://www.itu.int/ITU-D/ict/statistics>.

Teasing out the effects of each of these contributors (the GSM standard, lower relative price versus wireline, and calling party pays regulation), as well as others that might be adduced is not a trivial task. But we would suggest that the impact of the single standard is far less than typically implied, and certainly is not the principal factor in explaining higher mobile phone penetration rates in Europe versus North America.

CHAPTER SIX

HOW TO AVOID COMMODITIZATION

What causes commoditization? Is it the inevitable end-state of all companies in competitive markets? Can companies take action at any point in their development that can arrest its onset? Once the tide of commoditization has swept through an industry, can the flow reverse back toward proprietary, differentiated, profitable products? How can I respond to this?

Many executives have resigned themselves to the belief that, no matter how miraculous their innovations, their inevitable fate is to be "commoditized." These fears are grounded in painful experience. Here's a frightening example: The first one-gigabyte 3.5-inch disk drives were introduced to the world in 1992 at prices that enabled their manufacturers to earn 60 percent gross margins. These days, disk drive companies are struggling to eke out 15 percent margins on drives that are sixty times better. This isn't fair, because these things are mechanical and microelectronic marvels. How many of us could mechanically position the head so that it stored and retrieved data in circular tracks that are only 0.00008 inch apart on the surface of disks, without ever reading data off the wrong track? And yet disk drives of this genre are regarded today as undifferentiable commodities. If products this precise and complicated can be commoditized, is there any hope for the rest of us?

It turns out that there *is* hope. One of the most exciting insights from our research about commoditization is that whenever it is at work somewhere in a value chain, a reciprocal process of de-commoditization is at work somewhere else in the value chain.[1] And whereas commoditization destroys a company's ability to capture profits by undermining differentiability, de-commoditization affords opportunities to create and capture potentially enormous wealth. The reciprocality of these processes means that the locus of the ability to differentiate shifts continuously in a value chain as new waves of disruption wash over an industry. As this happens, companies that position themselves at a spot in the value chain where performance is not yet good enough will capture the profit.

Our purpose in this chapter is to help managers understand how these processes of commoditization and de-commoditization work, so that they can detect when and where they are beginning to happen. We hope that this understanding can help those who are building growth businesses to do so in a place in the value chain where the forces of de-commoditization are at work. We also hope it helps those who are running established businesses to reposition their firms in the value chain to catch these waves of de-commoditization as well. To return to Wayne Gretzky's insight about great hockey playing, we want to help managers develop the intuition for skating not to where the money presently is in the value chain, but to where the money will be.[2]

The Processes of Commoditization and De-commoditization

The process that transforms a profitable, differentiated, proprietary product into a commodity is the process of overshooting and modularization we described in chapter 5. At the leftmost side of the disruption diagram, the companies that are most successful are integrated companies that design and assemble the not-good-enough end-use products. They make attractive profits for two reasons. First, the interdependent, proprietary architecture of their products makes differentiation straightforward. Second, the high ratio of fixed to variable costs that often is inherent in the design and manufacture of architecturally interdependent products creates steep economies of scale that give larger competitors strong cost advantages and create formidable entry barriers against new competitors.

This is why, for example, IBM, as the most integrated competitor in the mainframe computer industry, held a 70 percent market share but made 95 percent of the industry's profits: It had proprietary products, strong cost advantages, and high entry barriers. For the same reasons, from the 1950s through the 1970s, General Motors, with about 55 percent of the U.S. automobile market, garnered 80 percent of the industry's profits. Most of the firms that were suppliers to IBM and General Motors, in contrast, had to make do with subsistence profits year after year. These firms' experiences are typical. Making highly differentiable products with strong cost advantages is a license to print money, and lots of it.[3]

We must emphasize that the reason many companies don't reach this nirvana or remain there for long is that it is the not-good-enough circumstance that enables managers to offer products with proprietary architectures that can be made with strong cost advantages versus competitors. When that circumstance changes—when the dominant, profitable companies overshoot what their mainstream customers can use—then this game can no longer be played, and the tables begin to turn. Customers will not pay still-higher prices for products they already deem too good. Before long, modularity rules, and commoditization sets in. When the relevant dimensions of your product's performance are determined not by you but by the subsystems that you procure from your suppliers, it becomes difficult to earn anything more than subsistence returns in a product category that used to make a lot of money. When your world becomes modular, you'll need to look elsewhere in the value chain to make any serious money.

The natural and inescapable process of commoditization occurs in six steps:

1. As a new market coalesces, a company develops a proprietary product that, while not good enough, comes closer to satisfying customers' needs than any of its competitors. It does this through a proprietary architecture, and earns attractive profit margins.

2. As the company strives to keep ahead of its direct competitors, it eventually overshoots the functionality and reliability that customers in lower tiers of the market can utilize.

3. This precipitates a change in the basis of competition in those tiers, which . . .

4. . . . precipitates an evolution toward modular architectures, which . . .

5. . . . facilitates the dis-integration of the industry, which in turn . . .

6. . . . makes it very difficult to differentiate the performance or costs of the product versus those of competitors, who have access to the same components and assemble according to the same standards. This condition begins at the bottom of the market, where functional overshoot occurs first, and then moves up inexorably to affect the higher tiers.

Note that it is overshooting—the more-than-good-enough circumstance—that connects disruption and the phenomenon of commoditization. Disruption and commoditization can be seen as two sides of the same coin. A company that finds itself in a more-than-good-enough circumstance simply can't win: Either disruption will steal its markets, or commoditization will steal its profits. Most incumbents eventually end up the victim of both, because, although the pace of commoditization varies by industry, it is inevitable, and nimble new entrants rarely miss an opportunity to exploit a disruptive foothold.

There can still be prosperity around the corner, however. The attractive profits of the future are often to be earned elsewhere in the value chain, in different stages or layers of added value. That's because the process of commoditization initiates a reciprocal process of de-commoditization. Ironically, this de-commoditization—with the attendant ability to earn lots of money—occurs in places in the value chain where attractive profits were hard to attain in the past: in the formerly modular and undifferentiable processes, components, or subsystems.[4]

To visualize the reciprocal process, remember the steel minimills from chapter 2. As long as the minimills were competing against integrated mills in the rebar market, they made a lot of money because they had a 20 percent cost advantage relative to the integrated mills. But as soon as they drove the last high-cost competitor out of the rebar market, the low-cost minimills found themselves slugging it out against equally low-cost minimills in a commodity market, and competition among them caused pricing to collapse. The assemblers of modular products generally receive the same reward for victory as the minimills did whenever they succeed in driving the higher-cost competitors and their proprietary architectures out of a tier in their market: The victorious disruptors are left to slug it out against equally low-cost disruptors who are assembling modular components procured from a common supplier base. Lacking any basis for competitive differentiation, only subsistence levels of profit remain. A low-cost strategy works only as long as there are higher-cost competitors left in the market.[5]

The only way that modular disruptors can keep profits healthy is to carry their low-cost business models up-market as fast as possible so that they can keep competing at the margin against higher-cost makers of proprietary products. Assemblers of modular products do this by finding the best performance-defining components and subsystems and incorporating them in their products faster than anyone else.[6] The assemblers need the very best performance-defining components in order to race up-market where they can make money again. Their demand for improvements in performance-defining components, as a result, throws the suppliers of those components back to the not-good-enough side of the disruption diagram.

Competitive forces consequently compel suppliers of these performance-defining components to create architectures that, within the subsystems, are increasingly interdependent and proprietary. Hence, the performance-defining subsystems become de-commoditized as the result of the end-use products becoming modular and commoditized.

Let us summarize the steps in this reciprocal process of de-commoditization:

1. The low-cost strategy of modular product assemblers is only viable as long as they are competing against higher-cost opponents. This means that as soon as they drive the high-cost suppliers of

proprietary products out of a tier of the market, they must move up-market to take them on again in order to continue to earn attractive profits.

2. Because the mechanisms that constrain or determine how rapidly they can move up-market are the performance-defining subsystems, these elements become not good enough and are flipped to the left side of the disruption diagram.

3. Competition among subsystem suppliers causes their engineers to devise designs that are increasingly proprietary and interdependent. They must do this as they strive to enable their customers to deliver better performance in their end-use products than the customers could if they used competitors' subsystems.

4. The leading providers of these subsystems therefore find themselves selling differentiated, proprietary products with attractive profitability.

5. This creation of a profitable, proprietary product is the beginning, of course, of the next cycle of commoditization and de-commoditization.

Figure 6-1 illustrates more generally how this worked in the product value chain of the personal computer industry in the 1990s. Starting at the top of the diagram, money flowed from the customer to the companies that designed and assembled computers; as the decade progressed, however, less and less of the total potential profit stayed with the computer makers—most of it flowed right through these companies to their suppliers.[7]

As a result, quite a bit of the money that the assemblers got from their customers flowed over to Microsoft and lodged there. Another chunk flowed to Intel and stopped there. Money also flowed to the makers of dynamic random access memory (DRAM), such as Samsung and Micron, but not much of it stopped at those stages in the value chain in the form of profit. It flowed through and accumulated instead at firms like Applied Materials, which supplied the manufacturing equipment that the DRAM makers used. Similarly, money flowed right through the assemblers of modular disk drives, such as Maxtor and Quantum, and tended to lodge at the stage of value added where heads and disks were made.

FIGURE 6-1

Where the Money Was Made in the PC Industry's Product Value Chain

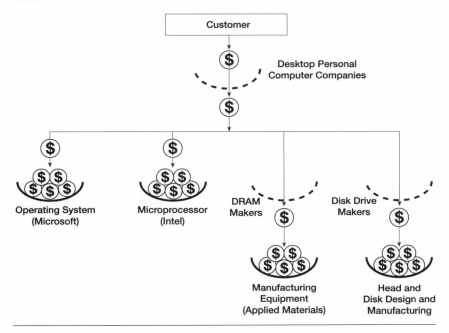

What is different about the baskets in the diagram that held money, versus those through which the money seemed to leak? The tight baskets in which profit accumulated for most of this period were products that were not yet good enough for what their immediate customers in the value chain needed. The architectures of those products therefore tended to be interdependent and proprietary. Firms in the leaky-basket situation could only hang onto subsistence profits because the functionality of their products tended to be more than good enough. Their architectures therefore were modular.

If a company supplies a performance-defining but not-yet-good-enough input for its customers' products or processes, it has the power to capture attractive profit. Consider the DRAM industry as an example. While the architecture of their own chips was modular, DRAM makers could not be satisfied even with the very best manufacturing equipment available. In order to succeed, DRAM makers needed to make their products at ever-higher yields and ever-lower costs. This rendered the functionality of equipment made by firms such as Applied Materials not good enough. The architecture of this equipment became interdependent and proprietary as a consequence, as the equipment makers strove to inch closer to the functionality that their customers needed.

It is important never to conclude that an industry such as disk drives or DRAMs is inherently unprofitable, whereas others such as microprocessors or semiconductor manufacturing equipment are inherently profitable. "Industry" is usually a faulty categorization scheme.[8] What makes an industry appear to be attractively profitable is the circumstance in which its companies happen to be at a particular point in time, at each point in the value-added chain, because the law of conservation of attractive profits is almost always at work (see the appendix to this chapter). Let's take a deeper look at the disk drive industry to see why this is so.

For most of the 1990s, in the market tiers where disk drives were sold to makers of desktop personal computers, the capacity and access times of the drives were more than adequate. The drives' architectures consequently became modular, and the gross margins that the nonintegrated assemblers of 3.5-inch drives could eke out in the desktop PC segment declined to around 12 percent. Nonintegrated disk drive assemblers such as Maxtor and Quantum dominated this market (their collective market share exceeded 90 percent) because integrated manufacturers such as IBM could not survive on such razor-thin margins.

The drives had adequate capacity, but the assemblers could not be satisfied even with the very best heads and disks available, because if they maximized the amount of data they could store per square inch of disk space, they could use fewer disks and heads in the drives— which was a powerful driver of cost. The heads and disks, consequently, became not good enough and evolved toward complex, interdependent subassemblies. Head and disk manufacturing became so profitable, in fact, that many major drive makers integrated backward into making their own heads and disks.[9]

But it wasn't the disk drive industry that was marginally profitable—it was the modular circumstance in which the 3.5-inch drive makers found themselves. The evidence: The much smaller 2.5-inch disk drives used in notebook computers tended not to have enough capacity during this same era. True to form, their architectures were interdependent, and the products had to be made by integrated companies. As the most integrated manufacturer and the one with the most advanced head and disk technology in the 1990s, IBM made 40 percent gross margins in 2.5-inch drives and controlled 80 percent of that market. In contrast, IBM had less than 3 percent of the unit volume in drives sold to the desktop PC market, where its integration rendered it uncompetitive.[10]

At the time we first published our analysis of this situation in 1999, it appeared that the capacity of 2.5-inch disk drives was becoming more than good enough in the notebook computer application as well—presaging, for what had been a beautiful business for IBM, the onset of commoditization.[11] We asserted that IBM, as the most integrated drive maker, actually was in a very attractive position if it played its cards right. It could skate to where the money would be by using the advent of modularity to decouple its head and disk operations from its disk drive design and assembly business. If IBM would begin to sell its most advanced heads and disks to competing 2.5-inch disk drive makers—aggressively putting them into the business of assembling modular 2.5-inch drives—it could eventually de-emphasize the assembly of drives and focus on the more profitable head and disk components. In so doing, IBM could continue to enjoy the most attractive levels of profit in the industry. In other words, on the not-good-enough side of the disruptive diagram, IBM could fight in the war and win. On the more-than-good-enough side, a better strategy is to sell bullets to the combatants.[12]

IBM made similar moves several years earlier in its computer business, through its decisions to decouple its vertical chain and to sell its technology, components, and subsystems aggressively in the open market. Simultaneously it created a consulting and systems integration business in the high end and moved to de-emphasize the design and assembly of computers. As IBM skated to those points in the value-added chain where complex, nonstandard integration needed to occur, it led to a remarkable—and remarkably profitable—transformation of a huge company in the 1990s.

The bedrock principle bears repeating: The companies that are positioned at a spot in a value chain where performance is not yet good enough will capture the profit. That is the circumstance where differentiable products, scale-based cost advantages, and high entry barriers can be created.

To the extent that an integrated company such as IBM can flexibly couple and decouple its operations, rather than irrevocably sell off operations, it has greater potential to thrive profitably for an extended period than does a nonintegrated firm such as Compaq. This is because the processes of commoditization and de-commoditization are continuously at work, causing the place where the money will be to shift across the value chain over time.

Core Competence and the ROA-Maximizing Death Spiral

Firms that are being commoditized often ignore the reciprocal process of de-commoditization that occurs simultaneously with commoditization, either a layer down in subsystems or next door in adjacent processes. They miss the opportunity to move where the money will be in the future, and get squeezed—or even killed—as different firms catch the growth made possible by de-commoditization. In fact, powerful but perverse investor pressure to increase returns on assets (ROA) creates strong incentives for assemblers to skate away from where the money will be. And having failed to recognize their modular, commoditized circumstance, the firms turn to attribute-based core competence theory to make decisions they may later regret.

How can firms that assemble modular products meet investors' demands that they improve their return on assets or capital employed? They cannot improve the numerator of the ROA ratio because differentiating their product or producing it at lower costs than competitors is nearly impossible. Their only option is to shrink the denominator of the ROA ratio by getting rid of assets. This would be difficult in an interdependent world that demanded integration, but the modular architecture of the product actually facilitates dis-integration. We will illustrate how this happens using a disguised example of the interactions between a component supplier and an assembler of modular personal computers. We'll call the two firms Components Corporation and Texas Computer Corporation (TCC), respectively.

Components Corporation begins by supplying simple circuit boards to TCC. As TCC wrestles with investor pressure to get its ROA up, Components Corp. comes up with an interesting proposition: "We've done a good job making these little boards for you. Let us supply the whole motherboard for your computers. We can easily beat your internal costs."

"Gosh, that would be a great idea," TCC's management responds. "Circuit board fabrication isn't our core competence anyway, and it is very asset intensive. This would reduce our costs and get all those assets off our balance sheet." So Components Corp. takes on the additional value-added activity. Its revenues increase smartly, and its profitability improves because it is utilizing its manufacturing assets better. Its stock price improves accordingly. As TCC sheds those assets, its revenue line is unaffected. But its bottom line and its return on assets improve—and its stock price improves accordingly.

A short time later Components Corp. approaches TCC's management again. "You know, the motherboard really is the guts of the computer. Let us assemble the whole computer for you. Assembling those products really isn't your core competency, anyway, and we can easily beat your internal costs."

"Gosh, that would be a great idea," TCC's management responds. "Assembly isn't our core competence anyway, and if you did our product assembly, we could get all those manufacturing assets off our balance sheet." Again, as Components Corp. takes on the additional value-added activity, its revenues increase smartly and its profitability improves because it is utilizing its manufacturing assets better. Its stock price improves accordingly. And as TCC sheds its manufacturing assets, its revenue line is unaffected. But its bottom line and its return on assets improve—and its stock price improves accordingly.

A short time later Components Corp. approaches TCC's management again. "You know, as long as we're assembling your computers, why do you need to deal with all the hassles of managing the inbound logistics of components and the outbound logistics of customer shipments? Let us deal with your suppliers and deliver the finished products to your customers. Supply chain management really isn't your core competence, anyway, and we can easily beat your internal costs."

"Gosh, that would be a great idea," TCC's management responds. "This would help us get those current assets off our balance sheet." As Components Corp. takes on the additional value-added activity, its revenues increase smartly and its profitability improves because it is pulling higher value-added activities into its business model. Its stock price improves accordingly. And as TCC sheds its current assets, its revenue line is unaffected. But its profitability improves—and its stock price gets another bounce.

A short time later Components Corp. approaches TCC's management again. "You know, as long as we're dealing with your suppliers, how about you just let us design those computers for you? The design of modular products is little more than vendor selection anyway, and since we have closer relationships with vendors than you do, we could get better pricing and delivery if we can work with them from the beginning of the design cycle."

"Gosh, that would be a great idea," TCC's management responds. "This would help us cut fixed and variable costs. Besides, our strength really is in our brand and our customer relationships, not in product design." As Components Corp. takes on the additional value-added activity, its revenues increase further and its profitability improves because it is pulling higher value-added activities into its business model. Its stock price improves accordingly. And as TCC sheds cost, its revenue line is unaffected. But its profitability improves—and its stock price gets another nice little pop—until the analysts realize that the game is over.

Ironically, in this Greek tragedy Components Corp. ends up with a value chain that is actually more highly integrated than TCC's was when this spiral began, but often with the pieces reconfigured to allow Components Corp. to deliver against the new basis of competition, which is speed to market and the ability to responsively configure what is delivered to customers in ever-smaller segments of the market. Each time TCC off-loaded assets and processes to Components Corp., it justified its decision in terms of its own "core competence."

It did not occur to TCC's management that the activities in question weren't Components Corporation's core competencies, either. Whether or not something is a core competence is not the determining factor of who can skate to where the money will be.

This story illustrates another instance of asymmetric motivations—the component supplier is motivated to integrate forward into the very pieces of value-added activity that the modular assembler is motivated to get out of. It is not a story of incompetence. It is a story of perfectly rational, profit-maximizing decisions—and because of this, the ROA-maximizing death spiral traps many companies that find themselves assembling modular products in a too-good world. At the same time, it offers another avenue for creating new-growth businesses, in addition to the disruptive opportunities described in chapter 2. The assembler rids itself of assets, but it retains its revenues and often temporarily improves its bottom-line profit margins when it decides to outsource its back-end operations to contract suppliers. It feels good. When the supplier takes on the same pieces of business that the assembler was motivated to get out of, it also feels good, because it increases the back-end supplier's revenues, profits, and stock price. For many suppliers, eating their way up the value chain creates opportunities to design subsystems with increasingly optimized internal architectures that become key performance drivers of the modular products that its customers assemble.

This is how Intel became a vendor of chipsets and motherboards, which constitute a much more critical proportion of a computer's added value and performance than did the bare microprocessor. Nypro, Inc., a custom injection molder of precision plastic components whose history we will examine later in this book, has followed a similar growth strategy and has become a major manufacturer of ink-jet printer cartridges, computers, handheld wireless devices, and medical products. Nypro's ability to precision-mold complex structures is interdependent with its abilities to simplify assembly.

Bloomberg L.P. has done the same thing, eating its way up Wall Street's value chain. It started by providing simple data on securities prices and subsequently integrated forward, automating much of the analytics. Bloomberg has disruptively enabled an army of people to access insights that formerly only highly experienced securities analysts could derive. Bloomberg has continued to integrate forward from the back end, so that portfolio managers can now execute most trades from their Bloomberg terminals over a Bloomberg-owned electronic communications network (ECN) without needing a broker or a stock exchange. Issuers of certain government securities can now even auction their securities to institutional investors within Bloomberg's proprietary system. Back-end suppliers such as First Data and State Street enjoy a similar position vis-à-vis commercial banks. Venerable Wall Street institutions are being disrupted and hollowed out—and they don't even realize it because outsourcing the asset-intensive back end is a compelling mandate that feels good once the front end has become modular and commoditized.

Core competence, as it is used by many managers, is a dangerously inward-looking notion. *Competitiveness is far more about doing what customers value than doing what you think you're good at.* And staying competitive as the basis of competition shifts necessarily requires a willingness and ability to learn new things rather than clinging hopefully to the sources of past glory. The challenge for incumbent companies is to rebuild their ships while at sea, rather than dismantling themselves plank by plank while someone else builds a new, faster boat with what they cast overboard as detritus.

What can growth-hungry managers do in situations like this? In many ways, the process is inevitable. Assemblers of modular products must, over time, shed assets in order to reduce costs and improve returns—financial market pressure leaves managers with few alternatives. However, knowing that this is likely to happen gives those same managers the opportunity to own or acquire, and manage as separate growth-oriented businesses, the component or subsystem suppliers that are positioned to eat their way up the value chain. This is the essence of skating to where the money will be.[13]

Good Enough, Not Good Enough, and the Value of Brands

Executives who seek to avoid commoditization often rely on the strength of their brands to sustain their profitability—but brands become commoditized and de-commoditized, too. Brands are most valuable when they are created at the stages of the value-added chain where things aren't yet good enough. When customers aren't yet certain whether a product's performance will be satisfactory, a well-crafted brand can step in and close some of the gap between what customers need and what they fear they might get if they buy the product from a supplier of unknown reputation. The role of a good brand in closing this gap is apparent in the price premium that branded products are able to command in some situations. For similar logic, however, the ability of brands to command premium prices tends to atrophy when the performance of a class of products from multiple suppliers is manifestly more than adequate.

When overshooting occurs, the ability to command attractive profitability through a valuable brand often migrates to those points in the value-added chain where things have flipped into a not-yet-good-enough situation. These often will be the performance-defining subsystems within the product, or at the retail interface when it is the speed, simplicity, and convenience of getting exactly what you want that is not good enough. These shifts define the opportunities in branding.

For example, in the early decades of the computer industry, investment in complex and unreliable mainframe computer systems was an unnerving task for most managers. Because IBM's servicing capability was unsurpassed, the brand of IBM had the power to command price premiums of 30 to 40 percent, compared with comparable equipment. No corporate IT director got fired for buying IBM. Hewlett-Packard's brand commanded similar premiums.

How did the brands of Intel and Microsoft Windows subsequently steal the valuable branding power from IBM and Hewlett-Packard in the 1990s? It happened when computers came to pack good-enough functionality and reliability for mainstream business use, and modular, industry-standard architectures became predominant in those tiers of the market. At that point, the microprocessor inside and the operating system became not good enough, and the locus of the powerful brands migrated to those new locations.

The migration of branding power in a market that is composed of multiple tiers is a process, not an event. Accordingly, the brands of companies with proprietary products typically create value mapping upward from their position on the improvement trajectory—toward those customers who still are not satisfied with the functionality and reliability of the best that is available. But mapping downward from that same point—toward the world of modular products where speed, convenience, and responsiveness drive competitive success— the power to create profitable brands migrates away from the end-use product, toward the subsystems and the channel.[14]

This has happened in heavy trucks. There was a time when the valuable brand, Mack, was on the truck itself. Truckers paid a significant premium for Mack the bulldog on the hood. Mack achieved its preeminent reliability through its interdependent architecture and extensive vertical integration. As the architectures of large trucks have become modular, however, purchasers have come to care far more whether there is a Cummins or Caterpillar engine inside than whether the truck is assembled by Paccar, Navistar, or Freightliner.

Apparel is another industry in which the power to brand has begun to migrate to a different stage of the value-added chain. As elsewhere, it has happened because a changed basis of competition has redefined what is not good enough. A generation ago most of the valuable brands were on the products. Levi's brand jeans and Gant brand shirts, for example, enjoyed strong and profitable market shares because many of the competing products were not nearly as sturdily made. These branded products were sold in department stores, which trumpeted their exclusive ability to sell the best brands in clothing.

Over the past fifteen years, however, the quality of clothing from a wide range of manufacturers has become assured, as producers in low-labor-cost countries have improved their capabilities to produce high-quality fabrics and clothing. The basis of competition in the apparel industry has changed as a consequence. Specialized retailers have stolen a significant share of market from the broad-line department stores because their focused merchandise mix allows the customers they target to find what they want more quickly and conveniently. What is not good enough in certain tiers of the apparel industry has shifted from the quality of the product to the simplicity and convenience of the purchasing experience. Much of the ability to create and maintain valuable brands, as a consequence, has migrated away from the product and to the channel because, for the present, it is the channel that addresses the piece of added value that is not yet good enough.[15] We don't even question who makes the dresses in Talbot's, the sweaters for Abercrombie & Fitch, or the jeans at Gap and Old Navy. Much of the apparel sold in those channels carries the brand of the channel, not the manufacturer.[16]

A View of the Automobile Industry's Future Through the Lenses of This Model

Most of our examples of commoditization and de-commoditization have been drawn from the past. To show how this theory can be used to look into the future, this section discusses how this transformation is under way in the automobile industry, initiating a massive transfer of the ability to make attractive profits in the future away from automobile manufacturers and toward certain of their suppliers. Even the power to cultivate valuable brands is likely to migrate to the subsystems. This transformation will probably take a decade or two to fully accomplish, but once you know what to look for, it is easy to see that the processes already are irreversibly under way.

The functionality of many automobiles has overshot what customers in the mainstream markets can utilize. Lexus, BMW, Mercedes, and Cadillac owners will probably be willing to pay premium prices for more of everything for years to come. But in market tiers populated by middle- and lower-price-point models, car makers find themselves having to add more and better features just to hang onto their market share, and they struggle to convince customers to pay higher prices for these improvements. The reliability of models such as Toyota's Camry and Honda's Accord is so extraordinary that the cars often go out of style long before they wear out. As a result, the basis of competition—what is not good enough—is changing in many tiers of the auto market. Speed to market is important. Whereas it used to take five years to design a new-model car, today it takes two. Competing by customizing features and functions to the preferences of customers in smaller market niches is another fact of life. In the 1960s, it was not unusual for a single model's sales to exceed a million units per year. Today the market is far more fragmented: Annual volumes of 200,000 units are attractive. Some makers now promise that you can walk into a dealership, custom-order a car, and have it delivered in five days—roughly the response time that Dell Computer offers.

In order to compete on speed and flexibility, automakers are evolving toward modular architectures for their mainstream models. Rather than uniquely designing and knitting together individual components procured from hundreds of suppliers, most auto companies now procure subsystems from a much narrower base of "tier one" suppliers of braking, steering, suspension, and interior cockpit subsystems. Much of this consolidation in the supplier base has been driven by the cost-saving opportunities that it affords—opportunities that often were identified and quantified by analytically astute consulting firms.

The integrated American automakers have been forced to disintegrate in order to compete with the speed, flexibility, and reduced overhead cost structure that this new world demands. General Motors, for example, spun off its component operations into a separate publicly traded company, Delphi Automotive, and Ford spun off its component operations as Visteon Corporation. Hence, the same thing is happening to the auto industry that happened to computers: Overshooting has precipitated a change in the basis of competition, which precipitated a change in architecture, which forced the dominant, integrated firms to dis-integrate.

At the same time, the architecture is becoming progressively more interdependent within most of the subsystems. The models at lower price points in the market need improved performance from their subsystems in order to compete against higher-cost models and brands in the tiers of the market above them. If Kia and Hyundai used their low-cost Korean manufacturing base to conquer the subcompact tier of the market and then simply stayed there, competition would vaporize profits. They must move up, and once their architectures have become modular the only way to do this is to be fueled by ever-better subsystems.

The newly interdependent architectures of many subsystems are forcing the tier-one suppliers to be less flexible at their external interface. The automobile designers are increasingly needing to conform their designs to the specifications of the subsystems, just as desktop computer makers need to conform the designs of their computers to the external interfaces of Intel's microprocessor and Microsoft's operating system. As a consequence, we would expect that the ability to earn attractive profits is likely to migrate away from the auto assemblers, toward the subsystem vendors.[17]

In chapter 5 we recounted how IBM's PC business outsourced its microprocessor to Intel and its operating system to Microsoft, in order to be fast and flexible. In the process, IBM hung on to where the money had been—design and assembly of the computer system—and put into business the two companies that were positioned where the money would be. General Motors and Ford, with the encouragement of their consultants and investment bankers, have just done the same thing. They had to decouple the vertical stages in their value chains in order to stay abreast of the changing basis of competition. But they have spun off the pieces of value-added activity where the money will be, in order to stay where the money has been.[18]

These findings have pervasive implications for managers seeking to build successful new-growth businesses and for those seeking to keep current businesses robust. The power to capture attractive profits will shift to those activities in the value chain where the immediate customer is not yet satisfied with the performance of available products. It is in these stages that complex, interdependent integration occurs—activities that create steeper scale economics and enable greater differentiability. Attractive returns shift away from activities where the immediate customer is more than satisfied, because it is there that standard, modular integration occurs. We hope that in describing this process in these terms, we might help managers to predict more accurately where new opportunities for profitable growth through proprietary products will emerge. These transitions begin on the trajectories of improvement where disruptors are at work, and proceed upmarket tier by tier. This process creates opportunities for new companies that are integrated across these not-good-enough interfaces to thrive, and to grow by "eating their way up" from the back end of an end-use system. Managers of industry-leading businesses need to watch vigilantly in the right places to spot these trends as they begin, because the processes of commoditization and de-commoditization both begin at the periphery, not the core.

Appendix: The Law of Conservation of Attractive Profits

Having described these cycles of commoditization and de-commoditization in terms of products, we can now make a more general statement concerning the existence of a general phenomenon that we call the law of conservation of attractive profits. Our friend Chris Rowen, CEO of Tensilica, pointed out to us the existence of this law, whose appellation was inspired by the laws of conservation of energy and matter that we so fondly remember studying in physics class. Formally, the law of conservation of attractive profits states that in the value chain there is a requisite juxtaposition of modular and interdependent architectures, and of reciprocal processes of commoditization and de-commoditization, that exists in order to optimize the performance of what is not good enough. The law states that when modularity and commoditization cause attractive profits to disappear at one stage in the value chain, the opportunity to earn attractive profits with proprietary products will usually emerge at an adjacent stage.[19]

We'll first illustrate how this law operates by examining handheld devices such as the RIM BlackBerry and the Palm Pilot, which constitute the latest wave of disruption in the computing industry. The functionality of these products is not yet adequate, and as a consequence their architectures are interdependent. This is especially true for the BlackBerry, because its "always on" capability mandates extraordinarily efficient use of power. Because of this, the BlackBerry engineers cannot incorporate a one-size-fits-all Intel microprocessor into their device. It has far more capability than is needed. Rather, they need a modular microprocessor design—a system-on-a-chip that is custom-configured for the BlackBerry—so that they do not have to waste space, power, or cost on functionality that is not needed.

The microprocessor must be modular and conformable in order to permit engineers to optimize the performance of what is not good enough, which is the device itself. Note that this is the opposite situation from that of a desktop computer, where it is the microprocessor that is not good enough. The architecture of the computer must therefore be modular and conformable in order to allow engineers to optimize the performance of the microprocessor. Thus, one side or the other must be modular and conformable to allow for optimization of what is not good enough through an interdependent architecture.

In similar ways, application software programs that are written to run on Microsoft's Windows operating systems need to be conformed to Windows' external interface; the Linux operating system, on the other hand, is modular and conformable to optimize the performance of software that runs on it.

We have found this "law" to be a useful way to visualize where the money will migrate in the value chain in a number of industries. It is explored in greater depth in a forthcoming book by Clayton Christensen, Scott Anthony, and Erik Roth, *Seeing What's Next* (Boston: Harvard Business School Press, 2004).

This law also has helped us understand the juxtaposition of modular products with interdependent services, because services provided with the products can go through similar cycles of commoditization and de-commoditization, with consequent implications for where attractive profitability will migrate.

We noted previously that when the functionality and reliability of a product become more than good enough, the basis of competition changes. What becomes not good enough are speed to market and the rapid and responsive ability to configure products to the specific needs of customers in ever-more-targeted market segments. The customer interface is the place in the value chain where the ability to excel on this new dimension of competition is determined. Hence, companies that are integrated in a proprietary way across the interface to the customer can compete on these not-good-enough dimensions more effectively (and be rewarded with better margins) than can those firms that interface with their customers only in an arm's-length, "modular" manner. Companies that integrate across the retail interface to the customer, in this circumstance, can also earn above-average profits.

We would therefore not say that Dell Computer is a nonintegrated company, for example. Rather, Dell is integrated across the not-good-enough interface with the customer. The company is not integrated across the more-than-good-enough modular interfaces among the components within its computers. Figure 6-2 summarizes in a simplified way how the profitable points of proprietary integration have migrated in the personal computer industry.

On the left side of the diagram, which represents the earliest years of the desktop computer industry when product functionality was extremely limited, Apple Computer, with its proprietary architecture and integrated business model, was the most successful firm and was attractively profitable. The firms that supplied the bare components and materials to Apple, and the independent, arm's-length retailers that sold the computers, were not in nearly as attractive a position. In the late 1990s, the processes of commoditization and de-commoditization had transferred the points at which proprietary integration could build proprietary competitive advantage to

FIGURE 6-2

The Shifting Locus of Advantage in the PC Industry's Process Value Chain

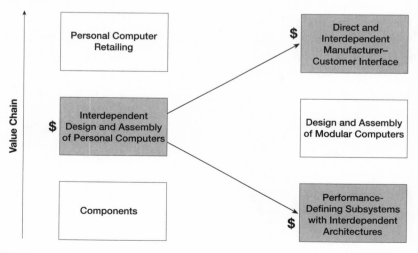

the retail interface with the customer (Dell) and to the interfaces within the subsystems (Intel and Microsoft).

We believe that this is an important factor that explains why Dell Computer was more successful than Compaq during the 1990s. Dell was integrated across an important not-good-enough interface, whereas Compaq was not. We also would expect that a proper cost accounting would show that Dell's profits from retailing operations are far greater than the profits from its assembly operations.

Notes

1. There are two ways to think of a product or service's value chain. It can be conceptualized in terms of its processes, that is, the value-added steps required to create or deliver it. For example, the processes of design, component manufacture, assembly, marketing, sales, and distribution are generic processes in a value chain. A value chain can also be thought of in terms of components, or the "bill of materials" that go into a product. For example, the engine block, chassis, braking systems, and electronic subassemblies that go into a car are components of a car's value chain. It is helpful to keep both ways of thinking about a value chain in mind, since value chains are also "fractal"—that is, they are equally complex at every level of analysis. Specifically, for a given product that goes through the processes that define its value chain, various components must be used. Yet every component that is used has its own sequence of processes through which it must pass. The complexity of analyzing a product's value chain is essentially irreducible. The question is which level of complexity one wishes to focus on.

2. This discussion builds heavily on Professor Michael Porter's five forces framework and his characterization of the value chain. See Michael Porter, *Competitive Strategy* (New York: Free Press, 1980) and *Competitive Advantage* (New York: The Free Press, 1985). Analysts often use Porter's five forces framework to determine which firms in a value-added system can wield the greatest power to appropriate profit from others. In many ways, our model in chapters 5 and 6 provides a dynamic overlay on his five forces model, suggesting that the strength of these forces is not invariant over time. It shows how the power to capture an above-average portion of the industry's profit is likely to migrate to different stages of the value chain in a predictable way in response to the phenomena we describe here.

3. As a general observation, when you examine what seems to be the hey-day of most major companies, it was (or is) a period when the functionality and

reliability of their products did not yet satisfy large numbers of customers. As a result, they had products with proprietary architectures, and made them with strong competitive cost advantages. Furthermore, when they introduced new and improved products, the new products could sustain a premium price because functionality was not yet good enough and the new products came closer to meeting what was needed. This can be said for the Bell telephone system; Mack trucks; Caterpillar earthmoving equipment; Xerox photocopiers; Nokia and Motorola mobile telephone handsets; Intel microprocessors; Microsoft operating systems; Cisco routers; the IT consulting businesses of EDS or IBM; the Harvard Business School; and many other companies.

4. In the following text we will use the term *subsystem* to mean, generally, an assembly of components and materials that provides a piece of the functionality required for an end-use system to be operational.

5. Once again, we see linkages to Professor Michael Porter's notion that there are two viable "generic" strategies: differentiation and low cost (see chapter 2, note 12). Our model describes the mechanism that causes neither of these strategies to be sustainable. Differentiability is destroyed by the mechanism that leads to modularization and dis-integration. Low-cost strategies are viable only as long as the population of low-cost competitors does not have sufficient capacity to supply what customers in a given tier of the market demand. Price is set at the intersection of the supply and demand curves—at the cash cost of the marginal producer. When the marginal producer is a higher-cost disruptee, then the low-cost disruptors can make attractive profits. But when the high-cost competitors are gone and the entire market demand can be supplied by equally low-cost suppliers of modular products, then what was a low-cost strategy becomes an equal-cost strategy.

6. Not all the components or subsystems in a product contribute to the specific performance attributes of value to customers. Those that drive the performance that matters are the "performance-defining" components or subsystems. In the case of a personal computer, for example, the microprocessor, the operating system, and the applications have long been the performance-defining subsystems.

7. Analysts' estimates of how much of the industry's money stayed with computer assemblers and how much "leaked" through to back-end or subsystem suppliers are summarized in "Deconstructing the Computer Industry," *BusinessWeek*, 23 November 1992, 90–96. As we note in the appendix to this chapter, we would expect that much of Dell's profit comes from its direct-to-customer retailing operations, not from product assembly.

8. With just a few seconds' reflection, it is easy to see that the investment management industry suffers from the problem of categorization along industry-

defined lines that are irrelevant to profitability and growth. Hence, they create investment funds for "technology companies" and other funds for "health care companies." Within those portfolios are disruptors and disruptees, companies on the verge of commoditization and those on the verge of de-commoditization, and so on. Michael Mauboussin, chief investment strategist at Credit Suisse First Boston, recently wrote an article on this topic. It builds on the model of theory building that we have summarized in the introduction of this book, and its application to the world of investing is very insightful. See Michael Mauboussin, "No Context: The Importance of Circumstance-Based Categorization," *The Consiliant Observer,* New York: Credit Suisse First Boston, 14 January 2003.

9. Those of our readers who are familiar with the disk drive industry might see a contradiction between our statement that much of the money in the industry was earned in head and disk manufacturing and the fact that the leading head and disk makers, such as Read-Rite and Komag, have not prospered. They have not prospered because most of the leading disk drive makers—particularly Seagate—integrated into their own head and disk making so that they could capture the profit instead of the independent suppliers.

10. IBM did have profitable volume in 3.5-inch drives, but it was at the highest-capacity tiers of that market, where capacity was not good enough and the product designs therefore had to be interdependent.

11. A more complete account of these developments has been published in Clayton M. Christensen, Matt Verlinden, and George Westerman, "Disruption, Disintegration and the Dissipation of Differentiability," *Industrial and Corporate Change* 11, no. 5 (2002): 955–993. The first Harvard Business School working papers that summarized this analysis were written and broadly circulated in 1998 and 1999.

12. We have deliberately used present- and future-tense verbs in this paragraph. The reason is that at the time this account was first written and submitted to publishers, these statements were predictions. Subsequently, the gross margins in IBM's 2.5-inch disk drive business deteriorated significantly, as this model predicted they would. However, IBM chose to sell off its entire disk drive business to Hitachi, giving to some other company the opportunity to sell the profitable, performance-enabling components for this class of disk drives.

13. We have written elsewhere that the Harvard Business School has an extraordinary opportunity to execute exactly this strategy in management education, if it will only seize it. Harvard writes and publishes the vast majority of the case studies and many of the articles that business school professors have used as components in courses whose architecture is of interdependent design. As on-the-job management training and corporate universities

(which are nonintegrated assemblers of modular courses) disrupt traditional MBA programs, Harvard has a great opportunity to flip its business model through its publishing arm and sell not just case studies and articles as bare-bones components but also value-added subsystems as modules. These should be designed to make it simple for management trainers in the corporate setting to custom-assemble great material, deliver it exactly when it is needed, and teach it in a compelling way. (See Clayton M. Christensen, Michael E. Raynor, and Matthew Verlinden, "Skate to Where the Money Will Be," *Harvard Business Review,* November 2001.)

14. This would suggest, for example, that Hewlett-Packard's branding power would be strong mapping upward to not-yet-satisfied customers from the trajectory of improvement on which its products are positioned. And it suggests that the HP brand would be much weaker, compared with the brands of Intel and Microsoft, mapping downward from that same point to more-than-satisfied customers.

15. We are indebted to one of Professor Christensen's Harvard MBA students, Alana Stevens, for many of these insights, which she developed in a research paper entitled "A House of Brands or a Branded House?" Stevens noted that branding power is gradually migrating away from the products to the channels in a variety of retailing categories. Manufacturers of branded food and personal care products such as Unilever and Procter & Gamble, for example, fight this battle of the brands with their channels every day, because many of their products are more than good enough. In Great Britain, disruptive channel brands such as Tesco and Sainsbury's have decisively won this battle after first starting at the lower price points in each category and then moving up. In the United States, branded products have clung more tenaciously to shelf space, but often at the cost of exorbitant slotting fees. The migration of brands in good-enough categories is well under way in channels such as Home Depot and Staples. Where the products' functionality and reliability have become more than good enough and it is the simplicity and convenience of purchase and use that is not good enough, then the power to brand has begun migrating to the channel whose business model is delivering on this as-yet-unsatisfied dimension.

   Procter & Gamble appears to be following a sensible strategy by launching a series of new-market disruptions that simultaneously provide needed fuel for its channels' efforts to move up-market, and preserve P&G's power to keep the premium brand on the product. Its Dryel brand do-it-yourself home dry cleaning system, for example, is a new-market disruption because it enables individuals to do for themselves something that, historically, only a more expensive professional could do. Do-it-yourself dry cleaning is not yet good enough, so the power to build a profitable brand is likely to reside in the product for some time. What is more, just as Sony's solid-state electronics products enabled discount merchandisers to compete against appliance stores, so P&G's Dryel gives Wal-Mart a vehicle to move up-market and begin competing against dry cleaning establishments. P&G is doing the same thing with its introduction of its Crest brand do-it-yourself teeth whitening system, a new-market disruption of a service that historically could only be provided by professionals. We thank one of Professor Christensen's former students, David Dintenfass, a global brand manager at Procter & Gamble, for pointing this out to us.

16. As we have shared these hypotheses with students, some of the more stylishly dressed among them have asked whether this applies also to the highest-fashion brands, such as Gucci, and in product categories such as cosmetics. Those who know us probably have observed that dressing ourselves in fashionable, branded merchandise just isn't a job that we have been trying to get done in our lives. We confess, therefore, to having no intuition about the world of high fashion. It will probably persist profitably forever. Who are we to know?

17. Remaining competitive at the level of the process-defined value chain that the current auto assemblers dominate is likely to require that they move toward new distribution structures—an integration of supply chains and customer interfaces in a way that effectively exploits the modularity of the product itself. How this can be done and its performance implications are explored at length in the Deloitte Research study "Digital Loyalty Networks," available for download at <http://www.dc.com/research>, or upon request from delresearch@dc.com.

18. Those of our readers who believe in the efficiency of capital markets and the abilities of investors to diversify their portfolios will see no tragedy in these decisions. After these divestitures the shareholders of the two auto giants found themselves owning stock in companies that design and assemble cars, and in companies that supply performance-enabling subsystems. It is because we are writing this book for the benefit of managers in firms like General Motors and Ford that we characterize these decisions as unfortunate.

19. We say "usually" here because there are exceptions (most, but not all, of which prove the rule). We note in the text of this chapter, for example, that two modular stages of added value can be juxtaposed—as DRAM memory chips fit in modular personal computers. And there are instances where two interdependent architectures need to be integrated, such as when enterprise resource planning software from companies such as SAP needs to be interleaved into companies' interdependent business processes. The fact that neither side is modular and configurable is what makes SAP implementations so technically and organizationally demanding.

CHAPTER SEVEN

IS YOUR ORGANIZATION CAPABLE OF DISRUPTIVE GROWTH?

Who should we chose to run new-growth businesses? Which organizational unit in the company will do the best job of building a successful growth business around this particular idea, and which units will likely botch it? What is the best way to structure the team that develops and launches this product? When is creating an autonomous organization important for success, and when is it folly? How can we predict precisely what an organizational unit is capable and incapable of accomplishing? How can we create new capabilities?

A surprising number of innovations fail not because of some fatal technological flaw or because the market isn't ready. They fail because responsibility to build these businesses is given to managers or organizations whose capabilities aren't up to the task. Corporate executives make this mistake because most often the very skills that propel an organization to succeed in sustaining circumstances systematically bungle the best ideas for disruptive growth. An organization's *capabilities* become its *disabilities* when disruption is afoot.[1] This chapter offers a theory to guide executives as they choose a management team and build an organizational structure that together will be capable of building a successful new-growth business. It also outlines how the choices of managers and structure ought to vary by circumstance.

Resources, Processes, and Values

What does this awfully elastic term *capability* really mean? We've found it helpful to unpack the concept of capabilities into three classes or sets of factors that define what an organization can and cannot accomplish: its resources, its processes, and its values—a triptych we refer to as the RPV framework. Although each of these terms requires careful definition and analysis, taken together we've found that they provide a powerful way to assess an organization's capabilities and disabilities in ways that can make disruptive innovation much more likely to succeed.[2]

Resources

Resources are the most tangible of the three factors in the RPV framework. Resources include people, equipment, technology, product designs, brands, information, cash, and relationships with suppliers, distributors, and customers. Resources are usually people or things— they can be hired and fired, bought and sold, depreciated or built. Most resources are visible and often are measurable, so managers can readily assess their value. They tend to be quite flexible as well: It is relatively easy to transport them across the boundaries of organizations. An engineer who is a valuable contributor in a large company can quickly become a valuable contributor in a start-up. Technology that was developed for telecommunications can be valuable in health care. Cash is a very flexible resource.

Of all the resource choices required to successfully build new-growth businesses, the one that most often trips a venture up is the choice of its managers. We have examined innumerable failed efforts to create new-growth business and would estimate that in as many as half of these cases, those close to the situation judge that, in retrospect, the wrong people had been chosen to lead the venture.[3] Why is the selection process for key managerial resources so vexingly unpredictable?

Why Those with the Right Stuff Are Often the Wrong People

We suspect that the mistakes happen when firms choose managers at any level—from CEO to business unit head to project manager—

based on what we call "right stuff" thinking, borrowing the term from Tom Wolfe's famous book and the 1983 movie of the same name.[4] Many search committees and hiring executives classify candidates by right-stuff attributes. They assume that successful managers can be identified using phrases such as "good communicator," "results oriented," "decisive," and "good people skills." They often look for an uninterrupted string of past successes to predict that more successes are in store. The theory in use is that if you find someone with a track record and with the right-stuff attributes, then he or she can successfully manage the new business venture. But in the parlance of this book, right-stuff thinking gets the categories wrong.[5]

An alternative, circumstance-based theory articulated by Professor Morgan McCall can, in our view, serve as a much more reliable guide for executives who are attempting to get the right people in the right positions at the right time.[6] McCall asserts that the management skills and intuition that enable people to succeed in new assignments were shaped through their experiences in previous assignments in their careers. A business unit therefore can be thought of as a school, and the problems that managers have confronted within it constitute the "curriculum" that was offered in that school. The skills that managers can be expected to have and lack, therefore, depend heavily upon which "courses" they did and did not take as they attended various schools of experience.

Managers who have successfully worked their way up the ladder of a stable business unit—for example, a division that manufactures standard high-volume electric motors for the appliance industry—are likely to have acquired the skills that were necessary to succeed in that context. The "graduates" of this school would have finely honed operational skills in managing quality programs, process improvement teams, and cost-control efforts. Even the most senior manufacturing executives from such a school would likely be weak, however, in starting up a *new* plant, because one encounters very different problems in starting up a new plant than in running a well-tuned one.

When a slowly growing firm's leaders decide they need to launch a new-growth business to restore their company's vitality, who should they tap to head the venture? A talented manager from the core business who has demonstrated a record of success? An outsider who has started and grown a successful company? The school-of-experience view suggests that both of these managers might be risky hires. The internal candidate would have learned how to meet budgeted numbers, negotiate major supply contracts, and improve operational efficiency and quality, but might not have attended any "courses" on starting a new business in his or her prior career assignments. An outside entrepreneur might have learned a lot about building new fast-moving organizations, but would have little experience competing for resources and bucking inappropriate processes within a stable, efficiency-oriented operating culture.

In order to be confident that managers have developed the skills required to succeed at a new assignment, one should examine the sorts of problems they have wrestled with in the past. It is not as important that managers have succeeded with the problem as it is for them to have wrestled with it and developed the skills and intuition for how to meet the challenge successfully the next time around. One problem with predicting future success from past success is that managers can succeed for reasons not of their own making—and we often learn far more from our failures than our successes. Failure and bouncing back from failure can be critical courses in the school of experience. As long as they are willing and able to learn, doing things wrong and recovering from mistakes can give managers an instinct for better navigating through the minefield the next time around.

To illustrate how powerfully managers' prior experiences can shape the skills that they bring to a new assignment, let us continue chapter 4's discussion of Pandesic, the high-profile joint venture between Intel and SAP that was launched in 1997 to create a new-market disruption selling enterprise resource planning (ERP) software to small businesses. Intel and SAP hand-picked some of their most successful, tried-and-true executives to lead the venture.

Pandesic ramped to 100 employees in eight months, and quickly established offices in Europe and Asia. Within a year it had announced forty strategic partnerships with companies such as Compaq, Hewlett-Packard, and Citibank. Pandesic executives boldly announced their first product in advance of launch to warn would-be competitors to stay away from the small business marketspace. The company inked distribution and implementation agreements with the same IT consulting firms that had served as such capable channel partners for SAP's large-company systems. The product, initially intended to be simple ERP software delivered to small businesses via the Internet, evolved into a completely automated end-to-end solution. Pandesic was a spectacular failure. It sold very few systems and shut its doors in February 2001 after having spent more than $100 million.

It is tempting to use 20/20 hindsight to explain this failure. Pandesic's channel partners weren't motivated to sell the product because it was disruptive to their economic model. The company quickly ramped up expenses to establish a global presence, hoping to build a steeper ramp to volume. But this increased dramatically the volume required to break even. The product evolved into a complex solution instead of the simple small business software that originally was envisioned. Its features got specified and locked in before a single paying customer had used the product.

The Pandesic team did a lot of things wrong, certainly. But the truly interesting question isn't *what* they did wrong. It is how such capable, experienced, and respected managers—among the best that Intel and SAP had to offer—could have made these mistakes.

To see how managers with great track records could steer a venture so wrong, let's look at their qualifications for the task from the schools-of-experience point of view. This can be done in three steps. First, imagine yourself at Pandesic on day one, when the executives were agreeing to start this disruptive venture. With only foresight and no hindsight allowed, what challenges or problems could you predict with perfect certainty that this venture would encounter? Here are a few of the problems that we could know we would face:

- We know for sure that we aren't sure if our strategy is right—and yet we have to figure out the right strategy, develop consensus, and build a business around it.
- We don't know how this market ought to be segmented. "Small business" probably isn't right, and "industry vertical" probably isn't right. We have to figure out what jobs the customers are trying to get done, and then design products and services that do the job.

- We need to find or create a distribution channel that will be energized by the opportunity to sell this product.
- Our corporate parents will bequeath gifts upon us such as overhead, planning requirements, and budgeting cycles. We will need to accept some and fend off others.
- We need to become profitable, and we must manage perceptions and expectations so that our corporate parents will willingly continue to make the investments required to fuel our profitable growth.

Now, as the second step, let's apply McCall's theory. List the courses that we would want members of Pandesic's management team to have taken in earlier career assignments in the school of experience—experiences through which they would have developed the intuition and skill to understand and manage this set of foreseeable problems. This listing of experiences should constitute a "hiring specification" for the senior management team. Rather than specifying a set of right-stuff attributes, the first step specifies the circumstances in which the new team will be asked to manage. The second step matches those circumstances against the challenges with which the managers of the new venture need already to have wrestled.

We would, in Pandesic's instance, want a CEO who in the past had launched a venture thinking he or she had the right strategy, realized it wasn't working, and then iterated toward a strategy that did work. We'd want a marketing executive who had insightfully figured out how a just-emerging market was structured, had helped to shape a new product and service package that did an important job well for customers who had been nonconsumers, and so on.

With that list complete, our third step would be to compare that set of needed experiences and perspectives with the experiences on the resumés of the managers who led Pandesic. Despite their extraordinary track records in managing the global operations of very successful companies, none of the executives who were tapped to run this venture had faced any of these kinds of problems before. The schools of experience that they had attended taught them how to manage huge, complex, global organizations that served established markets with well-defined product lines. None of them had ever wrestled with establishing an initial market foothold with a disruptive product.[7]

One of the most vexing dilemmas that stable corporations face when they seek to rekindle growth by launching new businesses is that their internal schools of experience have offered precious few courses in which managers could have learned how to launch new disruptive businesses. In many ways, the managers that corporate executives have come to trust the most because they have consistently delivered the needed results in the core businesses cannot be trusted to shepherd the creation of new growth. Human resources executives in this situation need to shoulder a major burden. They need to monitor where in the corporation's schools of experience the needed courses might be created, and ensure that promising managers have the opportunity to be appropriately schooled before they are asked to take the helm of a new-growth business. When managers with the requisite education cannot be found internally, they need to ensure that the management team, as a balanced composite, has within it the requisite perspectives from the right schools of experience. We will return to this challenge later in this chapter.

Finding managers who have been appropriately schooled is a critical first step in assembling the capabilities required to succeed. But it is only the first step, because the capabilities of organizations are a function of resources other than people, and of elements beyond just resources, namely, processes and values. To these we now turn.

Processes

Organizations create value as employees transform inputs of resources—the work of people, equipment, technology, product designs, brands, information, energy, and cash—into products and services of greater worth. The patterns of interaction, coordination, communication, and decision making through which they accomplish these transformations are *processes*.[8] Processes include the ways that products are developed and made and the methods by which procurement, market research, budgeting, employee development and compensation, and resource allocation are accomplished.

Processes differ not only in their purpose, but also in their visibility. Some processes are "formal," in the sense that they are explicitly defined, visibly documented, and consciously followed. Other processes are "informal," in that they are habitual routines or ways of working that have evolved over time, which people adopt simply because they work or because ". . . that's the way we do things around here." Still other methods of working and interacting have proven so effective for so long that people unconsciously follow them—they constitute the culture of the organization. Whether they are formal, informal, or cultural, however, processes define how an organization transforms inputs into things of greater value.[9]

Processes are defined or evolve de facto to address specific tasks. When managers use a process to execute the tasks for which it was designed, it is likely to perform efficiently. But when the same, seemingly efficient process is employed to tackle a very different task, it often seems bureaucratic and inefficient. In other words, a process that defines a *capability* in executing a certain task concurrently defines *disabilities* in executing other tasks.[10] In contrast to the flexibility of many resources, processes by their very nature are meant not to change. They are established to help employees perform recurrent tasks in a consistent way, time after time. One reason that focused organizations perform so well is that their processes are always aligned to the tasks.[11]

Innovating managers often try to start new-growth businesses using processes that were designed to make the mainstream business run effectively. They succumb to this temptation because the new game begins before the old game ends. Disruptive innovations typically take root at the low end of markets or in new planes of competition at a time when the core business still is performing at its peak—when it would be crazy to revolutionize everything. It seems simpler to have one-size-fits-all processes for doing things, but *very* often the cause of a new venture's failure is that the wrong processes were used to build it.

The most crucial processes to examine usually aren't the obvious value-adding processes involved in logistics, development, manufacturing, and customer service. Rather, they are the enabling or background processes that support investment decisions. These include how market research is habitually done, how such analysis is translated into financial projections, how plans and budgets are negotiated and how those numbers are delivered, and so on. These processes are where many organizations' most serious disabilities in creating disruptive growth businesses reside.

Some of these processes are hard to observe, and it can therefore be quite difficult to judge whether the mainstream organization's processes will facilitate or impede a new-growth business. You can make a good guess, however, by asking whether the organization has faced similar situations or tasks in the past. We would not expect an organization to have developed a process for accomplishing a particular task if it has not repeatedly addressed a task like that before. For example, if an organization has repeatedly formulated strategic plans for established businesses in existing markets, then a process that planners follow in formulating such plans likely will have coalesced, and managers will instinctively follow that process. But if that organization has not repeatedly formulated plans for competing in markets that do not yet exist, it is safe to assume that no processes for making such plans exist.[12]

Values

The third class of factors that affect what an organization can or cannot accomplish is its values. Some corporate values are ethical in tone, such as those that guide decisions to ensure patient well-being at Johnson & Johnson or that guide plant safety at Alcoa. But in the RPV framework, *values* have a broader meaning. An organization's values are the standards by which employees make prioritization decisions—those by which they judge whether an order is attractive or unattractive, whether a particular customer is more important or less important than another, whether an idea for a new product is attractive or marginal, and so on.[13]

Employees at every level make prioritization decisions. At the executive tiers, these decisions often take the form of whether or not to invest in new products, services, and processes.[14] Among salespeople, they consist of on-the-spot, day-to-day decisions about which customers they will call on, which products to push with those customers, and which products not to emphasize. When an engineer makes a design choice or a production scheduler puts one order ahead of another, it is a prioritization decision.

The larger and more complex a company becomes, the more important it is for senior managers to train employees at every level, acting autonomously, to make prioritization decisions that are consistent with the strategic direction and the business model of the company. That is why successful senior executives spend so much time articulating clear, consistent values that are broadly understood throughout the organization. Over time, a company's values must evolve to conform to its cost structure or its income statement, because if the company is to survive, employees *must* prioritize those things that help the company to make money in the way that it is structured to make money.

Whereas resources and processes are often *enablers* that define what an organization *can* do, values often represent *constraints*—they define what the organization *cannot* do. If, for example, the structure of a company's overhead costs requires it to achieve gross profit margins of 40 percent, a powerful value or decision rule will have evolved that encourages employees not to propose, and senior managers to kill, ideas that promise gross margins below 40 percent. Such an organization would be *incapable* of succeeding in low-margin businesses—because you can't succeed with an endeavor that cannot be prioritized. At the same time, a different organization's values, shaped around a very different cost structure, might enable it to accord high priority to the very same project. These differences create the asymmetries of motivation that exist between disruptors and disruptees.

Over time, the values of successful firms tend to evolve in a predictable fashion in at least two dimensions. The first relates to acceptable gross margins. As companies upgrade their products and services to capture more attractive customers in premium tiers of their markets, they often add overhead cost. As a result, gross margins that at one point were quite attractive will seem unattractive at a later point. Companies' values change as they migrate up-market.[15]

The second dimension along which values can change relates to how big a business has to be in order to be interesting. Because a company's stock price represents the discounted present value of its projected earnings stream, most managers typically feel compelled not just to maintain growth but to maintain a constant *rate* of growth. For a $40 million company to grow 25 percent, it needs to find $10 million in new business the next year. For a $40 *billion* company to grow 25 percent, it needs to find $10 *billion* in new business the next year. An opportunity that excites a small organization simply isn't large enough to be interesting to a very large one. One of the bittersweet rewards of success is, in fact, that as companies become large, they literally lose the capability to enter small emerging markets. Their size and success put extraordinary resources at their disposal. Yet they cannot deploy those resources against the small disruptive markets of today that will be the large markets of tomorrow, because their values will not permit it.

Executives and Wall Street financiers who engineer mega-mergers among already huge companies in order to achieve cost savings need to account for the impact of these actions on the resultant companies' values. Although the merged corporations might have more resources to throw at new-product development, their commercial organizations tend to lose their appetites for all but the biggest blockbuster opportunities. Huge size constitutes a very real *disability* in creating new-growth businesses. But as we will show later in this chapter, when large corporations keep the flexibility to have small business units within them, they can continue to have decision makers who can become excited about emerging opportunities.

The Migration of Capabilities

In the start-up stages of a business, much of what gets done is attributable to its *resources*—particularly its people. The addition or departure of a few key people can have a profound influence on its success. Over time, however, the organization's capabilities shift toward its processes and values. As people work together successfully to address recurrent tasks, processes become defined. And as the business model takes shape and it becomes clear which types of business need to be accorded highest priority, values coalesce. In fact, one reason that many soaring young hot-product companies flame out after they go public is that the key initial resource—the founding team—fails to institute the *processes* or the *values* that can help the company follow up with a sequence of hot new products.

Success is easier to sustain when the locus of the capability to innovate successfully migrates from resources to processes and values. It actually begins to matter less which people get assigned to which project teams. In large, successful management consulting firms, for example, hundreds of new MBA's join the firm every year, and almost as many leave. But they are able to crank out high-quality work year after year because their capabilities are rooted in their processes and values rather than in their resources.

As a new company's processes and values are coalescing, the actions and attitudes of the company's founder typically have a profound impact. The founder often has strong opinions about the way employees ought to work together to reach decisions and get things done. Founders similarly impose their views of what the organization's priorities need to be. If the founder's methods are flawed, of course, the company will likely fail. But if those methods are useful, employees will collectively experience for themselves the validity of the founder's problem-solving methodologies and criteria for decision making. As they successfully use those methods of working together to address recurrent tasks, processes become defined. Likewise, if the company becomes financially successful by prioritizing various uses of its resources according to criteria that reflect the founder's priorities, the company's values begin to coalesce.

As successful companies mature, employees gradually come to assume that the priorities they have learned to accept, and the ways of doing things and methods of making decisions that they have employed so successfully, are the right way to work. Once members of the organization begin to adopt ways of working and criteria for making decisions by assumption, rather than by conscious decision, then those processes and values come to constitute the organization's *culture*.[16] As companies grow from a few employees to hundreds and thousands, the challenge of getting all employees to agree on what needs to be done and how it should be done so that the right jobs are done repeatedly and consistently can be daunting for even the best managers. Culture is a powerful management tool in these situations. Culture enables employees to act autonomously and causes them to act consistently.

Hence, the location of the most powerful factors that define the capabilities and disabilities of an organization migrates over time—from resources toward visible, conscious processes and values, and then toward culture. When the organization's capabilities reside primarily in its people, changing to address new problems is relatively simple. But when the capabilities have come to reside in processes and values and *especially* when they have become embedded in culture, change can become extraordinarily difficult.

Every organizational change entails a change in resources, processes, or values, or some combination of these. The tools required to manage each of these types of change are different. Moreover, established organizations typically face the opportunity to create new growth businesses—and the consequent requirement to utilize different resources, processes, and values—at a time when the mainstream business is still very healthy—when executives must *not* change the resources, processes, and values that enable core businesses to sustain their success. This requires a much more tailored approach to managing change than many managers have felt to be necessary, as we will discuss next.[17]

Selecting the Right Organizational Home for a New Disruptive Business

We noted in chapter 2 that the incumbent leaders in an industry almost *always* emerge victorious in sustaining-technology battles, whereas historically they have almost always *lost* the battles of disruption. The RPV framework of organizational capabilities helps us see why the leading firms' track records differ so markedly across these two tasks. The industry leaders develop and introduce sustaining technologies over and over again: In the study of the computer disk drive industry that was the foundation of *The Innovator's Dilemma,* 111 of the 116 new technologies were sustaining ones. Year after year, as established companies introduce new and improved products in order to gain an edge over the competition, they refine processes for evaluating the technological potential and assessing their customers' needs for alternative sustaining technologies. In other words, the organizations develop a *capability* for sustaining innovation that resides in their processes. Sustaining-technology investments also fit the values of the leading companies, because they promise improved profit margins from better or cost-reduced products.[18]

On the other hand, disruptive innovations occur so intermittently that no company has a practiced process for handling them. Furthermore, because disruptive products typically promise lower gross profit dollars per unit sold and cannot be used by the best customers, disruptions are inconsistent with the leading companies' values. Established companies have the *resources*—the engineers, money, and technology—required to succeed at both sustaining and disruptive technologies. But their processes and values constitute *disabilities* in their efforts to succeed at disruptive innovation.

In contrast, smaller, disruptive companies are actually more capable of pursuing emerging growth markets. They lack resources, but that doesn't constrain them. Their values can embrace small markets, and their cost structures can accommodate lower margins per unit sold. Their less formal market research and resource allocation processes allow managers to proceed intuitively rather than having to be backed up by careful research and analysis. All of these advantages add up to enormous opportunity or looming disaster, depending on your perspective. Executives who are building new-growth businesses therefore need to do more than assign managers who have been to the right schools of experience to the problem. They must ensure that responsibility for making the venture successful is given to an organization whose processes will facilitate what needs to be done and whose values can prioritize those activities. The theory is that the requirements of an innovation need to fit with the host organization's processes and values, or the innovation will not succeed.

In many ways, the RPV framework is a way of thinking through the management of change of *any* sort. A change involves the creation of new resources, new processes, or new values. It is rare that whole-sale change on any of these dimensions is warranted in a successful company, because usually the existing resources, processes, and values are capably supporting established, healthy businesses, even as new resources, processes, and values are needed to support new ones. If executives can stop using one-process- and one-organization-fits-all policies for all types of innovations, they can greatly improve the probabilities that their growth ventures will succeed.

Figure 7-1 offers a framework to help managers decide when they can exploit current organizational capabilities and when they should create or acquire new capabilities to launch a new-growth business. The left vertical axis in figure 7-1 measures the extent to which the existing processes—the patterns of interaction, communication, coordination, and decision making currently used in the organization—are the ones that will get the new job done effectively. If the fit is good (toward the lower end of the scale), the project manager can exploit the organization's existing processes and coordinate work that is done within the existing functional units. If not, new processes and new types of team interactions will be required.

FIGURE 7-1

A Framework for Finding the Right Organizational Structure and Home

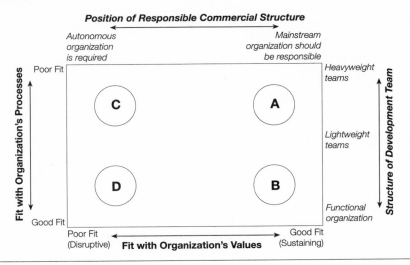

The lower horizontal axis asks managers to assess whether the organization's values will allocate to the new initiative the resources it will need in order to become successful. If there is a poor fit, then the mainstream organization's values will accord low priority to the project; that is, the project is potentially disruptive relative to its business model. The upper horizontal axis in figure 7-1 captures on a continuum the level of autonomy needed by an organizational unit attempting to exploit an innovation. For disruptive innovations, setting up an autonomous organization to develop and commercialize the venture will be absolutely essential to its success. At the other extreme, however, if there is a strong sustaining fit, then the manager can expect that the energy and resources of the mainstream organization will coalesce behind it because the project is sustaining. There is no reason for skunkworks or spin-offs in such cases.

The right vertical axis maps three types of organizational structures that can be used to either exploit or overcome existing processes. The development team charged with shepherding an innovation to market can be either *heavyweight, lightweight,* or *functional* (all defined later in this chapter). The four regions in figure 7-1 integrate the challenges of dealing with different types of fit with the mainstream organization's processes and values. Region A depicts a situation in which a manager is faced with a breakthrough but sustaining technological change. It fits the organization's values, but it presents the organization with different types of problems to solve and therefore requires new types of interaction and coordination among groups and individuals. This circumstance mandates a heavyweight project team (described later). In region B, where the project fits the company's processes as well as its values, the new venture can easily be developed by coordinating across functional boundaries within the existing organization. Region C denotes a disruptive technological change that fits neither the organization's existing processes nor its values. To ensure success in such instances, the managers should create an autonomous organization. Region D typifies projects in which products or services similar to those in the mainstream need to be sold within a fundamentally lower-overhead business model. These ventures can leverage the main organization's logistics management processes, but they need very different budgeting, management, and profit and loss profiles.[19]

In using figure 7-1, it is important to remember that disruption is a relative term. What is disruptive to one company might have a sustaining impact on another. For example, Dell Computer began by selling computers over the telephone. For Dell, the initiative to begin selling over the Internet was a *sustaining* innovation. It helped Dell make more money in the way it was already structured to make money. Not surprisingly Dell adopted Internet retailing very successfully. For Compaq, Hewlett-Packard, and IBM, however, marketing directly to customers was decidedly disruptive because of its impact on their retail channel partners. They couldn't make room for Internet distribution within their existing organizations, and so their attempts to incorporate this new channel were far less successful. The only way they could have succeeded at becoming leaders in marketing computers directly to customers was to have done it within an autonomous business unit, and possibly with a new brand.

Similarly, the Internet is a sustaining technology relative to catalog retailers such as Lands' End, and so we would expect them to incorporate it into their existing processes. But it is disruptive relative to bricks-and-mortar retailers such as Macy's, which would require autonomous units in order to exploit on-line retailing in a way that could create truly disruptive growth.[20] Similarly, the Internet is a sustaining technology to discount stockbrokers such as Ameritrade, and a disruptive technology to full-service brokers such as Merrill Lynch.

Organizations cannot disrupt themselves. So when Merrill Lynch implemented Internet-based equities trading within its mainstream brokerage organization, the effect was essentially to bring better information to Merrill's full-service brokers, to help them do an even better job servicing the needs of their high-net-worth clients. The Internet system was shaped as a sustaining technology relative to Merrill Lynch—and no other outcome would be possible. Furthermore, this was a wise thing for Merrill Lynch to do. Its brokerage business for wealthy clients is a beautiful, profitable business, and Merrill would be crazy not to make it even better and even more profitable.[21] But Merrill's executives should not conclude that they have addressed the threat and opportunity of discount online brokerage that is posed by Charles Schwab. They could only do that if they acquired or created an autonomous unit whose values or cost structure helps them earn attractive profits at discount prices.

This is an important reason for our observation in chapter 4 that established companies are prone to cram disruptive ideas into the mainstream market, forcing them to compete against consumption on a sustaining-technology basis. As long as the strategies for developing and commercializing these disruptive innovations are developed within the mainstream organization, this is the only outcome that we can expect. An organization's processes and values ensure that it can only implement sustaining innovations.

Creating New Capabilities

The RPV model can be a useful guide for executives who determine that they need to create new capabilities because those that their organization presently has aren't well suited for building new-growth businesses. This can be framed as a make-or-buy decision. We typically frame make-or-buy decisions as relating to resources, such as training managers internally or hiring them from outside. But processes and values can also be made or bought, as the following discussion describes.

Creating Management Bench Strength

In many ways, building the management bench strength required to launch a sequence of new-growth businesses is a chicken-or-the-egg problem. Maximizing the probabilities of success means identifying managers who are able, here and now, to grapple successfully with the challenges of building new businesses. But to develop managers for the future, organizations need to put up-and-coming managers into situations and responsibilities for which they are not yet qualified. It is the only way they can learn the skills required to succeed. You need to be creating successful businesses in order to have the right curriculum within your internal schools of experience in which next-generation managers can learn. And yet having capable managers in place is a prerequisite to building these growth businesses. Successfully wrestling with these dimensions of the innovator's dilemma is a critical responsibility of a director of human resources.

By the time a company reaches substantial size, most executives have established processes to identify a set of early-career, high-potential managers who should be prepared, ready and waiting, with the skills to succeed in the situations that will confront the company in the future. In many companies, employees are chosen for this high-potential management track based on early evidence of right-stuff attributes. In these firms, recruiting and promoting up-and-coming leaders entails sifting through lots of people in order to find those few who possess the desired end-state attributes in some nascent form.

The school-of-experience theory, however, says that potential should not be measured by attributes, but rather by the ability to *acquire* the attributes and skills needed for future situations. The talent to be sought, in other words, is the ability to learn what needs to be learned from the experiences in which the high-potential employee will be schooled in the future. By focusing on ability to learn, it is possible to avoid the trap of assuming that the finite list of competencies important for today are those that will be required in the future. A performance appraisal form targeted at identifying high-potential people would certainly cover basic technical and cognitive requirements, but would *not* ask for a ranking on right-stuff attributes. It would focus on learning-oriented measures such as "seeks opportunities to learn," "seeks and uses feedback," "asks the right questions," "looks at things from new perspectives," and "learns from mistakes." Some attributes of a good learner will show up as achievements, of course, but the quest is to determine whether an employee is willing to learn new skills.

Putting people in positions where they will learn, however, creates its own dilemma. Those who are "ready now," who are deemed to be fully qualified to handle a given job, by definition have the least to learn by doing it. And those who have the most to learn bring the least experience to the task. McCall notes that, as a result, many managers who are intensely focused on delivering ever-improving results often are the worst at developing next-generation management bench strength. It takes extraordinary discipline and vision on the part of senior executives to balance the tension between deploying fully qualified employees to deliver results now versus giving learning opportunities to high-potential employees who need further development. But strike this balance they must.

Some firms deal with this tension by turning repeatedly to the labor markets, raiding other companies for people with the requisite skills already in full flower. Harkening back to chapters 5 and 6, we believe that one reason why internal management training is becoming more pervasive is because managers don't yet perform well enough. In-house management development processes in many ways can create an optimized, interdependent interface between the skills of the manager and the processes and values of the company. In situations where management performance is not yet good enough, outsourcing "modular" managers and attempting to plug them into a company's complex, interdependent system of resources, processes, and values often does not work well.[22]

A company that works to develop a sequence of new-growth businesses can build a virtuous cycle in management development. Launching growth business after growth business creates a set of rigorous, demanding schools in which next-generation executives can learn how to lead disruption. Companies that only sporadically attempt to create new-growth businesses, in contrast, offer to their next-generation executives precious few of the courses they need to successfully sustain growth.

Making New Processes

The right vertical axis in figure 7-1 shows the kind of development team that is required to create appropriate processes for a new-growth business. When different processes need to be created, it requires what Harvard Business School Professors Kim Clark and Steven Wheelwright call a *heavyweight team*.[23] The term refers to a group of people who are pulled out of their functional organizations and placed in a team structure that allows them to interact over different issues at a different pace and with different organizational groups than they habitually could across the boundaries of functional organizations. Heavyweight teams are tools to create new processes, or new ways of working together. In contrast, *lightweight* or functional teams are tools to exploit existing processes.

We can use the concepts of interdependence and modularity from chapter 5 to visualize a heavyweight team and understand when it is important to create one. When there is a well-defined interface between the activities of two different people or organizational groups—meaning that you can clearly specify what each is supposed to deliver, you can measure and verify what they deliver, and there are no unanticipated interdependencies between what one does and what the other must do in response—then those people and groups can interface at arm's length and need not be on the same team. When these conditions are *not* met, then all unpredictable interdependencies should be incorporated within the boundaries of a heavyweight team. The team's external boundary can be drawn where there are modular interfaces. New methods of working together can coalesce within this team as it addresses its task. These can then become codified as processes if the team is kept intact and addresses a similar task repeatedly.[24]

To be successful, heavyweight teams should be co-located. Team members bring their functional *expertise* to the group, but they do not *represent* their functional group's "interests" on the team. Their responsibilities are simply to do what needs to be done in order for the project to be successful—even if that course of action is not optimal for their functional group. Many companies have used heavyweight teams successfully as a method for creating new processes. Chrysler, for example, historically structured its product development groups around specific components, such as electrical systems. When the changing basis of competition in its industry forced Chrysler to accelerate the development of new automobiles in the early 1990s, Chrysler organized its development teams around platforms like the minivan, instead of the technical subsystems. The heavyweight teams that Chrysler created were consequently not as good at focusing on component design, but the teams forged new processes that were much faster and more efficient in creating entirely new car designs. This was a critical achievement as the basis of competition changed. Companies as diverse as Medtronic in cardiac pacemakers, IBM in disk dives, and Eli Lilly with its schizophrenia drug Zyprexa have used heavyweight teams as vehicles for creating different, faster processes.[25]

Drawing flow diagrams does not create radically different processes. Rather, executives build processes by giving a group of people in a heavyweight team a new problem that the organization has not confronted before. After the team has successfully addressed the challenge, the team needs to confront a similar problem again, and then again. Ultimately, this new way of working will become ensconced within the team and then can diffuse throughout the organization.

Creating New Values

Companies can create new prioritization criteria, or values, only by setting up new business units with new cost structures. Charles Schwab, for example, set up its disruptive online brokerage venture as a completely autonomous organization. It priced online trades at $29.95, compared with the average price of nearly $70 that Schwab had been charging for trades executed through its telephone and office-based brokers. The separate unit was indeed disruptive to the mainstream. It grew so fast that within eighteen months the company decided to fold what had been the mainstream business into the new disruptive organization. The corporation's values, which in our model are synonymous with its cost structure, were thereby transformed by launching a successful disruptive enterprise. Schwab's corporate values changed when the disruptive business displaced the old organization, whose values were incapable of prioritizing the disruptive growth business.

The reason an organization cannot disrupt itself is that successful organizations can *only* naturally prioritize innovations that promise improved profit margins relative to their current cost structure. For Schwab, therefore, it was far more straightforward to create a new business model that could view $29.95 as a profitable proposition than it would have been to hack enough cost out of the original organization so that it could make money at the disruptive price point. This is the best way to change values because the new, disruptive game almost always must begin while the established business still has substantial, profitable sustaining potential.

What does *autonomous* mean? Our research suggests that geographical separation from the core business is not a critical dimension of autonomy. Nor is ownership structure. There is no reason why a disruptive venture cannot be wholly owned by its parent. The key dimensions of autonomy relate to processes and values. The disruptive business needs to have the freedom to create new processes and to build a unique cost structure in order to be profitable as it makes and sells even its earliest products. Making the judgment calls about which of the mainstream businesses' processes and overhead costs the new venture should and should not accept is a key role of the CEO in building new-growth businesses. We will return to this in chapter 10.

Buying Resources, Processes, and Values

Managers often think that acquiring rather than developing a set of capabilities makes competitive and financial sense. Unfortunately, companies' track records in developing new capabilities through acquisition are frighteningly spotty. The RPV framework can be a useful way to frame the challenge of integrating acquired organizations. Every time one company acquires another, it buys its resources, its processes, and its values. Acquiring managers therefore need to begin by asking, "What is it that really made this company that I just bought so expensive? Did I justify the price because of its *resources*— its people, products, technology, or market position? Or was a substantial portion of its worth created by its processes and values—its unique ways of working and decision making that have enabled the company to understand and satisfy customers; develop, make, and deliver new products in a timely way; and to do so within a cost structure that gave it disruptive potential?"

If the acquired company's processes and values are the real drivers of its success, then the last thing the acquiring manager wants to do is to integrate the company into the new parent organization. Integration will vaporize many of the processes and values of the acquired firm as its managers are required to adopt the buyer's way of doing business and have their new-growth proposals evaluated according to the decision criteria of the acquiring company. If its processes and values were the reason for its historical success, a better strategy is to let the acquired business stand alone, and for the parent to infuse its resources into the acquired firm's processes and values. This strategy, in essence, truly constitutes the acquisition of new capabilities.

If, on the other hand, the company's *resources* were the primary rationale for the acquisition, then integrating the firm into the parent makes a lot of sense—essentially plugging the acquired people, products, technology, and customers into the parent's processes as a way of leveraging the parent's existing capabilities.

The RPV model can illuminate Daimler-Benz's acquisition of Chrysler and its subsequent efforts to integrate the two organizations. Chrysler had few resources that could be considered unique in comparison to its competitors. Much of its success in the market of the 1990s was rooted in its processes—particularly in its heavyweight-team product design process, which could create classy new designs in twenty-four months. Chrysler's values were also worth a lot, because it could design and produce a car with one-fifth as many overhead employees as Daimler. What would have been the best way for Daimler to leverage the capabilities it acquired in Chrysler? By keeping it independent and infusing Daimler's resources into Chrysler's processes and its cost structure. Instead, as Wall Street began its demanding drumbeat for cost savings, analysts with little sense for processes and even less for values pressured Daimler management into consolidating the two organizations in order to cut costs. We suspect that integrating the two companies will compromise many of the key processes and the values that made Chrysler such an attractive acquisition.

In contrast, many of Cisco Systems' acquisitions worked well—because, we would argue, it has kept resources, processes, and values in the right perspective. Most of the companies that Cisco has acquired were small firms less than two years old: early-stage organizations whose market value was built primarily upon their resources, particularly their engineers and products. Cisco has a well-defined, deliberate process by which it essentially plugs these resources into the parent's processes and systems, and it has a carefully cultivated method of keeping the engineers of the acquired company happily on the Cisco payroll. In the process of integration, Cisco throws away whatever nascent processes and values came with the acquisition, because those weren't what Cisco paid for. On a couple of occasions when the company acquired a larger, more mature organization—notably its 1996 acquisition of StrataCom—Cisco did not integrate. Rather, it let StrataCom stand alone, and infused its substantial resources into the organization to help it grow at a more rapid rate.[26]

The Costs of Getting It Wrong

Great opportunities can be missed and millions of dollars wasted when managers have high-potential ideas but place them in an organizational context that is not suited to the task. Two high-profile examples of this are Bank One's effort to create WingspanBank.com in the late 1990s, and F. W. Woolworth's effort to build Woolco into a leading discount retailer in the 1960s. Let's look at them through the lens of this theory.

Bank One's Wingspan

Bank One's credit card division, First USA, worked with a leading management consulting firm to launch an online bank called Wingspan in the late 1990s. They set Wingspan up as a wholly owned but autonomous organization that would have separate customers and a separate brand; it therefore was free to pillage Bank One's business. The authors of the strategy apparently felt that the newness and disruptive nature of online banking meant that Wingspan had the best chance of success as a separate company.

The litmus tests in chapter 2, however, suggest that online banking is a *sustaining* innovation relative to the business models of the leading retail banks. Online banks cannot compete against nonconsumption, because almost all computer owners and users in the United States already have bank accounts. Hence, a new-market disruption just isn't possible: Online banking can only compete against consumption. The other disruptive alternative, crafting a low-end attack, would require first finding a set of customers who are overserved by the functionality and reliability of current banking products and services and, second, entail creating a business model that can earn attractive profits at the discount prices required to win the business of customers in the least-demanding tiers of the market. Given the high advertising costs of attracting customers and with no cost advantage in the cost of money, this also is not feasible.[27]

Because disruption is impossible, Internet banking can only be deployed as a sustaining technology relative to the business model of retail banks. A significant portion of their best customers in fact want the convenience, and in most instances the cost per transaction is lower when it is done over the Internet than when done in a branch or via an ATM. Hence, there was no reason why Bank One needed to set this effort up separately. Indeed, in a sustaining battle the established firms almost always win.

F.W. Woolworth and Discount Retailing

In 1962 F.W. Woolworth, one of the world's leading retailers, established its discount department store arm, Woolco, as a wholly owned but autonomously managed, free-standing division—and well it should have. Discount retailing was disruptive from a values standpoint, and it required fundamentally different operating processes. Woolworth's variety stores averaged 35 percent gross margins and turned inventories over about 3.4 times per year. Discount retailing entailed average gross margins of only 23 percent, and to earn acceptable returns these retailers needed to turn inventories about 5 times per year.[28]

In 1971, Woolworth's corporate executives decided to integrate the management, buying, and logistics functions of Woolco back into the mainstream of Woolworth in order to leverage these fixed costs across the volumes of both businesses. The result? Within a year, the values of the mainstream business had forced Woolco's margins up to 34 percent, and Woolco's inventory turns declined to four times—both mirroring the profit model of the F. W. Woolworth stores. Woolco ultimately had to be closed. Very quickly, just as we saw with Merrill Lynch's implementation of Internet brokerage, the business model of the potentially disruptive business simply had to conform itself to the processes and values of the organization in which it was housed. As a general law of organizational nature, there is no other possible outcome. Organizations cannot disrupt themselves. Managers can only do what makes sense to them, given the context in which they work. As a disruptive opportunity, Woolco needed to remain separate. As a sustaining opportunity, Internet banking needed to be integrated within Bank One's mainstream.

Managers whose organizations are confronting opportunities to grow must first determine that they have the people and other resources required to succeed. They then need to ask two further questions: Are the processes by which work habitually gets done in the organization appropriate for this new project? And will the values of the organization give this initiative the priority it needs? Established companies can improve their odds for success in disruptive innovation if they use functionally oriented and heavyweight teams where each is appropriate, and if they commercialize sustaining innovations in mainstream organizations but put disruptive ones in autonomous organizations.

A primary reason successful innovation seems difficult and unpredictable is that firms often employ talented people whose management skills were honed to address stable companies' problems. And often, managers are set to work within processes and values that weren't designed for the new task. Instead of accepting one-size-fits-all policies, if executives will spend time ensuring that capable people work in organizations with processes and values that match the task, they will create a major point of leverage in successfully creating new growth.

Notes

1. One of the most important studies on this topic is summarized in Dorothy Leonard-Barton, "Core Capabilities and Core Rigidities: A Paradox in Managing New Product Development," *Strategic Management Journal* 13 (1992): 111–125.
2. The concepts in this chapter attempt to build on a respected tradition of scholarship about the capabilities of organizations that is known in academic

circles as the "resource-based view" (RBV) of the firm. This tradition sees resources as the defining asset of a firm, and seeks to explain interfirm differences in performance and growth in terms of differences in resource complements. See, for example, K. R. Conner, "A Historical Comparison of Resource-Based Theory and Five Schools of Thought Within IO Economics: Do We Have a New Theory of the Firm?" *Journal of Management* 17, no. 1 (1991): 121–154. The seminal works in this stream are E. T. Penrose, *The Theory of the Growth of the Firm* (London: Basil Blackwell, 1959); and B. Wernerfelt, "A Resource-Based View of the Firm," *Strategic Management Journal* 5 (1984): 171–180. More recent work includes M. Peteraf, "The Cornerstones of Competitive Advantage: A Resource-Based View," *Strategic Management Journal* 14, no. 3 (1993): 179–192; and J. Barney, "The Resource-Based Theory of the Firm," *Organization Science* 7, no. 5 (1996): 469.

We have defined "resources" far more narrowly than many RBV researchers, using additional concepts—namely, processes and values—to capture other important constituent elements of firms' capabilities that some have chosen to include in the category of resources. See, for example, D. Teece and G. Pisano, "The Dynamic Capabilities of Firms: An Introduction," *Industrial and Corporate Change* 3, no. 3 (1994): 537–556; R. M. Grant, "The Resource-Based Theory of Competitive Advantage," *California Management Review* 33, no. 3 (1991): 114–135; and J. Barney, "Organizational Culture: Can It Be a Source of Sustained Competitive Advantage?" *Academy of Management Review* 11, no. 3 (1986): 656–665. Our belief is that what has become in many cases a debate over definitions of the phenomenon is actually a failure of categorization. The framework and theory presented in this chapter were summarized in preliminary form in a chapter added to the second edition of *The Innovator's Dilemma*. This model was initially published in Clayton Christensen and Michael Overdorf, "Meeting the Challenge of Disruptive Change," *Harvard Business Review,* March–April 2000.

3. Findings reported by managerial psychologists RHR International corroborate this estimate. RHR recently reported that up to 40 percent of newly hired senior executives either quit, significantly underperform, or are fired within two years of assuming their new positions (*Globe & Mail,* 1 April 2003, B1).

4. Tom Wolfe, *The Right Stuff* (New York: Farrar, Straus, and Giroux, 1979).

5. Consistent with our statements in chapter 1 about how robust theory can bring predictability to an endeavor, much early research about how to hire the right people into the right jobs has categorized potential managers by

their attributes. Remember that the early researchers in aviation observed a high correlation between the possession of attributes such as wings and feathers and the ability to fly. But they were only able to make statements about *correlation* or association, not causality. It is only when researchers identify the fundamental causal mechanism, and then understand the different circumstances in which practitioners might find themselves, that things can become highly predictable. In this case, possession of many right-stuff attributes might be quite highly correlated with success in an assignment, but it is not the fundamental causal mechanism of success.

6. Morgan McCall, *High Flyers: Developing the Next Generation of Leaders* (Boston: Harvard Business School Press, 1998). This book offers a refreshing, intellectually rigorous way of thinking about how managers learn, and of assessing whether a manager is capable of successfully addressing challenges that lie ahead. We highly recommend that practitioners who are interested in learning more about how to get the right people into the right place at the right time read the book in its entirety.

7. At a later point in the venture's development, of course, it will *need* executives who have taken these courses in the school of experience that relate to scaling a business—and later still, to efficiently operating an organization. One reason many new ventures flame out after an initial, single-product success is that the founders lack the intuition and experience in creating processes that can repeatedly create better products and produce and deliver them reliably.

8. The most logical, comprehensive characterization of processes that we have seen is in David Garvin, "The Processes of Organization and Management," *Sloan Management Review,* Summer 1998. When we use the term *processes,* we mean for it to include all of the types of processes that Garvin has defined.

9. Under various labels, many scholars have explored at length the notion of "processes" as the fundamental building block of organizational capability and competitive advantage. Perhaps among the most influential of such works is R. R. Nelson and S. G. Winter, An *Evolutionary Theory of Economic Change* (Cambridge, MA: Belknap Press, 1982). Nelson and Winter refer to "routines" rather than processes, but the fundamental concept is the same. They establish that firms build competitive advantage by developing better routines than other firms, and that superior routines are developed only through the faithful replication of effective behaviors. Once established, good routines are difficult to change. See, for example, M. T. Hannan and J. Freeman, "The Population Ecology of Organizations," *American Journal of Sociology* 82, no. 5 (1977): 929–964.

Subsequent work has explored and demonstrated the power of the concept of processes (called, variously, *organizational capabilities, dynamic capabilities,* and *core competencies*) as a source of competitive advantage. Examples of this work include D. J. Collis, "A Resource-Based Analysis of Global Competition: The Case of the Bearings Industry," *Strategic Management Journal* 12 (1991): 49–68; D. Teece and G. Pisano, "The Dynamic Capabilities of Firms: An Introduction," *Industrial and Corporate Change* 3, no. 3 (1994): 537–556; and C. K. Prahalad and G. Hamel, "The Core Competence of the Corporation," *Harvard Business Review,* May–June 1990, 79–91.

Our view is that although this stream of research has been extremely insightful, like the work on the resource-based view to which we referred in note 3, it suffers from the limitation either of expanding the definition of "process" to include all possible determinants of competitive advantage or, in the interests of intellectual integrity, of excluding important elements of firms' capabilities from its scope of analysis. For more on this, see A. Nanda, "Resources, Capabilities, and Competencies," in *Organizational Learning and Competitive Advantage,* eds. B. Moingeon and A. Edmondson (New York: The Free Press, 1996), 93–120.

10. See Leonard-Barton, "Core Capabilities and Core Rigidities."

11. See C. Wickham Skinner, "The Focused Factory," *Harvard Business Review,* May–June 1974.

12. Chet Huber, who was the founding president of General Motors' OnStar telematics service, reflected for us on how critical the distinction is between resources (people) and processes: "One of my biggest lessons has been realizing that the *company* needed to be entrepreneurial and not the *individuals* within the company. [The individuals] needed to act more like synchronized swimmers to keep the organization very well aligned." Clayton M. Christensen and Erik Roth, "OnStar: Not Your Father's General Motors (A)," Case 9-602-081 (Boston: Harvard Business School), 12.

13. The concept of values, as we define the term here, is similar to the constructs of "structural context" and "strategic context" that have emerged in scholarly work about the resource allocation process. Important works in this tradition include J. L. Bower, *Managing the Resource Allocation Process* (Homewood, IL: Richard D. Irwin, 1972), and R. Burgelman, "Corporate Entrepreneurship and Strategic Management: Insights from a Process Study," *Management Science* 29, no. 12 (1983): 1349–1364.

14. Chapter 8 examines in much greater depth the effect that values have on resource allocation and strategy making.

15. For example, Toyota entered the North American market with its Corona model, a product targeting the lowest-priced tiers of the market. As the entry-level tier of the market became crowded with look-alike models from Nissan,

Honda, and Mazda, competition among equally low-cost competitors drove down profit margins. Toyota developed more sophisticated cars targeted at higher tiers of the market in order to improve its margins. Its Corolla, Camry, 4-Runner, Avalon, and Lexus families of cars have been introduced in response to the same competitive pressures—Toyota kept its margins healthy by migrating up-market. In the process, Toyota has had to add costs to its operation to design, build, and support cars of this caliber. It subsequently decided to exit the entry-level tiers of the market, having found the margins it could earn there to be unacceptable given its changed cost structure.

Toyota recently introduced its Echo model in an attempt to reenter the entry-level tier with a $14,000 car—reminiscent of American automakers' periodic attempts to reestablish positions at the low end of the market. To be successful, Toyota management will have to swim against a very strong current. It is one thing for Toyota senior management to decide to launch this new model. But to implement this strategy successfully, many people in the Toyota system—including its dealers—will have to agree that selling more cars at lower margins is a better way for the company to boost profits and equity values than selling more Camrys, Avalons, and Lexuses. Only time will tell for certain whether Toyota will be successful at bucking the company's evolved values.

16. See Edgar Schein, *Organizational Culture and Leadership* (San Francisco: Jossey-Bass, 1988). Our description of the development of an organization's culture draws heavily from Schein's research.

17. Professors Michael Tushman of Harvard and Charles O'Reilly of Stanford have studied deeply the need to manage organizations in this way to create what they call "ambidextrous organizations." As we understand their work, they assert that it is not enough simply to spin off an autonomous organization to pursue important but disruptive innovations that don't match the mainstream organization's values. The reason is that too often, executives spin it off to get the disruption off their agenda so that they can focus on managing the core business. To create a truly ambidextrous organization, Tushman and O'Reilly assert that the two different organizations need to be located *within* a business unit. Responsibility for managing the disruptive and sustaining organizations needs to be at a level in the organization where the two are not treated as businesses in a portfolio. Rather, they should be within a group or business unit whose management has the bandwidth to pay careful attention to what should be integrated and shared across the groups, and what should be implemented autonomously. See Michael L. Tushman and Charles A. O'Reilly, *Winning Through Innovation: A Practical Guide to Leading Organizational Change and Renewal* (Boston: Harvard Business School Press, 2002).

18. Historically, some venture capital–backed start-ups, particularly in telecommunications and health care, have followed a strategy of developing a breakthrough sustaining innovation—leapfrogging ahead of the leader on the sustaining curve—and then quickly selling out to the larger established company that is moving up the trajectory behind them. This strategy works—not because the established companies' values constrain them from targeting the same innovation, but because their processes aren't as fast as those of the start-ups. This is a proven way to turn a profit, but it is not a route by which a new-growth business can be created. Either by acquiring the product or by outmuscling the entrant, the established company will in the end be offering the improved product as part of its product line, and the venture that developed it first will not exist. The start-ups essentially comprise heavyweight project teams, which develop products autonomously and then get disbanded when the products are ready for commercialization. It is a mechanism by which established companies with attractively priced equity can pay for research and development with equity, rather than expense.

19. Dow Corning Corporation's establishment of its Xiameter subsidiary is an example of exactly this situation. Xiameter is a high-dependability, low-overhead sales and distribution business model that allows the company to make attractive profits on commodity-level pricing of standard silicone products. Customers who need higher-cost services to guide their purchasing decisions can purchase their silicones through Dow Corning's mainstream sales and distribution structure.

20. We make this statement for illustrative purposes only. At the time of this writing, catalog and online retailing are so well established as a disruptive wave in retailing that if a department store were to attempt to create a major new online growth business, it would be following a sustaining strategy as an entrant, relative to the firms that created online retailing. Even a giant like Macy's would likely lose to the firms that are already on a sustaining march up the disruptive trajectory. Acquiring a firm that has a strong position on that disruptive trajectory—as Sears did when it bought Lands' End—is about the only way that department stores could now catch that wave.

21. Like Merrill Lynch, Goldman Sachs has also implemented Internet-based trading systems for their existing customers within their mainstream, full-service brokerage businesses. The technology was, as a consequence, implemented in a manner that sustained the values, or cost structure, of those business units. In fact, the implementation of Internet-based trading capabilities probably added cost to the companies' structures, because it was an additional option and did not displace the traditional broker-based trading channel. See Dennis Campbell and Frances Frei, "The Cost Structure and

Customer Profitability Implications of Electronic Distribution Channels: Evidence from Online Banking," working paper, Harvard Business School, Boston, 2002.

22. An interesting stream of research is coming to this same conclusion. See, for example, Rakesh Khurana, *Searching for a Corporate Savior: The Irrational Quest for Charismatic CEOs* (Princeton, NJ: Princeton University Press, 2003). Khurana has found that bringing into a company high-profile "superstar" managers—those who in our parlance have many of the most coveted right-stuff attributes in abundance—meets with failure far more frequently than many have supposed.

23. See Kim B. Clark and Steven C. Wheelwright, "Organizing and Leading Heavyweight Development Teams," *California Management Review* 34 (Spring 1992): 9–28. The concepts described in this article are extremely important. We highly recommend that managers interested in these problems study it thoughtfully. Clark and Wheelwright define a heavyweight team as one in which team members typically are dedicated and co-located. The charge of each team member is not to represent his or her functional group on the team, but to act as a *general manager*—to assume responsibility for the success of the entire project, and to be actively involved in the decisions and work of members who come from each functional area. As they work together to complete their project, they will work out new ways of interacting, coordinating, and decision making that will come to compose the new processes, or new capabilities, that will be needed to succeed in the new enterprise on an ongoing basis. These ways of getting work done then get institutionalized as the new business or product line grows.

24. The fundamental conceptual breakthrough that leads to the conclusions in this paragraph comes from the seminal study by Rebecca M. Henderson and Kim B. Clark, "Architectural Innovation: The Reconfiguration of Existing Systems and the Failure of Established Firms," *Administrative Science Quarterly* 35 (1990): 9–30. This is the research that, in our view, elevated the state of theory building in process research from attribute-based categories to circumstance-based categories. Their essential idea is that over a period of time, the patterns of interaction, communication, and coordination among those responsible for designing a new product (the product development process that a company follows) will come to mirror the pattern in which the components of the product interact within the architecture of the product. In the circumstance in which the architecture is unchanged from one generation to the next, this habitual process will facilitate the kinds of interactions that are necessary for success. But in the circumstance in which the development organization needs to change the architecture significantly, so that different

people need to interact with different people about different topics and with different timing, the same habitual process will impede success.

In many ways, the diagnosis and recommendations about process change that are on the vertical axes of figure 7-1 derive from Henderson and Clark's work. The diagnoses and recommendations on the horizontal axes that relate to the values of the organization derive from *The Innovator's Dilemma*, which in turn built on the work of Professors Bower and Burgelman that we have cited elsewhere. This body of research also seems to have lifted the state of theory from attribute-based categorizations to circumstance-based theory.

25. We have observed a frustrating tendency among managers to seek one-size-fits-all solutions to the challenges they face, rather than to develop a way of applying solutions that are appropriate to the problem. On this particular issue, some managers seem to have concluded in the 1990s that heavyweight teams were the "answer," and flipped their entire development organizations into using heavyweight development teams for *all* projects. After a few years, most of them decided that heavyweight teams, while they offered benefits in terms of speed and integration, were too expensive—and they then flipped their entire organizations back into the lightweight mode. Some of the companies cited in the text have suffered these problems, and have not learned how to employ the appropriate types of team in the appropriate circumstance.

26. See Charles A. Holloway, Steven C. Wheelwright, and Nicole Tempest, "Cisco Systems, Inc.: Acquisition Integration for Manufacturing," Case OIT26 (Palo Alto and Boston: Stanford University Graduate School of Business and Harvard Business School, 1998).

27. We recognize that this is a dangerous statement to make; probably a more accurate statement is that at the time of this writing, nobody seems to have been able to devise a viable disruptive strategy for online banking. It is possible, for example, that E*Trade Bank is successfully building a low-end disruptive bank. We cited in note 21 one of an ongoing series of papers that Professor Frances Frei of the Harvard Business School has been writing with various coauthors about the impact of providing new service channels to customers. When established banks have added ATM, telephone, and online services to customers, they have not been able to discontinue the old channels of service, such as live tellers and loan officers. As a consequence, Frei has have shown that the provision of lower-cost channels of service actually adds cost, because they are additive and not substitutive. It is possible that E*Trade Bank, without the legacy infrastructure and costs of in-person service, can actually create a business model whose costs are low enough that it

can earn attractive returns at the discount prices required to win the business of overserved customers.

28. A retailer's inventory turns are not simple to ratchet up (see chapter 2, note 18). When heading up, retailers carry a relatively rigid structure of inventory turns into higher margin products, resulting in an immediate improvement in ROI. Heading down-market entails carrying the same rigid turnover structure into lower-margin products, resulting in an immediate hit to ROI. This is a very asymmetric part of the world.

CHAPTER EIGHT

MANAGING THE STRATEGY DEVELOPMENT PROCESS

Don't just tell me that the right strategy is crucial for success. How do I come up with a strategy that works? What process for formulating strategy is most likely to generate a strategy that will lead to success? Is it better to be the pioneer in an emerging market, or to be a follower once the market's topography is clearer? When should we let innovations bubble up from within the company? When and why should we drive things from the top? Which aspects of strategy formulation do senior executives need to manage most closely?

Most questions about strategy that arise in building a new business concern the substance of the strategy. Managers are anxious that their strategy be the right one. There is an even more important strategy question, however, that most managers forget to ask—and it is the reason many ventures end up with flawed strategies. This crucial question relates to the *process* of strategy formulation that the venture's management team will use to develop and implement a winning plan. Although executives are understandably obsessed with finding the right strategy, they can actually wield greater leverage by managing the process used to develop the strategy—by making sure that the right process is used in the right circumstances.

Innovative ideas always emerge in a half-baked, partially formed condition, as we have noted. They subsequently go through a shaping process that transforms them into the fully fleshed-out business plan, complete with strategy, that is required to win funding. This chapter describes two simultaneous but fundamentally different processes of strategy development, and presents a circumstance-based theory that indicates which of these processes management should rely on as the most reliable source of strategic insight at different stages of business development. It then describes the workings of the resource allocation process, which is the filter through which all strategic actions must flow in order to affect the company's course. The chapter ends by describing some tools and concepts that executives can use to manage the ongoing processes of strategy formulation more effectively.

Two Processes of Strategy Formulation

In every company there are two simultaneous processes through which strategy comes to be defined. Figure 8-1 suggests that both of these strategy-making processes—deliberate and emergent—are always operating in every company.[1] The deliberate strategy-making process is conscious and analytical. It is often based on rigorous analysis of data on market growth, segment size, customer needs, competitors' strengths and weaknesses, and technology trajectories. Strategy in this process typically is formulated in a project with a discrete beginning and end, and then implemented "top down." We hope that the theories discussed in this book can help executives and their advisers devise even better deliberate strategies for creating and sustaining growth than have been possible through traditional methods of data analysis.

Deliberate strategies are the appropriate tool for organizing action if three conditions are met. First, the strategy must encompass and address correctly all of the important details required to succeed, and those responsible for implementation must understand each important detail in management's deliberate strategy. Second, if the organization is to take collective action, the strategy needs to make as much sense to all employees as they view the world from their own context as it does to top management, so that they will all act appropriately

FIGURE 8-1

The Process by Which Strategy Is Defined and Implemented

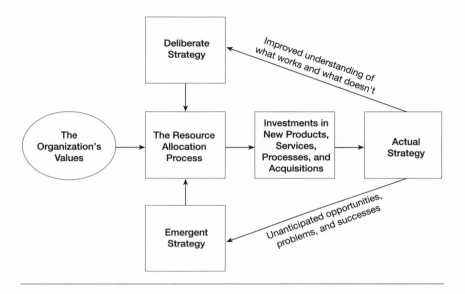

and consistently. Finally, the collective intentions must be realized with little unanticipated influence from outside political, technological, or market forces. Because it is difficult to find a situation in which all three of these conditions apply, the emergent strategy-making process almost always alters the strategy that the company actually implements.[2]

Emergent strategy, which as depicted in figure 8-1 bubbles up from within the organization, is the cumulative effect of day-to-day prioritization and investment decisions made by middle managers, engineers, salespeople, and financial staff. These tend to be tactical, day-to-day operating decisions that are made by people who are not in a visionary, futuristic, or strategic state of mind. For example, Sam Walton's decision to build his second store in another small town near his first one in Arkansas for purposes of logistical and managerial efficiency, rather than building it in a large city, led to what became Wal-Mart's brilliant strategy of building in small towns discount stores that were large enough to preempt competitors' ability to enter. Emergent strategies result from managers' responses to problems or opportunities that were unforeseen in the analysis and planning stages of the deliberate strategy-making process. When the efficacy of a strategy that was developed through an emergent process is recognized, it is possible to formalize it, improve it, and exploit it, thus transforming an emergent strategy into a deliberate one.

Emergent processes should dominate in circumstances in which the future is hard to read and in which it is not clear what the right strategy should be. This is almost always the case during the early phases of a company's life. However, the need for emergent strategy arises whenever a change in circumstances portends that the formula that worked in the past may not be as effective in the future. On the other hand, the deliberate strategy process should be dominant once a winning strategy has become clear, because in those circumstances effective execution often spells the difference between success and failure.[3]

The Crucial Role of Resource Allocation in the Strategy Development Process

Figure 8-1 charts the confluence of these deliberate and emergent decision-making processes in defining actual strategy. Ideas and initiatives, whether of deliberate or emergent origin, are filtered through the resource allocation process, as represented by the center-left box in the figure. The resource allocation process determines which of the deliberate and emergent initiatives get funded and implemented, and which are denied resources. Actual strategy is manifest only through the stream of new products, processes, services, and acquisitions to which resources are allocated.

The resource allocation process is typically complex and diffused, operating at every level and all the time. If the values that guide prioritization decisions in resource allocation are not carefully tied to the company's deliberate strategy (and often they are not), then significant disparities can develop between a company's deliberate strategy and its actual strategy. Actively monitoring, understanding, and controlling the criteria by which day-to-day resource allocation decisions are made at all levels of the organization are among the highest-impact challenges a manager can tackle in the strategy development process.

Initiatives that receive funding and other resources from the re-source allocation process can be called *strategic actions,* as opposed to strategic intentions. Intel chairman Andrew Grove has counseled, "To understand companies' actual strategies, pay attention to what they do, rather than what they say."[4] In our parlance, this means that a company's strategy is what comes out of the resource allocation process, not what goes into it.

As the company does these things, managers then confront and respond to unexpected crises and opportunities, and their experiences cycle back into the emergent process. As managers learn what works and what doesn't in the competitive marketplace, their improved understanding flows back into the deliberate strategy process. Each resource allocation decision, no matter how slight, shapes what the company actually does. This creates a new set of opportunities and problems and generates new deliberate and emergent inputs into the process.

How does this critical resource allocation process work? It is powerfully driven by the values of the organization, which, as noted in chapter 7, are the criteria by which managers and employees make prioritization decisions. Most of the ideas for developing new products, services, and businesses bubble up from employees within the organization. Middle managers cannot carry all of these ideas up to senior management for approval and funding, however. The values or criteria that middle managers use to decide which ideas they will promote and which they will allow to languish play a crucial role in determining what comes out of the resource allocation process. We noted in chapter 1 that once middle managers decide an idea has merit, they engage with the innovators in a process of shaping the idea into a fully fleshed-out business plan that can win funding. The values that senior management employ in these funding decisions therefore exert an equally powerful influence on the types of ideas that can and cannot emerge from the resource allocation process.[5]

Two factors exert a particularly important influence on the values that guide resource allocation decisions. The first is the company's cost structure, which determines the gross profit margins that it must earn to cover overhead costs and make a profit. Good managers have a very difficult time according priority in the resource allocation process to innovative proposals that will not maintain or improve the organization's profit margins.[6] The second factor is the size threshold that new opportunities must meet in order to get through the resource allocation filter. This threshold grows higher as a company becomes larger. Opportunities that were seen as energizing in a company's resource allocation process when the company was small get filtered out as "not big enough to be interesting" in the larger company.

In addition to these powerful, direct determinants of the values that guide senior executives' priorities in resource allocation, other criteria that are subtly embedded in diffused processes throughout the company influence what lower-level employees are able to prioritize. These combine to exert additional influence on which initiatives can pass through the resource allocation filter. An example of these factors is the short tenure in assignment that is typical in the career path of high-potential employees. Management development systems in most organizations move high-potential employees into new positions of responsibility every two to three years in order to help them master management skills in various parts of the business. This practice is critical in management development, but its effect is to influence midlevel managers to accord priority to projects that will pay off within the typical tenure that they expect in their jobs. They want to produce improved results that will merit attractive promotions.

Other factors are embedded within the sales force's incentive compensation system. Salespeople's decisions about which customers to focus on and which products to emphasize are critical elements of the diffused resource allocation process and are heavily influenced by how they are compensated. Customers also exert a powerful influence on the sorts of initiatives that survive the resource allocation process. You can't build a business around a product that your customers don't want, because the customers pay the bills. Although managers think that they control the resource allocation process, customers often exert even more powerful de facto control over how money can and cannot be spent. Competitors' actions likewise exert powerful influence. When a competitor's action threatens to steal customers or growth opportunities away, managers have almost no choice but to push a response through the resource allocation filter.

The resource allocation process, in other words, is a diffused, unruly, and often invisible process. Executives who hope to manage the strategy process effectively need to cultivate a subtle understanding of its workings, because strategy is determined by what comes out of the resource allocation process, not by the intentions and proposals that go into it.

An Illustration of Resource Allocation in Strategy Making: The Case of Intel

Intel began as a manufacturer of semiconductor memories, and its founding engineers developed the world's first commercially viable dynamic random access memory (DRAM) chips.[7] In 1971 an Intel engineer serendipitously invented the microprocessor during a funded development project for a Japanese calculator company, Busicom. Although DRAMs continued to account for the lion's share of company sales through the 1970s, Intel's sales of microprocessors grew gradually in a host of small, emerging applications.

Every month Intel's production schedulers met to allocate the available production capacity across their products, which ranged from DRAMs to EPROMs and microprocessors.[8] The sales department would bring to this meeting its forecast shipments by product, and accounting would bring a rank ordering of those products by gross margins per wafer start. The highest-margin product would then be allocated the production capacity needed to meet its forecast shipments. The next-highest-margin product would then get the capacity it needed in order to meet its forecast shipments, and so on, until the product line with the lowest gross margins was allocated whatever residual capacity remained. Gross margins per wafer start, in other words, constituted the values of the organization that were used in this critical resource allocation decision.

Japanese DRAM makers attacked the U.S. market in the early 1980s, causing pricing levels to drop precipitously and relegating DRAMs to the lowest ranking by gross margin of Intel's products. Because there was less intense competition, microprocessors consistently earned among the most attractive gross margins in Intel's product portfolio. The resource allocation process therefore systematically diverted manufacturing capacity away from DRAMs and into micro-processors. This occurred without any explicit management decision to change strategy. Senior management, in fact, continued to invest two-thirds of R&D dollars into the DRAM business even as the resource allocation process was executing a systematic exit from DRAMs.[9]

Finally, by 1984, when the company had plunged into financial crisis and DRAMs had contracted to just a fraction of Intel's volume, senior management recognized that Intel had become a microproces-sor company. They stopped DRAM R&D spending, and Gordon Moore and Andy Grove made their storied exit through the com-pany's revolving lobby door as managers of the old company, and re-entered as managers of the new company.[10] But it was the resource allocation process that transformed Intel from a DRAM company into a microprocessor company. Intel's remarkable strategy shift was not the result of an intended strategy articulated within the executive ranks; rather, it emerged through the daily decisions made by middle managers as they allocated resources.[11]

Once this new business opportunity had become clear, then it was time to manage strategy in an assertive, deliberate mode—which Intel management did masterfully. By keeping a strong and sometimes ruthless hand on the resource allocation filter, management screened out bubbling-up initiatives that did not directly support the micro-processor business. Both strategy processes were crucial. A viable strate-gic direction had to coalesce from the emergent side of the process, because nobody could foresee clearly enough the future of micro-processor-based desktop computers. But once the winning strategy became apparent, it was just as critical to Intel's ultimate success that the senior management then seized control of the resource allocation process and deliberately drove the strategy from the top.

Match the Strategy-Making Process to the Stage of Business Development

Intel's history illustrates that strategies rarely follow a simple se-quence from formulation to implementation. Furthermore, strategy is never static. Most companies must at the outset chart their course in a deliberate direction because they need to start going somewhere. We hope that the theories in this book will help those who create new businesses to deliberately target a viable strategy with much more accuracy than was possible in the past. But even with this guidance, there will be much to be discovered.

Research suggests that in over 90 percent of all successful new businesses, historically, the strategy that the founders had deliberately decided to pursue was not the strategy that ultimately led to the business's success.[12] Entrepreneurs rarely get their strategies exactly right the first time. The successful ones make it because they have money left over to try again after they learn that their initial strategy was flawed, whereas the failed ones typically have spent their resources implementing a deliberate strategy before its viability could be known. One of the most important roles of senior management during a venture's early years is to learn from emergent sources what is working and what is not, and then to cycle that learning back into the process through the deliberate channel. As Mintzberg and Waters advise, "Openness to emergent strategy enables management to act before everything is fully understood—to respond to an evolving reality rather than having to focus on a stable fantasy. . . . Emergent strategy itself implies learning what works—taking one action at a time in a search for that viable pattern or consistency."[13]

Effective managers eventually recognize the viable pattern that constitutes a successful strategy. At this point, with a firm hand on the criteria used as filters in the resource allocation process, managers need to make strategy formulation much more deliberate. Rather than continuing to feel their way into the marketplace, they need to boldly execute the strategy that they have learned will work. Intel, Wal-Mart, and a host of other companies each saw a viable strategy emerge that was substantially different than their founders had envisioned. But once the model was clear, they executed that strategy aggressively.

Managing Two Fundamentally Different Strategy Processes: A Rare and Tricky Skill

In most waves of disruptive growth, a host of competitors are drawn to the opportunity. Firms that do not emerge from the pack as leaders fail in one of two places. First, many of the initial entrants fail because they spend their money aggressively implementing a deliberate strategy in the nascent stages when the right strategy cannot be known. The second point of failure occurs after the market and its applications become clear to the firms that have managed the emergent strategy process most effectively. The firms that then get left in the dust are those whose executives do not seize deliberate control of resource allocation and focus all investments in executing the race up-market.

The switch from an emergent to a deliberate strategy mode is crucial to success in a corporation's initial disruptive business. But the CEO's job in managing this process does not end there, because the deliberate strategy process often becomes a subsequent impediment to a company's efforts to launch new waves of successful disruptive growth. This happens in two ways. First, the filters in the resource allocation process of successful companies become so well attuned to the successful strategy that they filter out all but the initiatives that sustain the existing business—causing them to ignore the disruptive innovations that create the next waves of growth. Just as important, once deliberate strategy processes have become embedded within organizations, they find it difficult to employ emergent processes again when launching new businesses.

A company's efforts to catch new waves of disruptive growth need to be guided through emergent processes. Simultaneously, however, because the corporation's established businesses typically have many years of profitability remaining even while the disruptive new-growth business is getting underway, the mainstream business needs to be driven by deliberate strategy processes to guide the sustaining innovations that will keep it competitive and profitable.

In our studies we have found a good number of companies whose executives have perceived the need to allocate resources to create new disruptive growth businesses before it is too late. But very, very rarely have we seen executives who have consistently demonstrated the ability to manage the strategy development process appropriately across a range of businesses in various stages of maturity. After they have entered a deliberate strategy mode they find it very difficult to let new businesses be guided through an emergent process.

For example, Prodigy Communications, a joint venture between Sears and IBM, was a pioneer in online services in the early 1990s. The managers of Sears and IBM were extraordinarily bold in resource allocation: They invested over a billion dollars in what was a very uncertain, potentially disruptive innovation. But they weren't as successful in managing the strategy process—in helping Prodigy define a viable strategy through emergent processes even while the parent companies were managing their mainstream businesses deliberately.

Prodigy's original business plan envisioned that consumers would use online services primarily to access information and make online purchases. In 1992, management realized that Prodigy's two million subscribers were spending more time sending e-mail than downloading information or making purchases online. The architecture of Prodigy's computer and communications infrastructure had been designed to optimize transactions processing and information delivery, and Prodigy consequently began charging extra fees to subscribers who sent more than thirty e-mail messages per month. Rather than seeing e-mail as an emergent strategy signal, the company tried to filter it out, because in a deliberate mode, management's job was to implement the original strategy.

America Online (AOL) luckily entered the market later, after customers had discovered that e-mail was a primary reason for subscribing to an online service. With a technology infrastructure tailored to messaging and its "You've got mail" signature, AOL became much more successful.

In light of our model, Prodigy's mistake was not that it entered the market early. Nor was it a mistake that management targeted online information retrieval and shopping as the primary attraction of an online service. Nobody could know at the outset precisely how online services would be used.[14] The executives' mistake was to employ a deliberate strategy process before the strategy's viability could be known. Had Prodigy kept strategic and technological flexibility to respond to emergent strategic evidence, the company could have had a huge lead over AOL and CompuServe (the third major online service provider). A similar challenge confronted the set of companies that responded in the early 1990s to the widely held view that a large market for handheld personal digital assistants was about to emerge. Many of the leading computer makers—including NCR, Apple, Motorola, IBM, and Hewlett-Packard—targeted this market, along with a few start-up firms such as Palm. All sensed that the market wanted a handheld computing device. Apple was one of the most aggressive of the innovators in this space. Its Newton cost $350 million to develop because of the technologies, such as handwriting recognition, that were required to build as much functionality into the product as possible. Hewlett-Packard also invested aggressively to design and build its tiny Kittyhawk disk drive for this market.

In the end, the products just weren't good enough to be a substitute for notebook computers, and each of the companies scrapped its effort—except Palm. Palm's original strategy was to provide an operating system for these personal digital assistants.[15] When its customers' strategies failed, Palm searched around for another application and came up with the concept of an electronic personal organizer.

What were the strategic mistakes here? The computer companies employed deliberate strategy processes from the beginning to the end. They invested massively to implement their strategies, and then wrote the projects off when the strategies proved wrong. Palm was the only firm that shifted to an emergent strategy process when its original deliberate strategy failed. When a viable strategy emerged, Palm shifted back toward a deliberate process as it migrated up-market.

Clearly, this is not simple stuff.

Points of Executive Leverage in the Strategy-Making Process

The resource allocation process is the filter through which all strategic actions must flow. Because it is so complex and diffused throughout a company, it is rare that senior executives can simply devise a new strategy and "implement" it. Rather, defining and implementing strategy entails managing the conditions under which the strategy and resource allocation processes operate so that the strategy process can work efficiently, given the circumstances that each of the company's organizations is in. Effective, appropriate processes will generate the needed strategic insights. The remainder of this chapter focuses on three points of executive leverage on the strategy process. Managers must:

1. Carefully control the *initial* cost structure of a new-growth business, because this quickly will determine the values that will drive the critical resource allocation decisions in that business.

2. Actively accelerate the process by which a viable strategy emerges by ensuring that business plans are designed to test and confirm critical assumptions using tools such as discovery-driven planning.

3. Personally and repeatedly intervene, business by business, exercising judgment about whether the circumstance is such that the business needs to follow an emergent or deliberate strategy-making process. CEOs must not leave the choice about strategy process to policy, habit, or culture.

Create a Cost Structure that Finds the Right Customers Attractive

Note that we didn't identify "memos from the executive office" as a way of influencing the organization's values. That is because the power of a venture's cost structure overwhelms "being strategically important" as a criterion that drives resource allocation decisions.[16] Executives must pay very careful initial attention to creating a cost structure and business model within which orders from the kinds of ideal customers we described in chapter 4 will appear to be profitable. Otherwise, it will be impossible to build a business with those customers as a foundation.[17]

Let us illustrate by bringing things close to home, recounting Clayton Christensen's own experience in running a venture capital–backed company that he founded with several MIT professors in the early 1980s, before he retreated to academia. The company was formed to exploit exciting technology to make products with a class of remarkable materials called advanced ceramics, and the history is recounted in a set of cases under the disguised name Materials Technology Corporation (MTC).[18]

MTC's strategy was to become a major manufacturer of products made from these advanced ceramic materials. Because the materials business is capital intensive, Christensen and his colleagues knew from the beginning that MTC would need lots of capital to carry the company to break-even—they estimated about $60 million. In the early 1980s this was a lot of money to raise. What drove the amount needed was not just the cost of the physical facilities, but also the length of the product development cycle. Because of MTC's position at the beginning of the value chain, it needed to win contracts to develop new components for its customers, who would then use those advanced components to make next-generation products of their own. Developing and testing the components easily took one to two years. When MTC succeeded, then and only then could the customers initiate their own cycle to design and test the new products that MTC's advanced materials had enabled. The customers' development processes typically took two to four additional years. In other words, MTC's strategy entailed enduring a lot of expense before the revenue could begin rolling in.[19]

Christensen decided to cover the cost of MTC's research and development staff by negotiating multimillion dollar joint development contracts from major corporate partners, in much the same way that many biotechnology companies have funded their protracted development processes. When MTC sold a major development contract to create the technology required to manufacture the products that its strategy envisioned, it then had to hire the scientists and engineers to do the work.

The strategy worked well for a couple of years. Then MTC's first major development contract was completed, and the funding that had covered the salaries of three Ph.D. scientists and five engineers came to an end. Given the slow ramp to volume production inherent in MTC's product development cycle, how could the company cover their salaries? These were some of the best materials scientists in the world, and they just couldn't be sent packing. So the company had to sell another development contract to whomever would pay MTC enough money to cover their salaries and overhead. When the next funded project reached its end, the firm had to sell another funded program to cover the company's high fixed costs, and so on. The company started with a strategy to be a volume product manufacturer. But very quickly and without intention, management began implementing a strategy to become a contract research house. There just wasn't any way that the gross margins generated by initial volumes of manufactured products could cover the overheads that had to be put in place to deliver what MTC sold to its first customers.

MTC's long development cycle and huge funding need represent an extreme example, but every new corporate venture experiences its own version of this challenge. It is the habit of large, established companies to ramp up expenses ahead of revenues, because in a world of deliberate strategy and sustaining innovation, these are safe bets. But these outlays define a cost structure very quickly, and before you know it you've got yourself a business model that defines the kind of business that does or does not look attractive. Ultimately MTC did become a manufacturing company, but only through wrenching layoffs and by restructuring the nature of its costs. It was only by creating a new cost structure that a new type of customer order could appear to be attractive and could thereby be accorded priority in resource allocation.

This example illustrates why executives need to pay careful attention to getting the initial conditions right. The only way that a new venture's managers can compete against nonconsumption with a simple product is to put in place a cost structure that makes such customers and products financially attractive. Minimizing major cost commitments enables a venture to enthusiastically pursue the small orders that are the initial lifeblood of disruptive businesses in their emergent years.

Accelerating the Emergent Strategy Process

Executives whose ventures are in a discovery mode need not passively watch what evolves in the emergent strategy process. They can employ a rigorous method called *discovery-driven planning* to help a viable strategy emerge much more quickly and purposefully than is likely to happen through less-structured trial and error.[20]

Most deliberate strategic planning processes go through four steps, as suggested in table 8-1. First, innovators make assumptions about the future and about the success that a new business idea will enjoy. These assumptions might be grounded in good predictive theory, but often they are grounded in the way things worked in the past. In the second step, the innovators make financial projections based on those assumptions, and third, senior executives approve the proposal based on the financial projections. Fourth, the team responsible for the new venture goes off to implement the strategy. There frequently is a loop from the second step back to the first in this deliberate process. Because the innovators and middle managers typically know how good the numbers have to look in order for the proposal to get funded, they often will cycle back and revise the assumptions that they are making in order to make the numbers work.

This process does not work badly in a world of sustaining improvements and deliberate strategy. But when it is used for decision making in the emergent world of disruption, this process causes bad decisions to be made because the assumptions upon which the projections and decisions are built often prove wrong.

Discovery-driven planning is a way to actively manage the emergent strategy process. As depicted in table 8-1, it involves reordering the four steps. The first step is to make the financial projections—the targeted or required financial performance of the venture. The logic behind this is quite compelling. If everybody knows how good the numbers must look in order to win funding, why go through the cyclical charade of making and revising assumptions in order to make the numbers look good enough? The required income statement and return on investment should just be the standard first slide in every

TABLE 8-1

A Discovery-Driven Method for Managing the Emergent Strategy Process

Sustaining Innovations: Deliberate Planning	Disruptive Innovations: Discovery-Driven Planning
(Note: decisions to initiate these projects can be grounded on numbers and rules.)	(Note: decisions to initiate these projects should be based on pattern recognition.)
1. Make assumptions about the future.	1. Make the targeted financial projections.
2. Define a strategy based on those assumptions, and build financial projections based on that strategy.	2. What assumptions must prove true in order for these projections to materialize?
3. Make decisions to invest based on those financial projections.	3. Implement a plan to learn—to test whether the critical assumptions are reasonable.
4. Implement the strategy in order to achieve the projected financial results.	4. Invest to implement the strategy.

presentation. The second step, where the real work begins, is to compile an assumptions checklist. It answers the question, "We all know how good the numbers need to be. So what assumptions need to prove true in order for us to realistically expect that these numbers will materialize?" The assumptions on this list should be rank-ordered from most to least crucial. The list must include assumptions related to each of the theories in this book: that low-end or new-market disruptions are possible, that the targeted customers will use the new product for the jobs they are trying to get done, that the new venture will lead the company to the point in the value chain where the money will be in the future, and so on.

The third and fourth steps in discovery-driven planning also reverse the order of the deliberate strategy process. The third step is to implement a plan. This is not a deliberate strategic plan, but rather a plan to test the validity of the most important assumptions. This plan needs to generate quickly, and with as little expense as possible, validating or invalidating information about the most critical assumptions. This enables innovators to revise the strategy prior to the fourth step—the decision to implement through significant investment. This can be done after the viability of various assumptions becomes more evident.

Innovators who are using the discovery-driven process frequently learn quite early that there just isn't a reasonable set of assumptions to support a plan that will achieve the numbers the organization requires. This might imply that the idea simply can't be shaped into a viable strategy at all. Or it might mean that the idea needs to be placed within a smaller business unit, whose values might not demand that it get prohibitively big prohibitively fast.

Managing the Mix of Emergent and Deliberate Strategies

Many processes in an organization can become so refined and effective that they simply keep chugging along with little top-management attention, freeing managers to worry about more nonstandard dimensions of the business. It is dangerous, however, to allow the strategy development process to operate on autopilot. At any given point in time, some businesses under a manager's care may need to be managed through aggressive, deliberate strategy processes, while others need emergent processes.

Executives cannot twist an on/off valve to start and stop the flow of opportunities and problems from deliberate and emergent directions. These are always flowing in, and the CEO's job is to manage constantly which direction should predominantly influence strategic thinking. The valve, which is the resource allocation process, can get really sticky—which is why CEOs need to keep their hands on the control constantly and consciously. When a viable strategy has emerged and it is time for execution, the CEO needs aggressively to switch to a deliberate strategy mode and stop funding emergent opportunities that might divert the company from its focus on the winning plan.

Once this has been done, however, executives often suffer amnesia and selectively remember only their success in deliberately implementing the successful strategy. They lose memory of the emergent process through which the successful strategy was discovered, and therefore forget to reset the strategy process to an emergent mode in those new organizations that are attempting to build the next growth businesses. Nearly all companies, as a result, employ one-size-fits-all deliberate strategy systems. This is a very common reason why new ventures launched by corporations and by many venture capital firms fail.[21] Managing the strategy process in ways that are appropriate to the circumstance can greatly improve the odds that a venture can succeed.

Simply seeking to have the right strategy doesn't go deep enough. The key is to manage the process by which strategy is developed. Strategic initiatives enter the resource allocation process from two sources —deliberate and emergent. In circumstances of sustaining innovation and certain low-end disruptions, the competitive landscape is clear enough that strategy can be deliberately conceived and implemented. In the nascent stages of a new-market disruption, however, it is almost impossible to get the details of strategy right. Rather than executing a strategy, managers in this circumstance need to implement a process through which a viable strategy can emerge.

There are three points of executive leverage in strategy making. The first is to manage the cost structure, or values of the organiza-

tion, so that orders of disruptive products from ideal customers can be prioritized. The second is discovery-driven planning—a disciplined process that accelerates learning what will and won't work. The third is to vigilantly ensure that deliberate and emergent strategy processes are being followed in the appropriate circumstances for each business in the corporation. This is a challenge that few executives have mastered, and is one of the most important contributors to innovative failure in established companies.

Notes

1. The notion that these two different processes coexist was articulated by Henry Mintzberg and James Waters in their classic paper "Of Strategies, Deliberate and Emergent," *Strategic Management Journal* 6 (1985): 257. Stanford Professor Robert Burgelman is probably the preeminent scholar in this field, and many of his papers are cited in this chapter. Two important papers of his are "Intraorganizational Ecology of Strategy Making and Organizational Adaptation: Theory and Field Research," *Organization Science* 2, no. 3 (August 1991): 239–262; and "Strategy as Vector and the Inertia of Coevolutionary Lock-in," *Administrative Science Quarterly* 47 (2002): 325–357. Burgelman's recent book, *Strategy Is Destiny* (New York: Free Press, 2002), summarizes many of his findings. Professors Rita McGrath and Ian MacMillan of the Columbia and Wharton Business Schools, respectively, have also studied these issues. We have found their article "Discovery-Driven Planning" (*Harvard Business Review,* July–August 1995) to be particularly helpful in understanding what processes of strategy development are appropriate in what circumstances. Finally, we have also drawn heavily on the work of Professor Amar Bhide, *The Origin and Evolution of New Business* (Oxford and New York: Oxford University Press, 2000).
2. Mintzberg and Waters, "Of Strategies," 258.
3. This, too, is a departure from the traditional approach to thinking about the "right" way to set strategy. Typically, business scholars have adopted an "either-or" approach to the process of strategy formulation, as (in)famously demonstrated in the highly visible arm wrestle between Henry Mintzberg ("bottom-up") and Igor Ansoff ("top-down") in the pages of the *Strategic Management Journal* (vol. 11, 1990, and vol. 12, 1991).
4. Andrew Grove, *Only the Paranoid Survive* (New York: Doubleday, 1996), 146.
5. Professors Joseph L. Bower of the Harvard Business School and Robert Burgelman of Stanford are the leading scholars who have described how

resources get allocated across competing alternative investments at all levels of the organization. See Joseph L. Bower, *Managing the Resource Allocation Process* (Boston: Harvard Business School Press, 1970); and Robert A. Burgelman and Leonard Sayles, *Inside Corporate Innovation* (New York: Free Press, 1986).

6. The effect that such a filtering mechanism can have on a company's strategy possibilities can be profound. 3M Corporation, for example, is one of the most innovative companies in modern history, in terms of its abilities to apply its core technological platforms to an array of market applications. Its insistence that all new products meet relatively high gross margin targets, however, has focused the company on a vast array of small, premium product niches and has prevented all but a few of its new products from becoming large mass-market businesses.

7. This history has been chronicled in Robert A. Burgelman, "Fading Memories: A Process Study of Strategic Business Exit in Dynamic Environments," *Administrative Science Quarterly* 29 (1994): 24–56; and in Grove, *Only the Paranoid Survive.*

8. EPROMs are erasable, programmable, read-only memory circuits. Like its microprocessors, Intel's EPROM product line also resulted from the emergent, rather than deliberate, process. See Burgelman, "Fading Memories."

9. There were strong reasons why senior management continued to invest in DRAMs. For example, management believed that DRAMs were the "technology driver" and that remaining competitive in DRAMs was essential in order to be competitive in other product lines.

10. Grove, *Only the Paranoid Survive.*

11. Microprocessors were a new-market disruptive technology in that they brought logic to applications where it previously had not been feasible, given the size and cost of the large printed wiring board logic circuitry that was used in the mainframe computers and minicomputers of the day. Relative to Intel's business model, however, microprocessors were a sustaining innovation. The product helped Intel make more money in the way that it was structured to make money, and therefore resources were readily allocated to it. This illustrates a very important principle—that disruptiveness can only be expressed relative to the business model of a company and its competitors.

12. Strong evidence for this is discussed in Amar Bhide, *The Origin and Evolution of New Businesses* (New York: Oxford University Press, 2000).

13. Mintzberg and Waters, "Of Strategies," 271.

14. In a number of speeches and articles, Dr. John Seeley Brown has made this point—that it is very hard to predict in advance how people will end up using the disruptive technologies that change the way we live and work. We recommend all of Dr. Brown's writings to our readers. He has influenced our

own thinking in profound ways. See, for example, J. S. Brown, ed., *Seeing Differently: Insights on Innovation* (Boston: Harvard Business School Publishing, 1997); J. S. Brown, "Changing the Game of Corporate Research: Learning to Thrive in the Fog of Reality," in *Technological Innovation: Oversights and Foresights,* eds. Raghu Garud, Praveen Rattan Nayyar, and Zur Baruch Shapira (New York: Cambridge University Press, 1997), 95–110; and J. S. Brown and Paul Duguid, *The Social Life of Information* (Boston: Harvard Business School Press, 2000).

15. In the parlance of chapter 4, most of these firms were trying to cram the disruptive innovation—handheld devices—into the large, obvious mainstream market, notebook computers. True to form, this strategy proved to be very expensive, and they all failed.

16. An important theoretical perspective called "resource dependence" asserts that it is the entities external to the organization that control what the organization can and cannot do. These entities—customers and investors—provide to the organization the resources that it needs to thrive. Managers cannot do things that are not in the interests of these external providers of resources, or they will withhold their resources and the company will die. See Jeffrey Pfeffer and Gerald R. Salancik, *The External Control of Organizations: A Resource Dependence Perspective* (New York: Harper & Row, 1978). *The Innovator's Dilemma* devoted significant space to this issue, noting that the mechanism for managing change in the face of resource dependence is to create independent organizations that can be dependent on other providers of resources, who value the disruptive products.

17. The distinguished sociologist Arthur Stinchcombe has written extensively on the importance of initial conditions in determining the subsequent chain of decisions and events.

18. Clayton Christensen, "Materials Technology Corp.," Case 9-694-075 (Boston: Harvard Business School, 1994); and Clayton Christensen, "Linking Strategy and Innovation: Materials Technology Corp.," Case 9-696-082 (Boston: Harvard Business School, 1996).

19. For Christensen, studying these problems as an academic has made it clear that MTC's technology was a breakthrough sustaining innovation: The company was trying to bring better products into established markets, and the breakthrough technology entailed extensive interdependencies in development and design. MTC made many of the choices described in this book incorrectly—and as a result, although the company has survived and is profitable, the path was absolutely tortuous.

20. See Rita Gunther McGrath and Ian C. MacMillan, "Discovery-Driven Planning," *Harvard Business Review,* July–August 1995, 44–56. Professors McGrath and MacMillan have written a number of very useful things about

managing the creation of new businesses, of which this article is representative. We encourage you to badger them in their offices at Columbia and Wharton, respectively, for more good ideas. In their article, they use the term "platform-based planning." We have instead called this process "deliberate strategic planning" to be consistent with the language used elsewhere in this chapter.

21. We are concerned that as venture capital firms have gradually become populated by less-experienced analysts who learned only about deliberate strategy in their MBA courses, they are subtly demanding more and more rigor, and data and evidence that the strategy of a business is right. They then pressure the management teams of their portfolio companies to "execute." They only revert to an emergent mode when the initial investment has been squandered and the founding managers sacked, and there is no alternative but to seek a viable strategy through emergent processes.

CHAPTER NINE

THERE IS GOOD MONEY AND THERE IS BAD MONEY

Does it matter whose money funds the business I want to grow? How might the expectations of the suppliers of my capital constrain the decisions I'll be able to make? Is there something about venture capital that does a better job nurturing disruptive businesses than corporate capital? What can corporate executives do to ensure that the expectations that accompany their funding will cause managers to correctly make the decisions that will lead to success?

Getting funded is an obsession for most innovators with a great idea; as a result, most research about raising capital has focused on how to get it. For corporate entrepreneurs, writers often describe the capital budgeting process as a cumbersome bureaucracy and recommend that innovators find a well-placed "champion" in the hierarchy who can work the system of numbers and politics in order to get funding. For start-ups seeking venture capital, much advice is focused on structuring deals that do not give away too much control, while still allowing them to benefit from the networks and acumen that venture capital firms offer.[1]

Although this advice is useful, it skirts an issue that we think is potentially more important: The *type* of money that corporate executives provide to new-growth businesses and the type of capital that managers of those businesses accept represent fundamental early choices when launching a new-growth business. These are critical fork-in-the-road decisions, because the type and amount of money that managers accept define the investor expectations that they'll have to meet. Those expectations then heavily influence the types of markets and channels that the venture can and cannot target. Because the process of securing funding forces many potentially disruptive ideas to get shaped instead as sustaining innovations that target large and obvious markets, the very process of getting the money to start a venture actually sends many of them on a march toward failure.

We have concluded that the best money during the nascent years of a business is *patient for growth* but *impatient for profit*. Our purpose in this chapter is to help corporate executives understand why this type of money tends to facilitate success, and to see how the other category of capital—which is *impatient for growth* but *patient for profit*—is likely to condemn innovators to a death march if it is invested at early stages. We also hope this chapter will help those who bankroll new businesses understand the forces that make their money good or bad for nurturing growth.

The most commonly used theories about good and bad money for new-growth ventures have been based on attributes rather than circumstances. Probably the most common attribute-based categorization is venture capital versus corporate capital. Other categories include public versus private capital, and friends and family versus professionally managed money. None of these categorization schemes supports a theory that can reliably predict whose money will best help new ventures to succeed. Sometimes money from each of these categories proves to be a boon, and sometimes it becomes the kiss of death.

We've already demonstrated why the money that funds a new-growth business needs to be patient for growth. Competing against nonconsumption and moving disruptively up-market are critical elements of a successful new-growth strategy—and yet by definition, these disruptive markets are going to be small for a time. The only way that a venture can instantly become big is for existing users of a high-volume product to be enticed to switch en masse to the new enterprise's product. This is the province of sustaining innovation, and start-ups rarely can win a sustaining-innovation battle. Money *should* be impatient for growth in later-stage, deliberate-strategy circumstances, after a winning strategy for the new business has emerged.

Money needs to be impatient for profit to accelerate a disruptive venture's initial emergent strategy process. When new ventures are expected to generate profit relatively quickly, management is forced to test as quickly as possible the assumption that customers will be happy to pay a profitable price for the product—that is, to see whether real products create enough real value for which customers will pay real money. If a venture's management can keep returning to the corporate treasury to fund continuing losses, managers can postpone this critical test and pursue the wrong strategy for a long time. Expectations of early profit also help a venture's managers to keep fixed costs low. A business model that can make money at low costs per unit is a crucial strategic asset in both new-market *and* low-end disruptive strategies, because the cost structure determines the type of customers that are and are not attractive. The lower it can start, the greater its upside. And finally, early profitability protects a growth venture from cutbacks when the corporate bottom line turns sour.[2]

In the following sections we describe in more detail how good money becomes bad. We recount this process from the point of view of corporate investors, with the hope that this telling of the story will help managers who are seeking funding to know good and bad money when they see it, and to understand the consequences of accepting each type. We hope also that venture capital investors and the entrepreneurs whom they fund will be able to see in these accounts parallel implications for their own operations. Bad money can come from venture and corporate investors—as can good money.

The Death Spiral from Inadequate Growth

Good money turns bad in a self-reinforcing downward spiral that makes it very difficult for even the best executives to do anything except preside over the company's demise. There are five steps in this spiral. Once a company has fallen into it, it becomes almost impossible not to take the subsequent steps.

Step 1: Companies Succeed

After using an emergent strategy process to find a successful formula, a young company hits its stride with a product that helps customers get an important job done better than any competitor. With the winning strategy now clear, the executive team wrestles control of the strategy-making process away from emergent influences and deliberately focuses all investments to exploit this opportunity.[3] Anything that would divert resources from the crucial, deliberate focus on growing the core business is stomped out. Such focus is an essential requirement for success at this stage.[4] However, it means that no new-growth businesses are launched while the core business is still thriving.

This focus propels the company up its sustaining trajectory ahead of competitors who are less aggressive and less focused. Because margins at the high end are attractive, the company barely notices when it begins losing low-end, price-sensitive business in what comes to be viewed as a "commodity segment." Exiting the lowest-margin products and replacing those revenues with higher-margin products at the top of the sustaining trajectory typically feels good, because overall gross profit margins improve.

Step 2: Companies Face a Growth Gap

Despite the company's success, its executives soon realize that they are facing a growth gap. This is caused by the pesky tendency of Wall Street investors to incorporate expected growth into the present value of a stock—so that meeting growth expectations results only in a market-average rate of stock price appreciation. The only way that managers can cause their companies' share prices to increase at a faster rate than the market average is to *exceed* the growth rate that investors have already built into the current price level. Hence, managers who seek to create shareholder value always face a growth gap—the difference between how fast they are expected to grow and how much faster they need to grow to achieve above-average returns for shareholders.[5]

As a rule, executives meet investor expectations through sustaining innovations. Investors understand the businesses in which companies presently compete and the growth potential that lies along the sustaining trajectory in those businesses—which they discount into the present value of the stock price. Sustaining innovation is therefore critical to *maintaining* a company's share price.[6]

It is the creation of new disruptive businesses that allows companies to exceed investor expectations, and therefore to create unusual shareholder value. For precisely the reasons why established companies are prone to underestimate the growth potential in disruptive businesses, investors likewise have consistently underestimated (and therefore have been pleasantly surprised by) the growth potential of disruptions. Creating new disruptive businesses is the only way in the long term to continue creating shareholder value.

When a company's revenues are denominated in millions of dollars, the amount of new business that managers need in order to close the growth gap—new revenues and profits from unknown and yet-to-be-discounted sources—also is denominated in the millions of dollars. But as a company's revenues grow into the billions, the size threshold of new business that is required to sustain its growth rate, let alone exceed investors' expectations, gets bigger and bigger and bigger. At some point the company will report slower growth than investors had discounted, and its stock price will take a hit as investors realize that they had overestimated the company's growth prospects.

To get the stock price moving again, senior management announces a targeted growth rate that is significantly higher than the realistic underlying growth rate of the core businesses. This creates a growth gap even larger than the company has ever faced before—a gap that must be filled by new-growth products and businesses that the company has yet to conceive. Announcing an unrealistic growth rate is the only viable course of action. Executives who refuse to play this game will be replaced by managers who are willing to try. And companies that do not attempt to grow will see their market capitalization decline until they get acquired by companies that are eager to play.

Step 3: Good Money Becomes Impatient for Growth

When confronted with a large growth gap, the corporation's values, or the criteria that are used to approve projects in the resource allocation process, will change. Anything that cannot promise to close the growth gap by becoming very big very fast cannot get through the re-source allocation gate in the strategy process. This is where the process of creating new-growth businesses comes off the rails. When the corporation's investment capital becomes impatient for growth, good money becomes bad money because it triggers a subsequent cascade of inevitable incorrect decisions.

Innovators who seek funding for the disruptive innovations that could ultimately fuel the company's growth with a high probability of success now find that their trial balloons get shot down because they can't get big enough fast enough. Managers of most disruptive businesses can't credibly project that the business will become very big very fast, because new-market disruptions need to compete against nonconsumption and must follow an emergent strategy process. Compelling them to project big numbers forces them to declare a strategy that confidently crams the innovation into a large, existing, and obvious market whose size can be statistically substantiated. This means competing against consumption.

After senior executives have approved funding for this inflated growth project, the company's managers cannot then back down and follow an emergent strategy that seeks to compete against nonconsumption. They are on the hook to deliver the growth that they projected. They therefore must ramp expenses according to plan.

Step 4: Executives Temporarily Tolerate Losses

It becomes clear that competing against consumption in a large and obvious market will be an expensive challenge, because if customers are to buy the product, it must perform better than the products that customers already are using. The team warns senior executives that stomaching huge losses is a prerequisite to winning the pot of gold. Determined to be visionary with the long-term interests of the company in mind, executives therefore accept the reality that the business will lose significant money for some time. There is no retreat. Executives convince themselves that investing for growth will *result* in growth, as if there were a linear relationship between the two—as if the more aggressively you invest to build the new business, the faster it will take off.[7]

In order to meet the budgeted timetable for rollout and ramp-up, the project managers put the cost structure in place before there are revenues—and because they must support a steep revenue ramp, these costs are substantial. But overfunding is hazardous to a new venture's health, because heavy expense levels in turn define the sorts of customers and market segments that will and will not provide adequate revenues to cover those costs. If this happens, then customers who come from nonconsumption in emerging applications and are therefore delighted with simple products—in short, the ideal customers for a disruptive venture—inevitably become unattractive to the business. The ideal channels—those that need something to fuel their own disruptive march up-market against *their* competition—also become unattractive. Only the largest channels that reach the largest populations appear to be capable of bringing in enough revenue fast enough.

This completes the character transformation of the corporation's money. It has become bad money for new-market disruption: Impatient for growth but patient for profit.

Step 5: Mounting Losses Precipitate Retrenchment

As the venture's managers try to succeed by competing against consumption, they find all sorts of reasons why customers prefer to continue buying the products they have always used from the vendors they have always trusted. Often these reasons entail the kinds of interdependencies we discussed in chapter 5. Breakthrough sustaining innovations can rarely be hot-swapped into existing systems of use. Typically, many other unanticipated things need to change in order for customers to be able to benefit from using the new product. While revenues fall far short, expenses are on budget. Losses mount. The stock price then gets hammered again, as investors realize anew that their expectations for growth cannot be met.

A new management team gets brought in to rescue the stock price. To stanch the bleeding, the new team stops all spending except what is required to keep the core business strong. Refocusing on the core is welcome news. It is a tried-and-true formula for performance improvement, because the company's resources, processes, and values have been honed exactly for this task. The stock price bounces in response, but as soon as the new price has fully discounted whatever growth potential exists in the core business, the new executives realize that they must invest to grow. But now the company faces an even greater growth gap, and the situation loops back to step 3, where the company needs new-growth businesses that can get *really* big *really* fast. That pressure then causes management to repeat the tragic sequence of wrong decisions again and again, until so much value has been destroyed that the company is acquired by another corporation, which itself had been unable to generate its own growth through disruption but saw in the acquisition a synergistic opportunity to wring cost out of the combination.

How to Manage the Dilemma of Investing for Growth

The dilemma of investing for growth is that the character of a firm's money is good for growth only when the firm is growing healthily. Core businesses that are still growing provide cover for new-growth businesses. Senior executives who are bolstered by a sense that the pipeline of new sustaining innovations in established businesses will meet or exceed investors' expectations can allow new businesses the time to follow emergent strategy processes while they compete against nonconsumption. It is when growth slows—when senior executives see that the sustaining-innovation pipeline is inadequate to meet investor expectations—that investing to grow becomes hard. The character of the firm's money changes when new things must get very big very fast, and it won't allow innovators to do what is needed to grow. When you're a corporate entrepreneur and you sense this shift in the corporate context occurring, you had better watch out.

This dilemma traps nearly every company and is the causal mechanism behind the findings in *Stall Points,* the Corporate Strategy Board's study that we cited in chapter 1.[8] This study showed that of the 172 companies that had spent time on *Fortune*'s list of the 50 largest companies between 1955 and 1995, 95 percent saw their growth stall to rates at or below the rate of GNP growth. Of the companies whose growth stalled, only 4 percent were able to successfully reignite their growth even to a rate of 1 percent above GNP growth.

Once growth had stalled, the corporations' money turned impatient for growth, which rendered it impossible to do the things required to launch successful growth businesses.

In recent years, the dilemma has become even more complex. If companies whose growth has stalled somehow find a way to launch a successful new-growth business, Wall Street analysts often complain that they cannot value the new opportunity appropriately because it is buried within a larger, slower-growing corporation. In the name of shareholder value, they demand that the corporation spin off the new-growth business to shareholders so that the full value of its exciting growth potential can be reflected in its own share price. If executives respond and spin it off, they may indeed "unlock" shareholder value. But after it has been unlocked they are left locked again in a low-growth business, facing the mandate to increase shareholder value.

In the face of this sobering evidence, chief executives—whose task it is to create shareholder value—*must* preserve the ability of their capital to nourish growth businesses in the ways that they need to be nourished. When executives allow the growth of core businesses to sag to lackluster levels, new-growth ventures must shoulder the whole burden of changing the growth rate of the entire corporation's top and bottom lines. This forces the corporation to demand that the new businesses become very big very fast. Their capital as a consequence becomes poison for growth ventures. The only way to keep investment capital from spoiling is to use it when it is still good—to invest it from a context that is still healthy enough that the money can be patient for growth.

In many ways, companies whose shares are publicly held are in a self-reinforcing vise. Their dominant shareholders are pension funds. Corporations pressure the managers of their pension fund investments to deliver strong and consistent returns—because strong investment performance reduces the amount of profits that must be diverted to fund pension obligations. Investment managers therefore turn around and pressure the corporations whose shares they own to deliver consistent earnings growth that is unexpectedly accelerating. Privately held companies are not subject to many of these pressures. The expectations that accompany their capital therefore can often be more appropriate for the building of new-growth businesses.

Use Pattern Recognition, Not Financial Results, to Signal Potential Stall Points

Because outsiders typically measure a company's success by its financial results, executives are tempted to rely on changes in financial results as signals that they should take comfort or take action. This is folly, however, because the financial outcomes of the most recent period actually reflect the results of investments that were made years earlier to improve processes and to create new products and businesses. Financial results measure how healthy the business was, not how healthy the business *is*.[9] Financial results are a particularly bad tool to manage disruption, because moving up-market feels good financially, as we have noted previously.

Executives should gingerly use data of *any* sort when looking into the future, because reliable data are typically available only about the past and will be an accurate guide only if the future resembles the past.[10] To illustrate the limitations of data in disruptive decision making, let us recount an experience that Clayton Christensen had in a recent MBA class. He had written a paper that worried that the leading business schools' traditional two-year MBA programs are being threatened by two disruptions. The most proximate wave, a low-end disruption, is executive evening-and-weekend MBA programs that enable working managers to earn MBA degrees in as little as a year. The most significant wave is a new-market disruption: on-the-job management training that ranges from corporate educational institutions such as Motorola University and GE's Crotonville to training seminars in Holiday Inns.

Christensen asked for a student vote at the beginning of class: "After reading the paper, how many of you think that the leading MBA programs are being disrupted?" *Three* of the 102 students raised their hands. The other 99 took the position that these developments weren't relevant to the venerable institutions' fortunes.

Christensen then asked one of the three who was worried to explain why. "There's a real pattern here," he responded, and he listed six elements of the pattern. These included MBA salaries overshooting what operating companies can afford; the disruptors competing against nonconsumption; people hiring on-the-job education to get a very different job done; a shift in the basis of competition to speed, convenience, and customization; and interdependent versus modular curricula. He concluded that the pattern fit: All of the things that had happened to other companies as they were disrupted were indeed under way in management education. "That's why I'd take this seriously," he concluded.

Christensen then turned to those who weren't concerned, and asked why. They tended to point to the data—the numbers of students still battling to be admitted into the leading schools, the attractive starting salaries of the graduates, the brand reputations of the programs, loyal alumni and great on-campus networking opportunities, and so on. None of the disruptive programs could come even close to competing on these dimensions.

Christensen then asked one of the most vocal defenders of the invincibility of the leading business schools, "What if you were dean of one of these schools. What data would convince you that this was something that you needed to address?"

"I'd look at the school's market share among the CEOs of the Global 1000 corporations," he responded. "If our market share started to drop, then I'd worry." Christensen then asked whether that data would be a signal that he should begin addressing the problem or that the game was over. "Oh, I guess the game would be over by then," he admitted.

"Anybody else?" Christensen pressed. "Imagine that you were dean. What data would convince you that you should take action?" Several proposed evidence that they would find convincing, but in every case, the class concluded that by the time convincing data became available, the game would be over for the high-quality two-year MBA programs.

When Christensen asked, "Should these schools view this as a threat or an opportunity?" there was another interesting reaction. There was little energy in the class regarding the growth opportunity that on-the-job management education presented for the leading business schools. We suspect that the reason for the students' indifference is related to the threat-versus-opportunity paradox highlighted in chapter 3. At the time of this writing, the leading business schools are at the top of their game, by any measure of financial, academic, and competitive performance.

They don't need growth to feel healthy. There is nothing yet in the measures of strength and organizational vitality to suggest that the world these programs have enjoyed is likely to change.[11]

Create Policies to Invest Good Money Before It Goes Bad

When you're driving a car, you can wait until the fuel gauge drops toward empty before you refill the tank, and once the tank is full again you can rev the car back up to full speed. It just isn't possible to manage growth in the same way—to wait until the growth gauge begins falling toward zero before you seek a fill-up from new-growth businesses. The growth engine is a much more delicate machine that must be kept running continuously by process and policy, rather than by reacting when the growth gauge reads empty. We suggest three particular policies for keeping the growth engine running. Taken together, the policies force the organization to *start early, start small,* and *demand early success.*

- Launch new-growth businesses regularly when the core is still healthy—when it can still be patient for growth—not when financial results signal the need.
- Keep dividing business units so that as the corporation becomes increasingly large, decisions to launch growth ventures continue to be made within organizational units that can be patient for growth because they are small enough to benefit from investing in small opportunities.
- Minimize the use of profit from established businesses to subsidize losses in new-growth businesses. Be impatient for profit: There is nothing like profitability to ensure that a high-potential business can continue to garner the funding it needs, even when the corporation's core businesses turn sour.

Start Early: Launch New-Growth Businesses Regularly While the Core Is Still Healthy

Establishing a policy that mandates the launch of new disruptive growth businesses in a predetermined rhythm is the only way that executives actually can avoid reacting after the growth engine has stalled. They *must* regularly launch or acquire new-growth businesses while their core businesses are still growing healthily, because when growth slows, the dramatic change in the company's values that ensues makes growth impossible. If executives do this, and continue to shape the strategies of those businesses to be disruptive, soon a new business or two will punch into the realm of major revenue every year, ready to sustain the total corporation's growth. If executives use their corporations' investment capital when they can be patient for growth, the money will not spoil. It remains fresh, able to fund new-growth businesses.

Acquire New-Growth Businesses in a Predetermined Rhythm

Some executives of large, successful companies fear that even if they develop high-potential ideas and business plans for disruptive growth businesses, they just won't be able to create the processes and values required to nurture them. They therefore are inclined to buy disruptive growth businesses, rather than to make them internally. Acquisition can be a very successful strategy if it is guided by good theory.

Many corporate acquisitions are triggered by the arrival of an investment banker with a business to sell. Decisions to acquire or not are often driven by discounted cash flow projections and an assessment of whether the business is undervalued or fixable or can yield cost savings through synergies with an existing business. Some of the theories that are used to justify these acquisitions prove to be accurate, and the acquisitions create great value. But most of them don't.[12]

Corporate business development teams can just as readily acquire disruptive businesses. If they wait until the growth trajectories of these companies are obvious to everyone, of course, the disruptive companies may be too expensive to acquire. But if a business development team identifies candidates through the lenses of the theories in chapters 2 through 6 rather than waiting for conclusive historical evidence, then acquiring early-stage disruptive growth businesses in a regular rhythm can be a great strategy for creating and sustaining a corporation's growth. In contrast to the acquisition of mature businesses that put a company on a higher but still flat revenue trajectory, acquiring early-stage disruptive companies can change the slope of the revenue trajectory.

One company whose fortunes have been heavily shaped by acquiring disruptive businesses has been Johnson & Johnson. For most of the 1990s, J&J was organized in three major operating groups—ethical pharmaceuticals, medical devices and diagnostics (MDD), and consumer products. Figure 9-1 shows that in 1993 the consumer and MDD groups were comparably sized, each generating just under $5 billion in sales. They subsequently grew at very different rates. The consumer business's intrinsic growth trajectory was essentially flat, and it grew by acquiring big new revenue platforms, such as Neutrogena and Aveeno, whose growth trajectories were similarly flat. Although these acquisitions put the revenue line of the consumer group on a higher platform, they did not change the *slope* of the platform—and remember that it is changes in the slope of the platform, not the level of the platform, that create shareholder value at an above-average rate. Even with the acquisitions, the consumer group's total revenues only grew at about a 4 percent annual rate over the decade.

In contrast, the MDD group of businesses grew at over 11 percent annually over the same period. This was driven by four disruptive businesses, each of which the company had acquired. J&J's Ethicon Endo-Surgery company makes instruments for endoscopic surgery, a disruption relative to conventional invasive surgery. Its Cordis division makes instruments for angioplasty, which is disruptive relative to open-heart cardiac bypass surgery. The company's Lifescan division makes portable blood glucose meters that enable patients with diabetes to test their own blood sugar levels instead of needing to go to hospital laboratories. And J&J's Vistakon disposable contact lenses were disruptive relative to traditional lenses made by companies such as Bausch & Lomb. The strategies of each of these businesses fit precisely the litmus tests for new-market disruption described in chapter 2. Together, they have grown at a 43 percent annual rate since 1993, and now account for about $10 billion in revenue. The group's overall growth rate was 11 percent because the other MDD group companies—those not on disruptive trajectories—grew in aggregate at a 3 percent annual rate. Both the consumer and MDD

FIGURE 9-1

Johnson & Johnson Consumer Products (CP) Versus Medical Devices & Diagnostics (MDD) Revenue and Operating Profit, 1992–2001

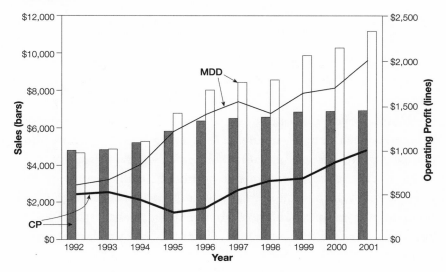

Sources: Johnson & Johnson financial statements; Deloitte Consulting analysis.

groups grew through acquisition. The growth rates of the two groups differed because MDD acquired businesses with disruptive potential, whereas the consumer group acquired premium businesses that were not disruptive.[13]

Hewlett-Packard also sustained its growth for nearly two decades after its core lines of business matured, using a hybrid strategy for finding disruptions. Its acquisition of Apollo Computer, a leading workstation maker, was the platform upon which HP built its microprocessor-based computer businesses, which disrupted minicomputer makers such as Digital Equipment. HP's ink-jet printer business, which today provides a significant portion of the corporation's total profit, was a disruption that was conceived and launched internally, but within an organizationally autonomous business unit.

GE Capital, which was the primary engine of value creation for GE shareholders in the 1990s, has been a massive disruptor in the financial services industry. It has grown through a hybrid strategy of incubating disruptive businesses in some segments of the industry and acquiring others.

Start Small: Divide Business Units to Maintain Patience for Growth

The second policy imperative is to keep operating units relatively small. A decentralized company can maintain the values required to see and enthusiastically pursue disruptive innovations far longer than can a monolithic, centralized one, because the size that a new disruptive venture must reach to make a difference to a small business unit is more consistent with the revenue ramp of a new disruptive business.

Compare the perspective in a monolithic $20 billion company that needs to grow 15 percent annually with the perspective in a $20 billion corporation that is composed of twenty business units. The managers of the monolithic company will have to look at every proposed innovation from the perspective of needing to find $3 billion in new revenues beyond what was done in the prior year. The average perspective of the twenty business unit managers in the decentralized company, in contrast, is that they need to bring in $150 million of new business in the next year. In the multiple-business-unit firm there are more managers seeking disruptive growth opportunities, and more opportunities will look attractive to them.

In fact, most of the companies that appear to have transformed themselves over the past thirty years or so—companies such as Hewlett-Packard, Johnson & Johnson, and General Electric, for example—have been composed of a large number of smaller, relatively autonomous business units. These corporations have not transformed themselves by transforming the business models of their existing business units into disruptive growth businesses. The transformation was achieved by creating new disruptive business units and by shutting down or selling off mature ones that had reached the feasible end of their sustaining-technology trajectories.[14]

One reason the mortality rate of independent disk drive companies measured in *The Innovator's Dilemma* was so high was that they all were single-business companies. As monolithic organizations—

even relatively small ones—they had never learned how to manage nascent disruptive growth businesses alongside larger, maturing businesses. There were no processes for doing this.

In following the policy we are recommending, managers again need to be guided by theory, not by the numbers. Accountants will argue that redundant overhead expenses can be eliminated when business units are consolidated into much larger entities. Such analysts rarely assess the impact that consolidation has on the consequent demands in those mega-units that any new businesses that are launched must get very big very fast.[15]

Demand Early Success: Minimize Subsidization of New-Growth Ventures

The third policy, which is to expect new-growth businesses to generate profit relatively quickly, does two important things. First, it helps accelerate the emergent strategy process by forcing the venture to test as quickly as possible the assumption that there are customers who will pay attractive prices for the firm's products. The fledgling business can then press on or change course based on this feedback. Second, forcing a venture to become profitable as soon as feasible helps protect it from being shut down when the core business turns sour.[16]

Honda: An Example of Forced Floundering

Not having much money proved to be a great blessing for Honda, for example, as it attacked the U.S. motorcycle market.[17] Founded in postwar Japan by motorcycle racing enthusiast Suchiro Honda, by the mid-1950s the company had become best known for its 50cc Super Cub, designed as a more powerful but easy-to-handle moped that could wind its way through crowded Japanese streets for use as a delivery vehicle.

When Honda targeted the U.S. motorcycle market in 1958, its management set a seat-of-the-pants sales target of 6,000 units a year, representing 1 percent of the U.S. market. Securing support for the U.S. venture was not merely a matter of convincing Mr. Honda. The Japanese Ministry of Finance also had to approve the release of the foreign currency needed to set up operations in America. Hard on the heels of

Toyota's failed introduction of the Toyopet car, the Ministry was loathe to give up scarce foreign exchange. Only $250,000 was released, of which only $110,000 was cash; the rest had to be in inventory.

Honda launched its U.S. operations with inventory in each of its 50cc, 125cc, 250cc, and 305cc models. The biggest bets were placed on the largest motorcycles, however, because the U.S. market was composed exclusively of large bikes. In our parlance, Honda set out to achieve a low-end disruption, hoping to pick off the most price-sensitive customers in the existing market with a low-price, full-sized motorcycle.

In 1960 Honda sold a few models of its larger machines, which promptly began to leak oil and blow their clutches. It turned out that Honda's best engineers, whose skills had been honed through developing products that performed well in short stop-and-go bursts in congested streets, didn't know what they didn't know about the demands of the constant, high-speed, over-the-road travel that was common among motorcyclists in the United States. Honda had little choice but to invest its precious currency in sending the defective bikes via air freight back to Japan. The problem almost broke Honda.

With almost all of its resources devoted to supporting and promoting the problematic larger machines against well-financed and successful incumbents, the Honda personnel in the United States turned to using the 50cc Super Cubs as their own transportation. They were reliable, cheap to run, and Honda figured they couldn't sell them anyway: There simply was no market for motorbikes that small. Right?

The exposure the Super Cub got from the daily use of the Honda management team in Los Angeles generated surprising interest from individuals and retailers—not motorcycle distributors, but sporting goods shops. Running low on cash thanks to the difficulties encountered in selling the big bikes, Honda decided to sell the Super Cubs just to stay afloat.

Little by little, continued success in selling the Super Cub and continued disappointment with the larger machines eventually redirected Honda's efforts toward the creation of an entirely new market segment—off-road motorbikes. Priced at one-fourth the cost of a big Harley, these were sold to people without leather jackets who never would have purchased deep-throated cycles from the established U.S.

or European makers. They were used for fun, not over-the-road transportation. Apparently a low-end disruption wasn't a viable strategy because there just weren't enough over-the-road bikers who were overserved by the brands and muscle of Harleys, Triumphs, and BMWs. What emerged was a new-market disruption, which Honda subsequently did a masterful job of deliberately exploiting.

What pushed Honda to discover this market was its *lack* of financial resources. This prevented its managers from tolerating significant losses and instead created an environment in which the venture's managers had to respond to unanticipated successes. This is the essence of managing the emergent strategy process.[18]

It is important to remember that this policy—to limit expenses and seek early profit in order to accelerate the emergent strategy process—is not a one-size-fits-all mandate. In circumstances in which a viable strategy needs to emerge—such as new-market disruptions—this is a helpful policy. In low-end disruptions, the right strategy often is much clearer much earlier. As soon as the market applications become clear, and a business model that can viably and profitably address that market has emerged, aggressive investment—impatience for growth—is appropriate.

Insurance for When the Corporation Refocuses on the Core

Another reason why turning an early profit is important to a new business's success is that funding for new ventures very often gets cut off not because the ventures are off-plan, but because the core business is sick and needs all of the corporation's resources to recover. When the downturn occurs, new-growth ventures that cannot play a significant and immediate role in the corporation's return to financial health simply get sacrificed, even though everybody involved knows that they are cutting off the road to the future in order to salvage the present. The need to survive trumps the need to grow.[19]

Dr. Nick Fiore, who periodically speaks to our students at the Harvard Business School, is a battle-scarred corporate innovator whose experiences illustrate these principles in action. Fiore was hired at different points in his career by the CEOs of two publicly traded companies to start new-growth businesses that would set their corporations on robust growth trajectories.[20] In both instances, the CEOs—powerful, reputable executives who were secure in their positions—had truthfully assured Fiore that the initiative to create new-growth businesses had the full and patient backing of the companies' respective boards of directors.

Fiore cautions our students that if they ever receive such assurances, even from the most powerful and deep-pocketed executives in their companies, they had better watch out.

> When you start a new growth business, there is a ticking clock behind you. The problem is that this clock ticks at a variable rate that is determined by the health of the corporate bottom line, not by whether your little venture is on plan. When the bottom line is healthy, this clock ticks patiently on. But if the bottom line gets troubled, the clock starts to tick real fast. When it suddenly strikes twelve, your new business had better be profitable enough that the corporate bottom line would look worse without you. You need to be part of the solution to the corporation's immediate profit problems, or the guillotine blade will fall. This will happen because the board and the chairman have no option but to refocus on the core—despite what they may have told you with the best and most honest of intentions.[21]

This is why being impatient for profit is a virtuous characteristic of corporate capital. It forces new-growth ventures to ferret out the most promising disruptive opportunities quickly, and creates some (always imperfect) insurance against the venture's getting zeroed out when the health of the larger organization becomes imperiled.

Figure 9-2 summarizes the virtues of policy-driven growth. It shows that appropriate policies, if well understood and appropriately implemented, can generate an upward spiral to replace the death spiral from inadequate growth that we described at the beginning of this chapter. When this happens, companies place themselves in a circumstance of continual growth. They invest their good money and avoid letting it go bad. This is the only way to avoid letting the growth engine stall and to sidestep the death spiral from inadequate growth.

FIGURE 9-2

Self-Reinforcing Spirals from Adequate and Inadequate Growth

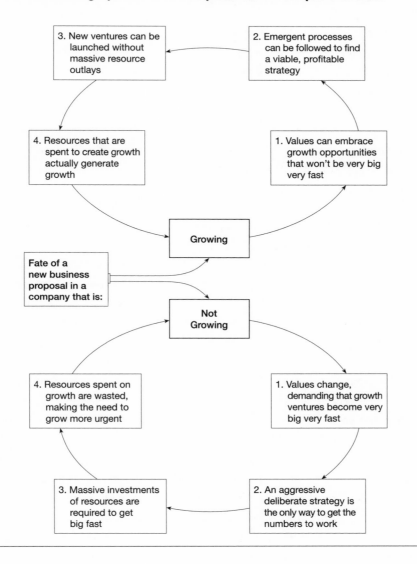

Good Venture Capital Can Turn Bad, Too

Those working to build disruptive growth businesses within established corporations sometimes look longingly at the green grass on the other side of the corporate fence, where innovators who build independent start-ups not only can avoid the encumbrances of corporate bureaucracy but also have the freedom to fund their ideas with venture capital. The belief that venture capitalists can fund start-ups much more effectively than corporate capitalists is so pervasive, in fact, that the venture capital investment arms of many corporations refuse to participate in a deal unless an independent venture capital firm will co-invest.

We would argue, however, that the corporate-versus-venture distinction isn't nearly as important as the willingness or inability to be patient for growth. Just like Honda, most successful venture capital firms had precious little capital to invest at the outset. The lack of money conferred on their ventures a superior capability in the emergent strategy process. When venture capitalists become burdened with lots of money, however, many of them seem to behave as corporate capitalists do in stages 3, 4, and 5 of the growth-gap spiral.

In the late 1990s venture investors plowed huge sums of capital into very early-stage companies, conferring extraordinary valuations upon them. Why would people with so much experience have done something so foolish as to invest all of that money in companies before they had products and customers? The answer is that they *had* to make investments of this size. Their small, early-stage investments had been so successful in the past that investors had shoveled massive amounts of capital into their new funds, expecting that they would be able to earn comparable rates of return on much larger amounts of money. The venture firms had not increased their number of partners in proportion to the increase in the assets that they were committed to invest. As a consequence, the partners simply could not be bothered with making little $2 million to $5 million early-stage investments of the very sort that had led to their initial success. Their values had changed. They *had* to demand that the ventures they invested in must become very big, very fast, just like their corporate counterparts.[22]

And just like their corporate counterparts, these funds then went through steps 3, 4, and 5 that were described at the beginning of this chapter. These venture funds weren't victims of the bubble—the collapse in valuations that occurred between 2000 and 2002. In many ways they were the cause of it. They had moved up-market into the magnitudes of investment that normally are meted out in later deliberate strategy stages, but the early-stage companies in which they continued to invest were in a circumstance that needed a different type of capital and a different process of strategy.[23] The paucity of early-stage capital that continues to prevent many entrepreneurs with great disruptive growth ideas from getting funding as of the writing of this book is in many ways the result of so many venture capital funds being in their equivalent of step 5 of the death spiral—retrenching and focusing all of their money and attention to fix prior businesses.

We often have been asked whether it is a good idea or bad idea for corporations to set up corporate venture capital groups to fund the creation of new growth businesses. We answer that this is the wrong question: They have their categories wrong. Few corporate venture funds have been successful or long-lived; but the reason is not that they are "corporate" or that they are "venture." When these funds fail to foster successful growth businesses, it is most often because they invested in sustaining rather than disruptive innovations or in modular solutions when interdependence was required. And very often, the investments fail because the corporate context from which the capital came was impatient for growth and perversely patient for profitability.

The experience and wisdom of the men and women who invest in and then oversee the building of a growth business are always important, in every situation. Beyond that, however, the context from which the capital is invested has a powerful influence on whether the start-up capital that they provide is good or bad for growth. Whether they are corporate capitalists or venture capitalists, when their investing context shifts to one that demands that their ventures become very big very fast, the probability that the venture can succeed falls markedly. And when capitalists of either sort follow sound theory—whether consciously or by intuition or happenstance—they are much more likely to succeed.

The central message of this chapter for those who invest and receive investment can be summed up in a single aphorism: Be patient for growth, not for profit. Because of the perverse dynamics of the death spiral from inadequate growth, achieving growth requires an almost Zen-like ability to pursue growth when it is not necessary. The key to finding disruptive footholds is to connect with a job in what initially will be small, nonobvious market segments—ideally, market segments characterized by nonconsumption.

Pressure for early profit keeps investors willing to invest the cash needed to fuel the growth in a venture's asset base. Demanding early profitability is not only good discipline, it is critical to continued success. It ensures that you have truly connected with a job in markets that potential competitors are happy to ignore. As you seek out the early sustaining innovations that realize your growth potential, staying profitable requires that you stay connected with that job. This profitability ensures that you will maintain the support and enthusiasm of the board and shareholders. Internally, continued profitability earns you the continued support and enthusiasm of senior management who have staked their reputation, and the employees who have staked their careers, on your success. There is no substitute. Ventures that are allowed to defer profitability typically never get there.

Notes

1. Many books have been written on the challenges of matching the right money with the right opportunity. Three that we have found to be useful are the following: Mark Van Osnabrugge and Robert J. Robinson, *Angel Investing: Matching Startup Funds with Startup Companies: The Guide for Entrepreneurs, Individual Investors, and Venture Capitalists* (San Francisco: Jossey-Bass, 2000); David Amis and Howard Stevenson, *Winning Angels: The Seven Fundamentals of Early-Stage Investing* (London: Financial Times Prentice Hall, 2001); and Henry Chesbrough, *Open Innovation: The New Imperative for Creating and Profiting from Technology* (Boston: Harvard Business School Press, 2003).

2. A stream of academic research explores the nature of "first-mover advantage" (for example, M. B. Lieberman and D. B. Montgomery, "First-Mover Advantages," *Strategic Management Journal* 9 [1988]: 41–58). This can manifest itself in "racing behavior" (T. R. Eisenmann, "A Note on Racing to Acquire Customers," Harvard Business School paper, Boston, 2002) in the context of "get big fast" (GBF) strategies (T. R. Eisenmann, *Internet Business Models: Text and Cases.* New York: McGraw-Hill, 2001). The thinking in this field is that in some circumstances it is preferable to pursue a particular strategy very aggressively, even at the risk of pursuing a suboptimal strategy, because of the benefits of establishing a significant market position quickly. The drivers of the benefits of a GBF strategy are strong network effects in customer usage (N. Economides, "The Economics of Networks," *International Journal of Industrial Organization* 14 [1996]: 673–699) or other forms of high customer switching costs. The arguments of this school of thought are well articulated and convincing, and suggest strongly that there are conditions when being patient for growth could undermine the long-run potential of a business.

Harvard Business School Professor William Sahlman, who also has studied this issue extensively, has noted in conversations with us that on occasion venture capital investors en masse conclude that a "category" is going to be "big"—even while there is no consensus which firms within that category are going to succeed. This results in a massive inflow of capital into the nascent industry, which funds more start-ups than can possibly survive, at illogical valuations. He notes that when investors and entrepreneurs are caught up in such a whirlwind, they almost have no alternative but to race to out-invest the competition. When the bubble pops, most of these investors and entrepreneurs will lose—and in fact in the aggregate, the venture capital industry loses money in these whirlwinds. The only way not to lose everything is to out-invest and out-execute the others.

The challenge is determining whether or not one is in such conditions. Compelling work by two scholars in particular suggests that network effects and switching costs that are sufficiently strong to overwhelm more prosaic determinants of success arise far *less* frequently than is generally asserted. See Stan J. Liebowitz and Stephen E. Margolis, *The Economics of QWERTY: History, Theory, Policy,* ed. Peter Lewin (New York: New York University Press, 2002.) As an example, Ohashi ("The Role of Network Externalities in the U.S. VCR Market 1976–86," University of British Columbia working paper, available from SSRN) argues that Sony under-invested in customer acquisition in the VCR market, suggesting that it could have been successful had it "raced" harder. Economic modeling suggests that indeed, controlling for product quality, it makes sense to invest more aggressively in customer acquisition when network effects are present than when they are not.

This *ceteris paribus* assumption with respect to product quality, however, is somewhat heroic, for it assumes away the very reason to be patient and avoid racing. As Liebowitz and colleagues (*The Economics of QWERTY*) have shown, in the case of the Betamax/VHS battle, a critical element driving customer choice was recording time: Although first to market and offering better video quality, Betamax did not permit two-hour recording times—the minimum typically required to record a movie being broadcast over network television. This turned out to be a critical driver of consumer adoption. JVC's VHS standard did enable this kind of recording, and met at least minimum acceptable standards for video fidelity. As a result, it was far better aligned with the job to be done, and this superior alignment overcame Betamax's first-mover advantage. It is doubtful that the incremental market share that a more aggressive marketing spend by Sony might have yielded for the Betamax standard would have beaten back the superior VHS product.

With these caveats in place, it is nevertheless important to recognize the possibility of powerful payoffs to optimal racing behavior, which, in our language, would capture a particular aspect of the job to be done by a given product or service. In the case of network effects, this is captured by the notion that in order for a product to do a job well for me, it must also be doing this same job for many other people. To the extent that such competitive requirements undermine profitability where racing behavior is called for, the need to be patient for profits can be mitigated.

Because the focus of this book is to help corporate managers launch new-growth businesses consistently, we anticipate that they will be caught in GBF racing situations less often than, for example, certain venture capital investors whose strategies might be to participate in big categories.

3. In the language of author and venture capitalist Geoffrey Moore, this is when the "tornado" happens. See Geoffrey A. Moore, *Inside the Tornado* (New York: HarperBusiness, 1995) and *Living on the Fault Line* (New York: HarperBusiness, 2000).

4. We refer the reader again to Stanford Professor Robert Burgelman's outstanding, book-length case study on the processes of strategy development and implementation at Intel, *Strategy Is Destiny* (New York: Free Press, 2002). In that account, Burgelman emphasizes how important it was that once the winning microprocessor strategy had emerged, Andy Grove and Gordon Moore very aggressively focused all of the corporation's investments into that strategy.

5. See Alfred Rappaport and Michael Mauboussin, *Expectations Investing: Reading Stock Prices for Better Returns* (Boston: Harvard Business School Press, 2001). We mentioned this point in chapter 1, but it merits repeating here. Because markets discount projected growth into the present stock price, companies that deliver what investors have foreseen and discounted will only earn market-average rates of return to shareholders. It is true that over the sweep of their histories, companies that grow at faster rates give higher returns to their shareholders than those that grow more slowly. But the particular shareholders in that history who realize above-average returns are those who find themselves holding the stock when the market realizes that its forecast of the company's growth was too low.

6. Cost reductions that enable a company to generate stronger cash flows than investors have expected also create shareholder value, of course. We classify these as sustaining innovations because they enable the leading companies to make more money in the way they are structured to make money. Because investors typically can expect ongoing efficiency improvements from any company, our statements here simply reflect the reality that generating shareholder value by exceeding investors' expectations for operational efficiency typically can only raise share prices to a higher but *flat* plateau. Tilting the slope of the share price graph upward requires disruptive innovation.

7. This is often true in sustaining situations—it is important to invest aggressively ahead of product launch to ensure that channels are filled and capacity exists to meet expected demand. But this is not the case in disruptive situations.

8. See Corporate Strategy Board, *Stall Points* (Washington, DC: The Corporate Strategy Board, 1998).

9. This is the theme of an important stream of work by Professor Robert Kaplan and his colleagues that has led them to advocate the use of a tool called the *Balanced Scorecard,* rather than financial statements, as a measure of an organization's long-term strategic health. See, for example, Robert S. Kaplan and David P. Norton, *The Strategy-Focused Organization* (Boston: Harvard Business School Press, 2001).

10. In asserting that managers ought to let theory guide their actions and not wait until convincing data have become available, we certainly hope that readers do not construe that we are advising managers to fly by the seat of their pants without numbers. Measuring in detail the operating performance of established lines of business, and making decisions based on such data, is crucial to profitable movement up the sustaining trajectory. When engaging in discovery-driven planning for a new disruptive business, the pro forma financial modeling of possible outcomes helps planners understand which assumptions are most important. Our case for theory-driven decisions is

grounded in a belief that sound theory can help executives assign strategic meaning to numbers that otherwise might appear to be inconclusive, and to sort the signal from the noise as the data come in.

11. As explored in chapter 6, we would expect that on-the-job management education, as a new-market disruption, will be a modular, nonintegrated industry where the ability to make attractive profits is unlikely to reside in the design and assembly of courses. And yet most of the business schools are attempting to compete in this market by designing and delivering custom executive education courses for large corporations. In our view, the business schools need a major dose of theory. Instead of simply selling cases and articles, a better strategy for them would be to create value-added curriculum modules that would enable tens of thousands of corporate training people to quickly slap together compelling content that helps employees learn exactly what they need to learn, when and where they need to learn it. It would also be critical to enable these trainers to teach these materials in such compelling and interesting ways that none of these on-the-job students has any desire ever to sit through a business school professor's class again. If history were any guide, if the publishing divisions of the business schools did this, they would ultimately have a far broader impact, and be far more profitable, than their existing on-campus teaching organizations.

12. The literature assessing the performance implications of merger and acquisition activity is enormous, and surprisingly unambiguous. Many studies have revealed that many, and perhaps even most, mergers destroy value in the acquiring firm; see, for example, Michael Porter "From Competitive Advantage to Competitive Strategy," *Harvard Business Review* 65, no. 3 (1987), 43–59, and J. B. Young, "A Conclusive Investigation into the Causative Elements of Failure in Acquisitions and Mergers," in *Handbook of Mergers, Acquisitions, and Buyouts,* ed. S. J. Lee and R. D. Colman (Englewood Cliffs, NJ: Prentice-Hall, 1981), 605–628. At best, the only winners appear to be the sellers; see, for example, G. A. Jarrell, J. A. Brickley, and J. M. Netter, "The Market for Corporate Control: The Empirical Evidence Since 1980," *Journal of Economic Perspectives* 2 (1988): 21–48, and M. C. Jensen and R. S. Ruback, "The Market for Corporate Control: The Scientific Evidence," *Journal of Financial Economics* 11 (1983): 5–50. Even if acquisition targets are "well-selected" from a conventional strategic point of view, there is significant evidence to suggest that implementation difficulties can derail the realization of any putative benefits; see, for example, Anthony B. Buono and James L. Bowditch, *The Human Side of Mergers and Acquisitions: Managing Collisions Between People, Cultures, and Organizations* (San Francisco: Jossey-Bass, 1988), and D. J. Ravenscraft and F. M.

Scherer, "The Profitabiliy of Mergers," *International Journal of Industrial Organization* 7 (1989): 101–116.

13. We wish to emphasize that our message is not that acquisitions can solve a company's growth problems. As we note in the text, even the successful acquisition of mature businesses does not change the growth trajectory of a corporation—it just places corporate revenues on a higher but flat plateau. In the late 1990s Cisco followed a very different acquisition strategy from the one we have described at J&J's MDD business. Cisco's packet-switching routers had created a powerful wave of disruption versus Lucent and Nortel, which made circuit-switching equipment for voice telephony. Most of Cisco's acquisitions were *sustaining* relative to its business model and market position, in that they helped the company move up-market better and faster. They did not constitute platforms for new disruptive growth businesses.

14. This is one of the conclusions of Professor Donald N. Sull's recent book, *Revival of the Fittest* (Boston: Harvard Business School Press, 2003).

15. We worry, in fact, that exactly this sort of reasoning has caused Hewlett-Packard's senior executives to combine the company's business units into a few massive organizations. The reorganization facilitated cost cutting, no doubt. But in our view, it can only exacerbate the company's battle with its values at a time when reigniting growth is very important. At the same time—and this is why good theory is so important—"smallness" versus "bigness" is not the right categorization scheme when thinking about the benefits of these kinds of mergers or the advantages of smallness achieved by organizational separation or spin-outs. Consolidation can yield important cost savings, but as we point out in this chapter, it can corrupt the values needed to pursue potential disruptive opportunities. Smaller organizations —or big organizations that are blown apart into a series of smaller organizations—might have an easier time dealing with the challenges of embracing disruption-friendly values, but as we point out in chapters 5 and 6, organizations must also cope with the demands of architectural interdependencies, which can often require larger, more integrated organizations. In our view, it's not so much about making trade-offs; that is, accepting inevitable compromises, as it is about recognizing the circumstances one is in and adopting the appropriate solution to the most pressing problem.

16. We have often been asked how much money a venture should be allowed to lose, and how much time it should take until profits should be expected. There can, of course, be no rigid rules, because the fixed-cost intensity of each business will vary. Mobile telephony was a disruptive growth business that entailed large fixed-cost investments, and hence more significant losses

than would many others. In making these recommendations, we simply hope to offer to executives the guiding principle that losing less is more.

17. Honda's experience is summarized on pages 153 to 156 of *The Innovator's Dilemma*. That account has been condensed from a case study by Evelyn Tatum Christensen and Richard Tanner Pascale, "Honda (B)," Case 9-384-050 (Boston: Harvard Business School, 1983).

18. Searching for unanticipated successes, rather than seeking to correct deviations from a plan, is one of the most important principles that Peter F. Drucker taught in his classic book *Innovation and Entrepreneurship* (New York: Harper & Row, 1985).

19. This tendency to refocus immediately on the core when things get bad, even at the expense of the long-term solutions to the problem that caused the core to get sick, is known among behavioral psychologists as "threat rigidity." See chapter 4 for more on this.

20. Fiore's experiences are detailed in Clayton M. Christensen and Tara Donovan, "Nick Fiore: Healer or Hitman? (A)" Case 9-601-062 (Boston: Harvard Business School, 2000).

21. Presentation by Dr. Nick Fiore to Harvard Business School students, 26 February 2003.

22. Professor William Sahlman of the Harvard Business School has studied the phenomenon of venture capital "bubble" investing for two decades. He observes that when many venture investors conclude that they need to have strong investment positions in a "category," investors develop "capital market myopia"—a view that does not consider the impact that other firms' investments will have on the probability that their individual investment will succeed. When massive amounts of available venture capital are focused on an industry where investors perceive steep scale economies and strong network effects, the funds and the companies in which they invest are compelled to engage in "racing" behavior. Firms seek to dramatically outspend the competition, because it is a company's *relative* spending rate and its *relative* execution capability that drive success. Sahlman notes that once a race like this has started, venture funds have no option but to engage in that behavior if they want to participate in that investment category. Sahlman has observed that between the mid-1980s and the early 1990s—the period following the first of these investment bubbles—the returns to venture capital were zero. We have seen a similar decline in venture returns in the years following the dot-com and telecommunications investment bubble in the late 1990s.

23. Big-ticket investing of money that is impatient for profit and growth is very appropriate in later stages of step 1 of the spiral, when the company needs to focus deliberately on a winning strategy that has become clear. Interestingly,

Bain Capital, which has been one of the most successful investment firms over the past decade, made this transition very effectively. Bain started out making rather small venture investments. It provided the start-up funding for Staples, the office superstore, for example. It was so successful with its first fund that investors simply poured as much money into subsequent funds as Bain would let them. This meant that the firm's values changed, and it could no longer prioritize small investments. In contrast to the behavior of the venture funds in the bubble, however, Bain stopped making early-stage investments as it got bigger. It became a later-stage private equity investor, and continued to perform magnificently. In the parlance of the model of theory building we presented in the introduction, as these investment funds grow, they find themselves in different circumstances. The strategies that led to success in one circumstance can lead to disaster in another. Bain Capital changed strategy as its circumstances changed. Many of the venture capital funds did not.

CHAPTER TEN

THE ROLE OF SENIOR EXECUTIVES IN LEADING NEW GROWTH

How should senior executives allocate their time and energy across all of the businesses and initiatives that demand their attention? How should their oversight of sustaining innovations differ from their mode of management in disruptive situations? Is the creation of new growth businesses inherently an idiosyncratic, ad hoc undertaking, or might it be possible to create a repeatable process that successfully generates wave after wave of disruptive growth?

The senior executives of a company that seeks repeatedly to create new waves of disruptive growth have three jobs. The first is a near-term assignment: personally to stand astride the interface between disruptive growth businesses and the mainstream businesses to determine through judgment which of the corporation's resources and processes should be imposed on the new business, and which should not. The second is a longer-term responsibility: to shepherd the creation of a process that we call a "disruptive growth engine," which capably and repeatedly launches successful growth businesses. The third responsibility is perpetual: to sense when the *circumstances* are changing, and to keep teaching others to recognize these signals. Because the effectiveness of any strategy is contingent on the circumstance, senior executives need to look to the horizon (which often is at the low end of the market or in nonconsumption) for evidence that the basis of competition is changing, and then initiate projects and acquisitions to ensure that the corporation responds to the changing circumstance as an opportunity for growth and not as a threat to be defended against.[1]

Standing Astride the Sustaining–Disruptive Interface

Because processes begin to coalesce within a group that is confronted repeatedly with doing the same task, the engine that propels accomplishment in well-run companies gradually becomes less dependent on the capabilities of individual people, and becomes instead embedded in processes, as we described in chapter 7. After successful companies find their initial disruptive foothold, the task that recurs repeatedly is sustaining innovation, not disruption. Well-oiled, capable processes for successfully addressing sustaining opportunities have therefore coalesced in most successful companies. We know of no companies, however, that as yet have built processes for dealing with disruption—because launching disruptive businesses has not yet been a recurrent task.[2]

At present, therefore, the ability to create growth businesses through disruption resides in companies' resources, and for reasons we'll explore in this chapter, the most critical of these resources is the CEO or another very senior executive with comparable influence. We say "at present" because it does not always need to be so. If a company tackles the task of creating disruptive growth again and again, the ability to create successful disruptive growth businesses can become ensconced in a process as well—a process that this chapter calls a *disruptive growth engine*. Although we know of no company that has yet developed such an engine, we believe it is possible and propose four critical steps that senior executives can take to do so. A company that succeeds in creating a disruptive growth engine will place itself on a predictable path to profitable growth, consistently skating to the money-making opportunities of the future.

A Theory of Senior Executive Involvement

Until processes that can competently manage disruptive innovation have coalesced, the personal oversight of a senior executive is one of the most crucial resources that disruptive businesses need to reach success. One of the most discouraging dimensions of senior executives' lives is the refrain by writers of many management books that they must be involved in order to fix whatever problem the book is about. Corporate ethics, shareholder value, business and product development, acquisitions, corporate citizenship, corporate culture, management development, and process improvement programs are all squeaky wheels that demand executive grease. Senior managers must pay close attention to managing the top line, the bottom line, and all the lines in between. Confronting such cacophony, executives need a good circumstance-based theory of executive involvement—a way to discern the circumstances in which their direct involvement actually *is* critical to success, and the circumstances in which they should delegate.

One of the most common theories of when senior executives should get involved in a decision and when they should not is based on an attribute of the decision, namely, the magnitude of money at stake. The theory asserts that lower-level managers can make small decisions or ones that involve minor changes, but that only senior executives have sufficient wisdom to make the big calls correctly. Almost every company enacts this theory through policies that give decision-making approval for smaller investments to lower-level executives and elevate big-ticket items for the scrutiny of the senior-most team.

Sometimes this theory accurately predicts the quality of decisions, but sometimes it doesn't.[3] One problem with systems that reflect the send-the-big-decisions-to-the-big-people theory is that the data are in the divisions: There is an asymmetry of information along the vertical dimension of every organization. Reporting systems can indeed elevate the information that senior managers ask for, but the problem is that sometimes senior management doesn't know what questions need to be asked.[4] Senior people in large organizations therefore typically can't know much beyond what the managers below them choose to divulge. Worse, when midlevel managers have been through a few senior management decision cycles, they learn what the numbers must look like in order for senior management to approve proposals, and they learn what information ought not be presented to senior management because it might "confuse" them. Hence, a good portion of middle managers' effort is spent winnowing the full amount of information into the particular subset that is required to win senior approval for projects that middle managers already have decided are important. Initiatives that don't make sense to the middle managers rarely get packaged for the senior people's consideration. Senior executives *envision* themselves as making the big decisions, but in fact they most often do not.

Because the senior-most executives in reality cannot participate when and where these decisions actually get made, decision-making processes that work well *without* senior attention are *critical* to success in circumstances of sustaining innovation. In the sustaining circumstance when capable processes exist—even in many big-ticket decisions—senior executives typically cannot improve the quality of the decision because of the asymmetry of information that exists.[5] This is when the gospel of "driving decisions down to the lowest level" and of "making the lowest level competent" is in fact good news.

Another version of the "size theory" states that large businesses require more active senior management involvement, whereas lower-level managers can cope with the demands of smaller organizational units. Fewer people and fewer assets, the belief goes, mean that less managerial skill is required. Sometimes this is the case, but sometimes it isn't. Potentially disruptive businesses are small. But with their ill-defined strategies and demanding profitability targets, make-or-break decisions arise with alarming frequency, and such businesses have no processes for making these decisions correctly. In contrast, larger businesses in successful organizations typically have established customers with clearly articulated needs, and have finely honed resource allocation and production processes to serve those needs. The decision-making requirements of these organizations typically transcend the involvement of any given individual, and are typically—and appropriately—met by the orderly functioning of established processes.

Both of these theories get the categories wrong. A better, circumstance-based theory can help managers decide which decisions ought to be made at which levels. For those decisions that the mainstream processes and values were designed to make effectively (sustaining innovations, primarily), less senior executive involvement is needed. It is when senior executives sense that the processes and values of the mainstream organization were *not* designed to handle important decisions in an organization (which is typically the case in disruptive circumstances) that a senior executive needs to participate. Because the plans for disruptive businesses by definition need to be shaped by different criteria, and because the values of the mainstream business have evolved to weed out the very sorts of ideas that have disruptive potential, disruptive innovation is the category of circumstance in which powerful senior managers must personally be involved. Sustaining innovation is the circumstance in which delegation works effectively. A senior-most executive is the only one who can endorse the use of corporate processes when they are appropriate, and break the grip of those processes and decision rules when they are not.

Another reason why senior executives need to stand astride the interface between sustaining innovations and disruption is that managers of the mainstream business units need to be fully informed of the technological and business model innovations that are developed in the new disruptive business, because disruption often is where the most important improvements for the future of the entire corporation are incubated. If senior managers have properly schooled themselves in sound theories of strategy and management, they can coach the managers of important growth businesses on both the sustaining and disruptive sides of the interface to take the actions that are appropriate to each particular circumstance. Ensuring that deliberate and emergent strategy processes are employed in the right circumstances and that managers are hired whose experience is a match for the problems at hand are ongoing challenges on both sides of the divide.

The Importance of Meddling

One of our favorite teaching case studies about Nypro, Inc., illustrates when and why a senior-most executive needs personally to shepherd the creation of disruptive growth businesses.[6] Nypro is an extraordinarily successful custom injection molder of precision plastic parts. Much of the company's innovative culture and financial success can be attributed to its owner and recently retired CEO, Gordon Lankton.

Nypro's customers are global manufacturers of health care and microelectronic products. They require worldwide sourcing of plastic components whose complexity and dimensional tolerances demand the most sophisticated molding process capabilities. Nypro seeks to offer a uniform capability from any of its twenty-eight plants—whether in North America, Puerto Rico, Ireland, Mexico, Singapore, or China—under the mantra "Nypro is your local source . . . world-wide." If Nypro sought to achieve this uniform capability by barring any plant from deviating from standard, company-wide procedures, it would kill innovation at the very level where it best occurs—the plants. Most of the important process innovations that help Nypro to make ever-better products are developed by engineering teams working to solve customer problems in far-flung individual plants, out of the eyesight and earshot of senior management. This situation is a stereotype of the dilemma that confronts most companies in one way or another: Companies need uniform capability but flexibility to change, and senior managers typically can't even *see* what innovations are being considered and developed, let alone decide which ones merit investment.

In response to this challenge, Lankton created a system to surface the most important and successful innovations so that he could evaluate which improvements should be adopted by all plants, thereby enabling Nypro to offer a uniform but ever-improving global manufacturing capability. A key element of this system was a monthly financial reporting system that rank-ordered the plants' performance along a number of important dimensions that Lankton judged to be the drivers of the company's near-term financial performance and its long-term strategic success. These reports showed, for all to see, which plants were doing better and which needed to improve. Plant managers were evaluated on the measures of plant performance in these reports, and their reputation vis-à-vis each other was affected by the relative ranking of their plants. The system, in other words, provided ample motivation for managers to search for any innovation that would improve their performance and relative ranking.

Lankton created interlocking boards of directors for each plant, so that each board was composed of managers and engineers from several other plants. This kept information flowing among plants.

The company augmented this with several global meetings each year for plant managers and engineers, in which they exchanged news about what process and product innovations each had implemented, and what the results had been. In time, there emerged a culture in which managers were intensely competitive to get ahead of each other, and yet were cooperative in sharing the process innovations each had developed.

Lankton watched carefully whenever one plant's successful innovation began to be adopted by managers at other plants. This was a signal to him that the idea had merit. After several respected managers had copied another plant's process innovation, Lankton had enough evidence to decide that the innovation should be implemented, and would then mandate that it become a standard practice worldwide. This method tested and validated sustaining innovations first, and then accelerated the implementation of those that had proved to be important.

By the mid-1990s it had become clear to Lankton that Nypro's world was changing. His engineers could mold millions of complicated plastic parts per month to extremely tight tolerances. Even though there were a few applications that needed even greater precision, Nypro's capabilities were more than good enough for the majority of the market, and other competitors had improved to compete favorably against Nypro's cost and quality. Lankton sensed, in other words, that the basis of competition in his markets was beginning to change. He noted that the type of business that had led to Nypro's success—very high-volume, high-precision molding—wasn't growing nearly as rapidly as the demand for a wider variety of parts with smaller volumes. Some of these parts demanded high precision as well, but it was the ability to respond quickly with that precision that loomed as the key to success.

Sensing a change of circumstance and crafting a response is a role that only the CEO can fill. Lankton sensed this shift masterfully—but when he left it to the organization to implement the required change, it couldn't. Here's what happened.

To prepare Nypro for this shift in the basis of competition, Lankton commissioned a project at the company's headquarters to develop a machine called "Novaplast" that could be set up in less than a minute.[7] The technology's unique mold design enabled economical, low-pressure molding of a variety of precision parts in short run lengths.

To be consistent with the company's practice, Lankton chose not to compel all plants to begin using the new machine. He made sure that all managers understood how the technology worked and what its strategic purpose was. He then made the machine available for plant managers to lease, hoping that this approach would minimize barriers to experimentation and adoption—and, as usual, to see whether those whose judgment he had learned to respect cast their votes for the technology. Six of Nypro's plants leased the machine, but within four months four of those had returned their machines to headquarters. The reason: They had concluded that there just wasn't any business that could be run economically on the machines. The two plants that kept the Novaplast machine had a long-standing order from a major manufacturer of AA-sized batteries to provide a thin-walled plastic liner that fit inside the metal casing of these batteries. The plants molded millions of these liners every month, and for unique reasons it turned out that the Novaplast machine could crank these parts out with higher yields and lower costs than could Nypro's conventional high-volume, high-pressure machines.

The end of the teaching case pictures Lankton puzzling about this outcome. Why was it that he had seen so clearly the growing demand for rapid delivery of a widening variety of short-run precision parts, and yet his plants hadn't been able to land any of that business for their Novaplast machines? Was it a victory or a failure that Novaplast's ultimate success came from a very high-volume, standard, high-precision part?

The answer is that this is exactly the result we would expect from the processes and values that supported the existing business model. Nypro's finely honed innovation engine shaped Novaplast as a sustaining technology, because this is exactly what the system was designed to do—to shape every investment to help the company make money in the way it was structured to make money. An organization cannot disrupt itself. It can only implement technologies in ways that sustain its profit or business model. The consequence for Nypro of allowing the standard process to remain in control is that (so far) the company has missed the chance to create a major new disruptive growth business.

To succeed at this disruption, Lankton would have needed to create a sales organization whose compensation structure energized salespeople to pursue this high-variety, low-volume-per-part business. He would have needed to build an operating organization whose processes were tuned to this work and to create measures of performance that were different from those that drove success in the core business. None of the processes of the core business could make these judgment calls correctly. This is why the CEO needs to stand astride the interface between mainstream business units and new disruptive growth businesses.[8]

Can Any Executive Lead Disruptive Growth?

Because the processes and values of the mainstream business by their very nature are geared to manage sustaining innovation, there is no alternative at the outset to the CEO or someone with comparable power assuming oversight responsibility for disruptive growth. Can only certain of these executives exercise this oversight effectively, or is it possible for *any* senior person to succeed? We noted in chapter 2 that most of the companies whose stock we wish we had owned in the past fifty years took root with a disruptive strategy. A few—but not many—of these companies subsequently caught or created other waves of disruption that kept the parent corporation growing at a robust pace for a time.

One of our most sobering realizations is that within the population of companies that successfully caught a subsequent wave of disruption and stayed atop their industries, the vast majority were still being run by the company's founder at the time they tackled the disruption. Only a few companies that were run by professional (non-founder) managers have succeeded in creating new disruptive growth businesses. Table 10-1, although not exhaustive, illustrates what we have sensed.[9]

TABLE 10-1

Founder-Led Companies That Launched New Disruptive Businesses

Company	Disruptive Growth Business	CEO/Founder
Bank One	Monoline credit cards (purchase of First USA)	John McCoy[a]
Charles Schwab	Online brokerage	Charles Schwab[b]
Dayton Hudson	Discount retailing (Target Stores)	The Dayton family
Hewlett-Packard	Microprocessor-based computers	David Packard
IBM	Minicomputers	Thomas Watson Jr.[c]
Intel	Low-end microprocessors (Celeron chip)	Andrew Grove
Intuit	QuickBooks small business accounting software; TurboTax personal tax assistance software; putting Quicken money management software online	Scott Cook
Microsoft	Internet-based computing; SQL and Access database software; Great Plains business solutions software	Bill Gates
Oracle	Centrally served software (applications service provider)	Larry Ellison
Quantum	3.5-inch disk drives	Dave Brown/ Steve Berkley
Sony	Transistor-based consumer electronics	Akio Morita
Teradyne	Integrated circuit testers based on CMOS processors	Alex d'Arbeloff
The Gap	Old Navy low-price-point casual clothing	Mickey Wexler
Wal-Mart	Sam's Club	Sam Walton

[a]McCoy was not the founder, but was the primary architect of the acquisition strategy that drove Bank One to its prominence.

[b]The company's co-CEO, David Pottruck, strongly assisted Charles Schwab in this effort.

[c]Again, Watson was the son of the founder, but was the primary driver of IBM's success in mainframe digital computing.

It's worth noting that these founder-led organizations were also essentially single-industry firms (that is, relatively undiversified when they faced the disruption), which, as chapter 9 noted, can make creating a new disruptive business even harder. We suspect that founders have an advantage in tackling disruption because they not only wield the requisite political clout but also have the self-confidence to override established processes in the interests of pursuing disruptive opportunities. Professional managers, on the other hand, often seem to find it difficult to push in disruptive directions that seem counterintuitive to most other people in the organization.

Table 10-2 shows, however, that there are some exceptions to the principle that only founders seem able to drive disruption. We know of five major companies that were run by professional managers at the time they launched successful disruptions. Of these, Johnson & Johnson, Procter & Gamble, and General Electric are all icons of diversification. IBM and Hewlett-Packard were relatively undiversified when their founders launched those companies' first successful disruptive businesses; hence, they are listed in table 10-1. Later, when professional managers were running the show, these two firms launched or acquired additional disruptive businesses, but did so when the firms had become much more broadly diversified.

We suspect that because the professional managers of the companies listed in table 10-2 undertook their new disruptions in the context of a diversified, multibusiness corporation, it was easier for them to succeed. Although their capabilities as managerial resources were undoubtedly important in these actions, there were precedents and processes for creating or acquiring new businesses and managing them appropriately that assisted the professional CEOs in creating disruptive growth.[10]

TABLE 10-2

Professionally Managed Companies That Launched New Disruptive Businesses

Company	Disruptive Growth Business
General Electric	GE Capital
Hewlett-Packard	Ink-jet printers
IBM	Personal computers
Johnson & Johnson	Glucose monitors, disposable contact lenses, equipment for endoscopic surgery and angioplasty
Procter & Gamble	Dryel home dry cleaning, inexpensive power toothbrushes, Crest brand tooth-whitening strips

Creating a Growth Engine: Embedding the Ability to Disrupt in a Process

Launching a single successful disruptive business can create years of profitable growth for a company, as GE Capital did for its parent during the years when Jack Welch was at its helm. Disruption blessed Johnson & Johnson's medical devices and diagnostics group, as we noted in chapter 9. Hewlett-Packard's disruptive ink-jet printer is now the profit driver of the entire corporation. If it feels so good to disrupt once, why not do it again and again?

If a company launches a *sequence* of growth businesses, if its leaders repeatedly use the litmus tests for shaping ideas or acquiring nascent disruptions, and if they repeatedly use sound theories to make the other key business-building decisions well, we believe that a predictable, repeatable process for identifying, shaping, and launching successful growth can coalesce. A company that embeds the ability to do this in a *process* would own a valuable growth engine.

Such an engine would have four critical components, as depicted in figure 10-1. First, it needs to operate rhythmically and by *policy,* rather than in response to financial developments. This would ensure that new businesses get launched while the corporation is still growing robustly, and that new businesses would not be pressured to grow too big too fast. Second, the CEO or another senior executive who has the confidence and the authority to lead from the top *when necessary* must lead the effort. This is particularly important in the early years, when success still depends more on resources than on processes. Third, it would establish a small corporate-level group—movers and shapers—whose members develop a practiced, repeatable system for shaping ideas into disruptive business plans that are funded and launched. Fourth, it would include a system for training and retraining people throughout the organization to identify disruptive opportunities and to take them to the movers and shapers.[11]

Step 1: Start Before You Need To

The best time to invest for growth is, as we noted in chapter 9, when the company is growing. To build what will be a respectable growth

FIGURE 10-1

The Disruptive Growth Engine

Disruptive Growth Engine

Start Before You Need To
- Best time to invest is when company is still growing
- Pressure to get big fast forces ventures to do many things wrong

A Senior Manager in Charge
- Senior managers monitor the resource allocation process
- Decide which corporate processes do and do not apply
- Keep communication flowing across disruptive–sustaining boundary

An Expert Team of Movers and Shapers
- Responsible for shaping ideas to fit the litmus tests of disruption
- Use theory to ensure that each action is appropriate to the circumstance

Train the Troops
- Engineers and salespeople who are closest to the market need to know what to look for
- If properly trained, can send the right ideas into the right process

business in five years, you have to start now. And you need to add new units to the portfolio of growth businesses in a rhythm that is dictated by the growth needs of the corporation five years hence. Companies that build while they are growing can shield their nascent high-potential businesses from Wall Street pressure, giving each one the time it needs to iterate toward a viable strategy and take off. Keep Wal-Mart in mind. In 2002 it generated nearly $220 billion in revenues. But from the time it opened its first discount store, it took a dozen years in today's dollars until it passed the billion-dollar revenue threshold. Disruptions need a longer runway before they take off to huge volumes, so you have to start them before your annual report suggests that you're leveling off.

The best way to do this is to budget for it—not just an amount of capital set aside to invest in disruptive growth, but a budgeted number of new businesses that need to be launched each year.[12] Remember that we are not advocating establishment of a corporate venture capital fund whose structure is predicated on the belief that one cannot predict which investments will and will not pan out. We believe that the process of creating successful growth is capable of much greater predictability if managers use sound theories to shape ideas properly. The needed number of new businesses can therefore be launched each year with not just the hope but the expectation that they will succeed.

Step 2: Appoint a Senior Executive to Shepherd Ideas into the Appropriate Shaping and Resource Allocation Processes

Creating a successful disruptive growth engine requires the careful coaching of the CEO or another senior manager who has the confidence and the power to exempt a venture from an established corporate process, to declare when different processes need to be created, and to ensure that the criteria being used in resource allocation are appropriate to the circumstance of each venture and the needs of the corporation. This executive must be well versed in disruptive innovation theory and should be able to separate ideas with disruptive potential from those that are best deployed on an established sustaining trajectory. The primary job of this manager is to make sure that ideas that are best used to create disruptive footholds are fed into a process that maximizes their chances of success.

As noted earlier, this executive role will change over time. At the outset it will entail monitoring and coaching individual decisions in individual growth businesses. Ultimately it will consist of monitoring the processes for collecting, shaping, and funding ideas; continued coaching and training; and monitoring the winds of changing circumstances in the company's environment.

Step 3: Create a Team and a Process for Shaping Ideas

We asserted in chapter 1 that lack of interesting growth ideas is rarely a problem in companies that are in danger of losing their growth. The problem is that ideas often lose their disruptive growth potential in the shaping process that they go through in order to get funded. The challenge for this third component of the growth engine is therefore to create a separately operating process through which ideas can be shaped into high-potential disruptions.

Processes like this can be diagrammed at a high level on paper, but they become tangible only as a stable group of people successfully solves similar problems again and again. Senior management should therefore create a core team at the corporate level that is responsible for collecting disruptive innovation ideas and molding them into propositions that fit the litmus tests outlined in chapters 2 through 6 of this book. The members of this team have to understand these theories at a deep level, stick together, and apply them frequently. This experience will help them sense which ideas can and cannot be shaped into exciting disruptions, and to distinguish these from ideas whose potential is sustaining and should be funneled through the shaping and resource allocation process of an established business.

Despite the guidance that we hope this book provides, many dimensions of the strategy that ultimately will prove successful for growth ventures cannot be known at the outset. This means that this core shaping group cannot use the company's standard strategic planning and budgeting processes when launching disruptive businesses. Chapter 8 detailed an equally rigorous discovery-driven planning process for use in disruptive circumstances.[13] Members of the core group could coach each new venture's management on these techniques for strategic planning and budgeting. We are confident that as they do this, their intuition and understanding of the ideas will improve far beyond what we now know and can convey in a limited book such as this.

Step 4: Train the Troops to Identify Disruptive Ideas

The fourth component of a well-functioning disruptive growth engine is the training of the troops, particularly sales, marketing, and engineering employees, because they are best positioned to encounter interesting growth ideas and to scout for small acquisitions with disruptive potential. They should be trained in the language of sustaining and disruptive innovation and absorb a deep understanding of the litmus tests, because it's crucial that they come to know what kinds of ideas they should channel into the sustaining processes of established business units, what kinds should be directed into disruptive channels, and what ideas have the potential for neither. This is truly a situation in which "making the lowest level competent" will pay off in spades. Capturing ideas for new-growth businesses from people in direct contact with markets and technologies can be far more productive than relying on analyst-laden corporate strategy or business development departments—as long as the troops have the intuition to do the first-level screening and shaping themselves.

Senior executives need to play four roles in managing innovation. First, they must actively coordinate action and decisions when no processes exist to do the coordination. Second, they must break the grip of established processes when a team is confronted with new tasks that require new patterns of communication, coordination and decision making. Third, when recurrent activities and decisions emerge in an organization, executives must create processes to reliably guide and coordinate the work of employees involved. And fourth, because recurrent cultivation of new disruptive growth businesses entails the building and maintenance of multiple simultaneous processes and business models within the corporation, senior executives need to stand astride the interfaces of those organizations—to ensure that useful learning from the new growth businesses flows back into the mainstream, and to ensure that the right resources, processes, and values are always being applied in the right situation.

When an established company first undertakes the creation of a new disruptive growth business, senior executives need to play the first and second roles. Disruption is a new task, and appropriate processes will not exist to handle much of the required coordination and decision making related to the initial projects. Certain of the mainstream organization's processes need to be pre-empted or broken because they will not facilitate the work that the disruptive team needs to do. To create a growth engine that sustains the corporation's growth for an extended period, senior executives need to play the third role masterfully, because launching new disruptive businesses needs to become a rhythmic, recurrent task. This entails repeated training for the employees involved, so that they can instinctively identify potentially disruptive ideas and shape them into business plans that will lead to success. The fourth task, which is to stand astride the boundary between disruptive and mainstream businesses, actively monitoring the appropriate flow of resources, processes, and values from the mainstream business into the new one and back again, is the ongoing essence of managing a perpetually growing corporation.

Notes

1. In this chapter we'll use the term *senior executives* to refer to men and women in positions such as chairman, vice chairman, CEO, and president. Senior executives who can perform well the leadership roles we describe in this chapter need to have the power and the confidence to declare that certain corporate rules will and will not be followed, given the circumstances that a growth venture is in.

2. As mentioned in chapter 8, Sony is the only example we know of that was a *serial* disruptor, having created a string of a dozen disruptive new-growth businesses between 1950 and 1982. Hewlett-Packard did it at least twice, when it launched microprocessor-based computers and ink-jet printers. More recently, our sense is that Intuit has been actively seeking to create new-growth businesses through disruptive means. But for the vast majority of companies, disruption has been at most a one-time event.

3. We again refer readers to Robert Burgelman's *Strategy is Destiny*, an extraordinarily insightful chronicle of how the *ex ante* and *ex post* quality of high-impact strategic decisions was distributed across the layers of management at Intel Corporation.

4. Practices such as "management by walking around," which was popularized by Thomas Peters and Robert Waterman in their management classic, *In Search of Excellence* (New York: Warner Books, 1982) are targeted at this challenge. The hope is that by walking around, senior managers might get a sense for what the important questions are, so that they can ask for the right information needed to make good decisions.

5. Some would assert that senior-most executives still need to be involved in decisions about major expenditures because of their fiduciary responsibility not to spend more than the company has to spend. Even decisions like these, however, can be made through capable processes.

6. This account summarizes a teaching case by Clayton Christensen and Rebecca Voorheis, "Managing Innovation at Nypro, Inc. (A)," Case 9-696-061

(Boston: Harvard Business School, 1995) and "Managing Innovation at Nypro, Inc. (B)," Case 9-697-057 (Boston: Harvard Business School, 1996).

7. In our account of this history, we are using the language of our models. Lankton did not know of our research and therefore was guided by his own intuition, not our advice. His intuition was stunningly consistent with how we would have viewed the situation, however.

8. Interestingly, despite the fact that the company has missed (so far) the opportunity to catch this wave of disruptive growth in high-variety, low-volume-per-model manufacturing, the company has done very well. It has followed the pattern outlined in chapter 6 of eating its way forward from the back end, integrating forward from component manufacturing into technologically interdependent subassemblies and even final product assembly. It (very profitably) *tripled* its revenues to nearly $1 billion between 1997 and 2002—a period in which several major competitors failed.

9. The nature of these companies' disruptions is analyzed in figure 2-4 and the appendix to chapter 2.

10. Something else worth noting is that we have not studied the relative success rates of founder-led versus agent-led disruptive initiatives. All we can say on the basis of the analysis we have done so far is that the relative incidence of successful founder-led disruption is higher than for agent-led disruption. Just who has a better batting average we can't yet say. For unfortunate but understandable reasons, data on failed business creation efforts are hard to come by.

11. Clayton M. Christensen, Mark Johnson, and Darrell K. Rigby, "Foundations for Growth: How to Identify and Build Disruptive New Businesses," *MIT Sloan Management Review*, Spring 2002, 22–31. We are grateful to Darrell Rigby for pointing out the possibility that an engine of growth might be created.

12. A good tool to use in this budgeting process is called aggregate project planning. Steven C. Wheelwright and Kim B. Clark described this method in their book *Revolutionizing Product Development* (New York: Free Press, 1992). Their concept has been extended to the corporate resource allocation process in a course note by Clayton Christensen, "Using Aggregate Project Planning to Link Strategy, Innovation, and the Resource Allocation Process," Note 9-301-041 (Boston: Harvard Business School, 2000).

13. See Rita G. McGrath and Ian MacMillan, "Discovery-Driven Planning," *Harvard Business Review*, July–August 1995, 44–54.

PASSING THE BATON

Managers rarely can exercise unbridled free agency. Powerful and predictable forces act upon them. These forces include the need to move up-market to maintain profit margins; the need to satisfy existing customers; the forces of commoditization and decommoditization; the mandate to grow from an ever-larger revenue base; and the fact that the processes and values that define the capabilities of one business model simultaneously define disabilities for other business models. These forces do not Calvinistically predestine managers to take a particular sequence of actions, but they strongly influence the types of choices that managers do and do not confront, and they shape the attractiveness of the different choices relative to the managers' situations. In this book we have tried to show that when companies face the wrong side of these forces, they lead to predictable growth pathologies. But when companies harness these same forces, they can put wind in their sails. The predictability of these forces makes it possible to capture them and turn them to your advantage in seeking, exploiting, and sustaining new growth opportunities.

If this were a book for mariners, it would be filled with discussions of sailing with or against tides and currents, and how to set sail in order to take advantage of the prevailing winds. Such a book would make it easy to see that where and when you start, relative to the direction that those forces want to carry you, can make a huge difference in how easy it is to get where you want to go.

Similarly, we hope that this book makes it easy to see that where you start, relative to the direction of the competitive, technological, and profit-seeking forces acting upon you, can make a huge difference in the probability that you will succeed. This view simplifies the challenge of creating new-growth businesses. It means that when you start a new business you do not need to envision accurately the details of your strategy or predict foresightedly how technology will evolve. Rather, you need to focus primarily on getting the initial conditions right. If you start from a good place, then *the choices that lead to success will look like the right choices*. In order to exploit these choices, you need to create a business model whose resources, processes, and values can harness these forces so that they propel you toward success rather than blow you away.

Accurately researched and written histories would reveal that many founders of successful companies—including many of the disruptive companies arrayed in figure 2-4—had the wrong strategy in mind when they started. But due to some combination of intuition and luck, they put themselves in a situation in which they were confronted with attractive choices. Doing what made sense led to a next set of attractive choices, and so on. The initial conditions under which they started and the business structures that they created allowed them to catch the trends and forces that subsequently propelled them toward successful growth.

The structures and initial conditions that are required for successful growth are enumerated in the chapters of this book. They include starting with a cost structure in which attractive profits can be earned at low price points and which can then be carried up-market; being in a disruptive position relative to competitors so that they are motivated to flee rather than fight; starting with a set of customers who had been nonconsumers so that they are pleased with modest products; targeting a job that customers are trying to get done; skating to where the money will be, not to where it was; assigning managers who have taken the right courses in the school of experience and putting them to work within processes and organizational values that are attuned to what needs to be done; having the flexibility to respond as a viable strategy emerges; and starting with capital that can be patient for growth. If you start in conditions such as these, you do not need to see deeply into the future. Attractive choices that lead to success will present themselves. It is when you start in conditions that are opposite to these that attractive options may not appear, and the right choices will be difficult to make.

We also believe that the overwhelming odds that corporations will stop growing and be unable to restart growth can be deferred much longer than has so far seemed possible. Executives who understand how these forces create growth pathologies can counteract them better when the tide of these forces begins to shift from opportunity toward threat.

A principal refrain in this book is that blindly copying the best practices of successful companies without the guidance of circumstance-contingent theory is akin to fabricating feathered wings and flapping hard. Replicating their success is not about duplicating their attributes; it's about understanding how to generate lift. Good theories are circumstance-based. They describe how managers need to employ different strategies as circumstances change in order to achieve the needed results. The use of one-size-fits-all processes and values historically has made the creation of growth torturous. One of the most valuable contributions you can make in the growth-creation process, therefore, is to keep watching for changes in circumstances. If you do this, you can understand when and why changes need to be made long before the evidence is clear to those whose vision is not clarified by theory.

Who? Me? Use Theory?

While *The Innovator's Dilemma* sought to *build* a theory, our purpose in writing *The Innovator's Solution* has been to teach you as a manager how to *use* theory. If your reaction has been that theory is too complicated—that you're an action-driven manager and are not a theory-driven person—think again. Reread the passage in Molière's *The Bourgeois Gentleman* in which Monsieur Jourdain finds the writing of poetry intimidating. Remember how delighted he is to learn that he can use the other option, which is to compose his love letter in prose, because he has unwittingly been speaking prose all his life? While you may not have known it, you have been using theory for the whole of your managerial life. Whenever you have taken an action or made a plan, it was predicated upon a theory in your mind that your actions would lead to the envisioned outcome. So using theory to create successful growth businesses needn't feel strange. You are—though perhaps unwittingly—a practiced theoretician.

We conclude with a summary of our advice to executives who seek solutions to the innovator's dilemma.

1. Never say yes to a strategy that targets customers and markets that look attractive to an established competitor. Keep sending the team back to the drawing board until they've identified a disruptive foothold that established competitors will be happy to ignore or be relieved to walk away from. If you create asymmetries of motivation, your competitors will help you win. Though you may not have done this before, it should feel good if you are accustomed to bloody fights of sustaining innovation against motivated competitors.

2. If your team targets customers who already are using pretty good products, send them back to see if they can find a way to compete against nonconsumption. When your customers are delighted to have a simple, inexpensive product because their alternative is to have nothing, all the techniques for pleasing customers that you learned in Marketing 101 will be easy and inexpensive. This also should spell welcome relief compared with the alternative, which is the massive investment typically required to make disruptive technologies preferable to the established products that customers already are comfortable using.

3. If there are no nonconsumers available, ask your team to explore whether a low-end disruption is feasible. They must devise a business model that can make attractive profits at the discount prices required to capture customers at the low end of the market, who can't use all the functionality for which they currently

must pay. If this isn't possible either, then don't invest—or at least, don't invest with the expectation that this will create a significant growth business.

4. If the project leader ever uses the phrase, "If we can just get the customer to . . . ," terminate the conversation. Send the team back to find a way to help customers get done more conveniently and inexpensively what they already are trying to get done. Competing wishfully against customers' manifest priorities has shortened the tenure-in-job of some pretty good people.

5. If the team's product or marketing plan focuses on market segments whose boundaries mirror your organization's boundaries, or if the targeted market is segmented along the lines for which data are readily available (by product type, price point, or demographic category), send the team back. Ask them to segment the market in ways that mirror the jobs that customers are trying to get done. Remind the team that you *still* have no alternative but to hire a one-size-fits-all milkshake for at least two different jobs that arise regularly in your life. The milkshake business is stalled because quick-service restaurants keep improving the shake's attributes rather than doing each job better and better—which would grow the category by helping shakes to steal share from the *real* competition.

6. If your team's product improvement road map assumes that the basis of competition won't change—that the types of improvements that merited good margins in the past will continue to merit those margins in the future—look at the low end. Often you can see there the opportunity to change the basis of competition.

7. If your disruptive product or service is not yet good enough and your team seems enthralled with industry standards and the attendant outsourcing and partnering deals, raise a big red flag. If you prematurely pursue modularity and open standards, or if you keep a proprietary architecture closed while the basis of competition changes, you'll struggle to succeed. Remember what made Wayne Gretzky so good. It is better to develop competencies where the money will be made in the future than to cling tenaciously to those skills that made you successful in the past.

8. If your team assures you that you'll succeed because a new venture fits your company's core competence, tell them that you can't deal in fuzzy concepts. Ask for answers to three specific questions:
   - Do we have the resources to succeed?
   - Will our processes—the ways we have learned to work together to succeed in our established businesses—facilitate what needs to be done to succeed in the new business?
   - Will our values, or the criteria that folks here use to prioritize one thing over another, enable the critical people to give the needed priority to this initiative when compared with the other initiatives that compete for their time, money, and talent?

   Use the answers to these questions to choose the right organizational structure and the right organizational home for this project.

9. Ask these three questions about each of the entities that constitute the venture's *channels* as well. It's not just you. The channel companies' processes and values—their methods and motivations—can cause your venture to come off the rails or even stall before leaving the station.

10. Unfortunately, you may need to distrust the managers whom you have learned to trust. The managers in your organization who have most consistently delivered results in the past may be the least skilled at delivering success in new-growth businesses. In choosing the management team for your new venture, don't look at the *attributes* that describe the people you might tap to lead a new-growth venture, or at the magnitude of their past responsibilities. Search their résumés for the problems they have grappled with, and compare them to the problems that you know this venture must confront.

11. Be sure that in the beginning years after a venture is launched, the development team remains convinced that they *aren't* sure what the best strategy is, in terms of products, customers, and applications. Insist that the team give you a plan to accelerate the emergence of a viable strategy. Call a halt to decisive plans to implement any strategy before there is evidence that it works.

12. Be impatient for profit. When someone tells you as a senior executive that you must endure years of substantial losses before a

new business will become huge and profitable, this flags a plan to cram a disruptive technology into a sustaining role in an established market. Some investments in sustaining technologies with extensive interdependencies across the value chain can indeed require years of massive investment. Let established competitors tackle those. In disruptive circumstances, patiently enduring years of losses generally allows a team to pursue the wrong strategy for a long time.

13. Keep your company growing so that you can be patient for growth. Disruption—and competing against nonconsumption in particular—requires a longer runway before a steep ascent is possible. If corporate growth slows and you then force the new businesses to attempt too fast a takeoff, you will force the management to make other fatal mistakes. The other side to this mandate is important as well. If you're slated to lead a new venture and corporate management says you need to become very big very fast, what you *really* are hearing is that management is going to make you cram your disruptive technology into an established market. When you sense this, don't take the job. You are *very* likely to fail.

Note that there is no mandate on this list that executives be brilliant strategists in order to supervise the building of new disruptive growth businesses. That's the whole point of this book. The disruptive companies listed in chapter 2 didn't succeed because their founders foresaw the entire strategy. If it depended on the brilliance of the founders and the correctness of their strategies, then success would be unpredictable indeed.

Many successful companies have disrupted once. A few, including IBM, Intel, Microsoft, Hewlett-Packard, Johnson & Johnson, Kodak, Cisco, and Intuit, have disrupted several times. Sony did it repeatedly between 1955 and 1982, before its engine of disruption got shut down. To our knowledge, no company has been able to build an engine of disruptive growth and keep it running and running. That reality has made this a risky book for us to write: Few business books say "Do this; no one's ever done it before." But there is little choice.

Creating and sustaining successful growth has, historically speaking, vexed some great managers.

Given the existence of principles but no precedent, we have simply done our best to suggest how successful growth can be created and sustained. We have offered an integrated body of theory derived from the successes *and* the failures of hundreds of different companies, each of which has illuminated a different aspect of the innovator's dilemma. And so we now pass the baton to you, in the hope that you will find our efforts to be a valuable foundation upon which to build your own innovator's solution.

INDEX

ABOUT THE AUTHORS

Clayton M. Christensen is the Robert and Jane Cizik Professor of Business Administration at Harvard Business School. He holds a joint appointment in the Technology and Operations Management and General Management faculty groups. His research and teaching interests center on the management of technological innovation and finding new markets for new technologies. Prior to joining the HBS faculty, Christensen served as Chairman and President of CPS Corporation, a materials science firm that he cofounded with several MIT professors. He was also a White House Fellow in the administration of President Ronald Reagan and was a member of the staff of the Boston Consulting Group.

Christensen's publications have received numerous academic awards, including the 1997 Global Business Book Award for his book *The Innovator's Dilemma.* He serves as a consultant to the management teams of many of the world's leading corporations and serves as a member of The Church of Jesus Christ of Latter-day Saints in as many ways as he can.

Christensen holds a B.A. in economics from Brigham Young University, an M.Phil. in economics from Oxford University, where he studied as a Rhodes Scholar, and an MBA and DBA from Harvard Business School. He and his wife, Christine, are the parents of five children.

Michael E. Raynor is a Director in Deloitte Research, the thought leadership arm of Deloitte, the global professional services firm. He has worked with some of the firm's most significant clients across many industries, including telecommunications, media, computer hardware and software, financial services, energy, and health care. He is also a professor at the Richard Ivey School of Business in London, Canada, where he teaches in the MBA and Executive Education programs. He focuses on innovation and corporate strategy in his research, writing, and client work, exploring the challenges of sustaining success through innovation and ways to cope with and exploit the constantly shifting demands of uncertain competitive environments.

Raynor is the author or coauthor of many book chapters and articles in a wide range of publications, including the *Harvard Business Review, Long-Range Planning,* the *Journal of Applied Corporate Finance,* the *Journal of Business Strategy,* and *Engineering Economist.*

Raynor holds an undergraduate degree in philosophy from Harvard University, where he was a John Harvard Scholar. He received his MBA from Ivey, where he received the Nelson M. Davis Memorial Scholarship for excellence, and his DBA from Harvard Business School, where he received the George S. Dively Memorial Award for research excellence. He is Annabel's husband, and they are Charlotte's parents.